ANTISEMITISM

A Channel Islander by birth, a graduate of both Oxford and Cambridge, and a Church of England clergyman, James Parkes is one of the world's foremost authorities on the history and nature of antisemitism. His attempt to understand the phenomenon has also led him to studies of Jewish history and of Judaism. His books include *The Jewish Problem in the Modern World*, *The Story of Jerusalem*, *The Foundations of Judaism and Christianity*, and *A History of the Jewish People*. Dr. Parkes lives in Dorset, England, and works at the Parkes Library, established to study relations between the Jewish and non-Jewish worlds.

ANTISEMITISM

JAMES PARKES

Q

QUADRANGLE PAPERBACKS

QUADRANGLE BOOKS/CHICAGO

Library of Congress Catalog Card Number: 64-10809

Second Printing and first QUADRANGLE PAPERBACK edition published 1969.

TO
DAVID ASTOR

CONTENTS

FOREWORD

In 1945 I wrote a *Penguin Special* entitled *An Enemy of the People :
Antisemitism*. It sold some hundred thousand copies in British and
American editions. It was translated into German and published by
the Ness Verlag in 1946, but it proved too early for German readers
to be able to tolerate a book on such a subject. It was a time when
paper was still short, and projects of editions in other languages
were adopted, and then abandoned for lack of it. The present work
is a new book but it has incorporated some chapters of that book.
In the main, however, it has been rewritten because of the new
factors and changed conditions which have had to be taken into
account. But it is sad to note that, in checking the original text, it
has only rarely been possible to say ' this is no longer a problem,'
for the usual comment has been that ' this problem has acquired
a new form of expression.'

Antisemitism is the oldest and most comprehensive of modern
political neuroses. In writing of it, three aspects will come in for
treatment ; there are the psychological motives which make men
hate, and which link antisemitism to all other expressions of group
prejudice ; there is the particular history of relations between the
Jewish and non-Jewish worlds, which are peculiar to this particular
problem, but which explain why Jews have been especially exposed
to prejudice and hatred ; and there is the extremely important fact
that antisemitism is a political weapon whose aim is the destruction
of responsible political judgement, the imposition of the Nazi or
fascist ' Fuehrer ' type of political leadership upon a people, and
the destruction of the democracy which we have slowly and
painfully built up in western Europe and elsewhere.

It is no accident that political antisemitism is anti-democratic.
It is, indeed, the most valuable and pervasive anti-democratic
weapon in the armoury of would-be National Socialists or Fascists.
It has this value for them that Hitler has made the world ' Jew-
conscious ' ; and that to call a thing ' Jewish ' is to arouse most
quickly an atmosphere of suspicion and distrust. In fact a confiden-

tial circular issued when the Nazis got into power to Nazi diplomatic and other officials abroad tells them always to label anything which is unfriendly to Germany as ' Jewish,' and to call ' Jewish ' anything which they wished to oppose. It was, of course, completely irrelevant whether Jews had anything to do with the matter or not. Thus the one thing which it is useless to attempt is the kind of apologetic or defence which hastens to explain carefully that this or that accusation is false or exaggerated, or that the Jewish community was not involved in this or that scandal. The antisemite is completely indifferent to the accuracy of his charge, so that defence can never keep up with this kind of attack. It requires only lack of scruple and a little imagination to invent a new one. It is surprising to see that even quite responsible political figures can sometimes stoop to the same trick. The Earl of Sandwich, in heading the opposition to British entry into the Common Market in the autumn of 1962, said that the entry was desired simply by merchants in the City of London ' whose origins were in Hamburg and Frankfurt.' The Frankfurt reference was obviously to the Rothschilds who came from that city about a hundred and fifty years ago. I have not troubled to guess to whom he referred in his first sneer. It obviously has nothing to do with serious argument whether the entry is good or bad.

If there is no precise defence against this kind of unscrupulous attack, it may be asked why so much of this book does discuss the history and character of the Jewish community. The answer is contained in the phrase used : *Hitler has made the world Jew-conscious.* The general answer to the Hitlerian picture is to give the real picture of the Jewish world and its relation to its neighbours, not to chase after his accusations, one by one, and deny them. For if we remain in ignorance of what the true story is, we are all the time liable to be caught by the innuendos and accusations. The Jews are an outstanding example of a minority, in that they have retained their identity through so many vicissitudes, and impinge on general history from so many angles and in so many continents and countries. In consequence odd facets of their story, odd incidents of their history, may so often be misunderstood or just unknown.

Jews are unhappily not the only group which has been subject to unjustified hostility ; and to understand this oldest and most pervasive expression of a widespread social evil is a help to understanding the same prejudice against people of a different colour, a different religion, a different social stratum. Because so much of it stems from a bygone age, it helps also to remind us that humanity has a long memory, and that men may be heirs to ancient enmities of whose origins they are themselves unaware.

The Oxford Dictionary defines the verb *prejudge* as ' to pass judgement, or pronounce sentence on, before trial, or without proper enquiry ; hence to judge (a person, cause, opinion, action, etc.) prematurely and without due consideration.' The definition is important, because it would be prejudice to decide in advance that no group could at any time be so damaging to another group that the hostility they aroused was unmerited and simply an expression of prejudice. There is a limit to the extent to which an established group can be expected to accept the transformation of its life by a minority, either an existing minority to which a new relationship has developed, or a new minority entering in. A determination to resist an innovation is not always ' prejudice.' We shall therefore, as this study proceeds, keep looking at the total situation in which group hostility to the Jews—antisemitism— manifested itself, before we can say that in this or that case it was group prejudice.

Nevertheless, prejudice is always dangerous. It is dangerous when it is individual and unorganised. For it blinds men to realities, and substitutes figments of their imagination. Its existence nearly always discloses a real problem, but the solution which prejudice proposes is scarcely ever the right one. Prejudice has always existed ever since men met each other and found that they were unlike. But Nazism and Fascism in our own day have taught us how many political ambitions can be satisfied, how many subconscious urges can be apparently alleviated, by the organising of prejudice on a national scale, and by sanctifying it with a gaggle of political *clichés*.

It has not been easy to arrange the order in which to present the material of this book. For the Jewish community attacked today is not the same as the Jewish community attacked by the Nazis after the First World War; and that Jewish community is itself different from the community which lay behind the beginnings of political antisemitism in the 19th century.

Modern antisemitism is a by-product of the vast electorates created by 19th-century democracy. Of course there was malice and hatred earlier, but it manifested itself in different ways. The anti-semitism of the 19th century depended for its efficacy on the human characteristic which likes to lay blame on a scapegoat, which prefers the short cuts of group prejudice to the hard road of under-standing. It was particularly effective in misleading the electorates of Europe in the first generations of their voting power. The book therefore begins with an analysis of group prejudice, and then goes on to recount its effective use in Germany, France, Austria-Hungary and Russia before the First World War. The Russian case is pin-pointed by a chapter on the Protocols of the Elders of Zion, a production of the Russian bureaucracy at the beginning of the 20th century.

Because all the cases quoted rested in large measure on suspicions, fears and enmities already aroused, and sometimes centuries old, there follows a chapter, *The Christian Roots of Antisemitism*, which traces antisemitism to its origin and distinguishes it from other group prejudices.

Russian antisemitism profoundly modified the structure of the Jewish people, by driving millions of Jews out of Russia to the United States and the rest of the world ; and it was on this new pattern of the Jewish people that the antisemitism of the Nazis and the inter-war years was vented. There follows then a chapter on *The Jewish World since* 1881, when the Russian exodus began.

The next two chapters deal with the antisemitism of the Nazis, first when they were openly in power, from 1933 to 1945, then when they were the secret influence and inspiration behind the scenes since 1945. They also, by their murder of some six million Jews—perhaps less than half the civilians whom they murdered in cold blood and who were not civilian victims of shelling or bombing —profoundly altered the demography of the Jews. There follows then a chapter describing contemporary Jewry. Jews today have to meet a new problem of group relations : the attitude of the Arab states to Israel, a problem which differs from the historic pattern of prejudice in that, beneath the hysteria and untruths of the propaganda of the Arabs and their European supporters, lies a real problem which demands a real solution.

But in the final example of antisemitism, we return in its simplest form to the examples of Chapter III, the unscrupulous exploitation of group prejudice in the use of Jews as a scapegoat in the Soviet Union.

In the first edition of the book the final chapter was called *The Elimination of Antisemitism*. As a reminder that this is only one of the examples of prejudice which we have currently to combat, and that its *political* manifestation is the present particular danger, the final chapter is called *The Sterilization of Prejudice*, a necessary step towards the more long-term goal of elimination by education and understanding.

In the preparation of the original edition, the Wiener Library, with its unique archives of the Nazi period, and its understanding of the problem elsewhere, gave the most generous assistance. The same is true of the present edition.

I

GROUP PREJUDICE TODAY

ALL THROUGH THE world men and societies are experiencing the tensions of an age of unrest. Two world wars in one generation have shattered any feeling of stability and security which may have existed in the past. They have destroyed the traditional values and disciplines which men once respected. Material developments and the possibilities inherent in scientific discovery have created for some favoured nations societies of unprecedented affluence ; but they have likewise undermined the ancient fatalisms of the under-privileged millions in the poorer countries and continents. Because of the breakdown of established barriers consequent upon the two world wars, all the imperfections and injustices of the past are clamouring simultaneously for redress or resolution. Because of the wealth which men see other men enjoy, all the dreams and potentialities of the future are demanding immediate attention.

It would be difficult enough to cope with all these issues at the same time if it were possible to examine each of them dispassion-ately, and to accept with equanimity the solution which reason and the facts of each case proposed. But human nature does not accept change so rationally and easily, whether it be a privileged position which has to be surrendered, or a long and patient period of travail which lies between men and some good object they desire. Everywhere it is easy for prejudice to enter in, to deny justice to a weaker party, to lay blame on other shoulders, or to justify the snatching of all in impatience at the delay it would involve to await an equable division.

Many of our urgent problems we have inherited from the past, and they are none of our own making. *Apartheid* in South Africa and segregation in the United States are consequences of an attitude to the African, which in 20th-century America goes back to the beginning of slavery in the West Indies or the southern States some three centuries ago, and in South Africa goes back even further to the original Dutch pioneers with their fierce Biblical fundamentalism and their conviction that the children of Ham, son of Noah, were divinely doomed to perpetual servitude. Wrong begets wrong, whether it be the wrong of material selfishness which led to the importation of African slaves, or wrong ideas and religious beliefs which denied the basic equality of black and white before God. In France and Algeria the terrorism of the OAS sought to justify itself today by the inequalities of the contributions of Frenchmen and Algerians to the French Algeria of yesterday, without reference to the changed climate of the present or the injustices of the past. Men remember for many generations the wrongs they have suffered; the wrongs they or their forbears inflicted they quickly forget.

There are also problems which we have not inherited from the past, but have created for ourselves by our scientific discoveries, by the progress in health or education which has been achieved in this century, and by the interchange of ideas which modern inventions have made possible. If the West has discovered that it is easier to acquire than to surrender an empire, Africa and the East are finding that political independence does not provide an immediate solution for every problem. It is easier and more popular to denounce ' Communism,' ' Colonialism ' and ' Imperialism,' even when these have nothing whatever to do with the issue. It is not only the new sovereign states which have grown up since 1945 which are beset by new problems. The democracies and the Communist *bloc* alike are beset by problems which existing formulas will not solve ; and both alike allow prejudice to complicate the issue. Faced by demands for cheaper medical services American medical associations are defending themselves by calling the British Health Service a form of Communism ; faced by the complex difficulties of large-scale centralised industries, the Soviet Union is trying to pretend that it is Jews who fail, and so rediscovers the convenience of Jews as scapegoats for a common evil.

In addition to the general problems of the Age, almost every country has its own particular problem into which group prejudice has been injected. In Britain the last decade has seen an immense increase of immigrants from the West Indies and Pakistan who are providing a number of real social problems, complicated and embittered by differences of colour, and by the fact that colour prejudice is never far below the surface in the British mind. The Far East has many different forms of the political, social and economic complications created by Chinese immigrants during the period when its ancient societies formed part of European empires. Every kind of religious, ethnic and social minority complicates existence in the vast Indian subcontinent and its two sovereign governments. There are few parts of the world in which some social malaise is not made more insoluble by our readiness to judge before we know the facts, and to decide before we have discovered what it is right and reasonable to do. Nations differ, but men and women are basically the same.

One might add that ' they have always been the same,' and there are people who reply to every subject which requires a little thought that ' you can't change human nature.' This is no answer to any problem ;   for human *nature* is so elastic a concept that it covers the widest possible variety of human *conduct*. But what is even more important, if we are to consider the practical issues which face us in the contemporary situation, is that whatever be true about human nature, human societies undoubtedly do change. A new factor with which we are faced today is the enormous power at the disposal of political executives and their instruments. The kind of rebellion or resistance to authority which was possible to our ancestors is not possible to their descendants over the greater part of the world today. It is therefore of immensely increased import- ance that the citizenry of a country reach that stage of political maturity where it can prevent wrong situations from emerging while it is still in a position to do so. That is why the institution of regular and properly held elections to a parliament which controls the executive is the most important of all the hard won victories of democracy and why the achievement of a comparable authority is the target towards which the many new political sovereignties of today will, one hopes, set their sights.

The evidence put before the court at the trial of Adolf Eichmann in Israel in 1961 emphasises the importance of the whole problem for *ordinary* citizens. It would be so much easier if one were able to say : ' But Eichmann and men like him were mad.' All over the world we could then all feel that we, and our country, were safe from any such terrible explosion of hatred and violence at the behest of our Government. But all the evidence is that Eichmann was as sane as any ordinary citizen. It is true that Adolf Hitler himself exhibited increasing signs of paranoia as his empire crashed around him. But Hitler was constitutionally elected to office in 1933 by the German people, and he did not execute his own policies. It is probable that his Jewish victims were little more, or even less, than half of the men, women, and children who perished in his gas chambers or were starved to death in his Concentration Camps. These human beings were collected, transported, deceived as to their destination, and then murdered in little more than three years, by the citizens of Germany and certain other countries while a great war was raging round them, and calling for all the services which the nation could muster.

Tens of thousands of men and women, armies of officials, transport desperately needed elsewhere, all these were mobilised for these terrible acts of mass murder. And of the human beings involved in their organisation very few would have been considered mentally unbalanced or insane by any normal medical examination. What is terrible about the mass murders ordered by sovereign states or dominant political parties today is that men and women will commit actions, when they are politically sanctioned, which they would turn from in horror if they were asked to commit them simply as individual human citizens.

Even then, something equally disturbing needs to be taken into account. It is said that of the Jewish victims a million were children and babies. Men and women like ourselves took these little ones, inflicted hideous sufferings of hunger, thirst, and fear upon them, and then murdered them in cold blood. They did so because they were told to do so by their Government. But it is still true that they could only do so because they had insulated themselves from feeling anything in common with their victims. These children did not, to them, appear identical with their own children. Something took the place of the innocence and defencelessness of childhood ; and that something was, in some form or other, created by group prejudice.

Events, comparable in quality if not in size, have been tragically common in this century, though more often at the behest of dominant political parties than on the orders of governments. But other governments, especially revolutionary governments, have been involved. The Bolshevik Revolution destroyed the professional classes in Russia because they were bourgeois. The revolution in Cuba was not bloodless. Terrible things were done in Ireland and

Cyprus before they reached independence. In the separation of India from Pakistan villagers killed each other, often though they were ancient neighbours, because some were ' Muslims ' and some were ' Hindus.' Frenchmen and Algerians have done the same in North Africa. Further south in the same continent there has been the Mau Mau terror against the whites, but in the Congo has also been black against black. The hideous tale is almost unending, and the violence increasingly appalling, not because of human nature but because of the new inventions put into men's hands.

The special features differ, but the lesson is the same, just as the danger is the same, for all : we need to understand, and so know how to control, that factor in our political thinking which sanctions such actions on the part of ordinary men and women. And part of the understanding will arise from awareness that we are being tempted to indulge in prejudice.

The prejudice with which this book deals is expressed when men visit on actual human beings, men, women and children, opinions which they hold of the whole group of which those individuals are thought to be part. Whatever their personal innocence, these humans become the scapegoats of a real or imagined group guilt. The book deals with the oldest and most universal victims of such prejudice, the Jewish people. It shows in their particular context the two elements which are essential to any exploitation of a scapegoat: the psychological needs which are satisfied by the impact of prejudice focused on a human group, and the manner in which the particular victim becomes the natural target of these needs by his history and his relationships. For both elements of the picture are essential. There is an old story that on an occasion when Hitler, not yet Chancellor of Germany, was laying the responsibility for all the ills on the Jews, a voice from the audience called out ' and the bicyclists.' In actual fact the Jews of Germany were just as innocent of responsibility for what Hitler was denouncing as the bicyclists. But in one case the innocence was obvious ; in the other the place of Jews in German life could be perverted, falsified, magnified and distorted, because of a particular history ; and, without that history, the distortions and downright falsifications would have been so glaringly obvious as to make the attempt to make them the scapegoat quite unconvincing. Anti-Jewish prejudice is thus both an individual evil, and an example of a general human weakness whose lessons are equally valuable in other fields.

In the matter of colour prejudice, there is also this similarity with antisemitism. In many fields the object of the prejudice may change his quality, or be held to have changed his quality. Today the Arab States lead the world in the shrill denunciation of ' colonialism ' and ' imperialism.' But these accusations are (in spite of Suez in 1956) largely inventions of the Arab States. They are not based on unchanging and unchangeable features of Arabs, Englishmen or Frenchmen. They depend on political needs in the Arab world or on reputed political activities in the West. They can change almost overnight. But if one is prejudiced against men of colour as such, or against Jews as such, then there is nothing that the victim can do. For the prejudice is against his existence itself, and against that in him which he can by no means change.

In saying that the prejudice is against ' that which he can by no means change,' I am distinguishing racial heredity from other human qualities. But no human group is unchanged by being the object of continuous prejudice in others. We are all affected by the behaviour of others towards us, even if its effects are not in the material sphere, but in the image of us in other people's minds. We shall not here be discussing the response of the inhabitants of Asia and Africa to the European concept of ' the nigger,' ' the Chink,' ' the Babu ' and so on. But we shall be considering the effects on members of the Jewish community of the hostile environment to which they have been exposed for so many centuries, effects which are both material and psychological. If there were no such effects it could only be because Jews had ceased to be human. But at this point it is well to remember the old witticism that ' Jews are just like other people only more so.' It was because Shakespeare realised this that the portrait of Shylock is so disturbing in *The Merchant of Venice*. The hideous story of Jewish martyrdom in Europe was only possible because medieval man and modern Nazi alike forgot that universal human quality in the Jew of which Shakespeare reminded his audience :

' I am a Jew. Hath not a Jew eyes ? Hath not a Jew hands, organs, dimensions, senses, affections, passions ? Fed with the same food, hurt with the same weapons, subject to the same diseases, healed by the same means, warmed and cooled by the same winter and summer, as a Christian is ? If you prick us, do we not bleed ? If you tickle us, do we not laugh ? If you poison us, do we not die ? And if you wrong us, shall we not revenge ? If we are like you in the rest, we will resemble you in that. If a Jew wrong a Christian, what is his humility ? Revenge. If a Christian wrong a Jew, what should his sufferance be by Christian example ? Why, revenge. The villainy you teach me, I will execute ; and it shall go hard but I will better the instruction ' (Act III, Sc. 1).

II

THE PSYCHOLOGY OF PREJUDICE

SOME TWENTY YEARS ago two organisations in Great Britain, the Society of Jews and Christians, and the Council of Christians and Jews, asked a group of psychologists and sociologists[1] to prepare them a report on the character of group prejudice, and almost simultaneously an American Symposium[2] on *The Jew in the Gentile World* appeared in which a similar group of American scholars presented a much fuller study of the same subject. Other studies have, of course, followed these pioneers, especially a series of volumes entitled *Studies in Prejudice* sponsored by the American Jewish Committee.[3] There is, then, adequate material to help us to under-

[1] The actual preparation of the report was entrusted to Dr. Charles S. Myers, late Principal of the National Institute of Industrial Psychology ; Dr. Morris Ginsberg, Professor of Sociology, University of London, London School of Economics ; Mr. Denys Harding, Lecturer in Psychology, University of Liverpool ; Dr. Alec Mace, Professor of Psychology, Birkbeck College, University of London ; Major Emmanuel Miller, of the Tavistock Clinic ; Major John Rickman, Editor of the British Journal of Medical Psychology ; Dr. R. H. Thouless, Head of the Teachers' Training Department, University of Cambridge ; Dr. Ranyard West, Department of Psychology, University of Edinburgh. I am grateful to this group for permission freely to make use of their report for the preparation of this section of the book, and a good deal of what follows, especially in the first section, is lifted bodily, or summarised, from their work. Most of the detailed studies of Group Prejudice seem to have appeared in the years 1935-1955. Technical language may have changed and refined itself since that time, but the studies in this and the following notes still seem to me the most important.

[2] The American study is edited by Dr. Isacque Graeber, formerly of the University of Paris, and Dr. Stuart Henderson Britt, Assistant Professor of Psychology, The George Washington University, in association with sixteen other psychologists and sociologists.

[3] *The Authoritarian Personality* : T. W. Adorno, Else Frenkel-Brunswik, Daniel J. Levinson and R. Nevitt Sanford. *Dynamics of Prejudice* : Bruno Bettelheim and Morris Janowitz. *Antisemitism and Emotional Disorder* : Nathan W. Ackerman and Marie Jahoda. *Rehearsal for Destruction* : Paul W. Massing. *Prophets of Deceit* : Leo Lowenthal and Norbert Guterman.

stand why the Jewish question has been so successfully exploited in modern political life and, at the same time, been the subject of so much exaggeration, anxiety and misunderstanding among normally reasonable people.

Fortunately the pattern of group relationships follows in large measure the pattern of individual relationships, so that it is possible to understand what happens between groups from our experience as individuals. We are all familiar with the range of emotional feelings which pass through the whole gamut from love to hate, with a neutral point of indifference in their graded path. In some cases we cannot say what it is that provokes these feelings, as for example when individuals fall in love at sight, or in the innate hostile attitude of a dog to a cat. But, fortunately for our present study, in other cases there is a rational explanation of these emotional feelings. For love and hate are closely associated with another individual or social range of feelings, those which pass from security to insecurity. The relevant point is that in many cases the feeling of insecurity is aroused by the presence of something unfamiliar, whether it be something wholly new, or something with which we are already in contact but in which we become aware of new qualities which we do not understand, or which we feel to be outside our control.

Towards this novelty men may express themselves in many ways. They may begin by curiosity. If their suspicions are not allayed by the results of their curiosity, then it is very likely that they will develop a feeling of anxiety and even fear for themselves. This is a situation which recurs again and again to poison industrial relations, when management introduces new methods, or when new potential workers appear in a locality. Then, simultaneously and proportionate to these feelings of insecurity, an attitude of suspicion, hatred and anger will be aroused against the novelty. It appears as a danger to be circumvented. That this is an almost inevitable and ' natural ' reaction we can see from the physical fact that our blood develops functionally anti-bodies to what is new and strange to it. In the case of our blood, once anti-bodies develop, the blood continues its normal activity and the danger is removed. The same may happen in various ways with regard to an individual or social novelty. If two individuals or groups are brought into contact with each other, and prove to be approximately equal in size and power, the result may be healthy competition accompanied by respect. If one proves definitely smaller or, even though more numerous, weaker than the other, then there may evolve an acceptable image of the master and employee relationship, with feelings of domination on one side and submission on the other. When such a situation is accepted by both sides, the social organism becomes again harmonious, as it was in this country when the ' peasant ' willingly accepted the superiority of the squire and the ' gentry'.

If any of these things happen it means that the ' minority ' has really ceased to be such. It has come to be incorporated in, or accepted by, the society to which it was once strange. But if the novelty continues to retain a separate identity, then the tendency is for the strange individual or group to continue to be regarded hostilely rather than co-operatively. Permanent differences in such things as language, race, religion, culture, dress or diet, can present obstacles, and signify differences in mental attitude, too deep and too unfavourable for friendly, sympathetic, communication. Isolation and rivalry or jealousy prove easier than intimate association and co-operation. The basic feeling of insecurity is still present, and the fear and anxiety of the majority are bound to be reflected in the minority. Then a typical minority situation emerges.

Once that has happened, new feelings come into play, based on the permanence of the minority and its distinctiveness, and new mechanisms of the human mind come into operation—feelings which can again be easily recognised in individual experience. The first of these is called by the psychologists *Projection*—the mechanism by which things in our own attitude and behaviour which we do not like, and do not wish to accept, are projected on to others. As a common example, one might cite that a quarrel is always the other man's fault. So a minority, which has not been harmoniously accepted, comes early to fulfil the function in the majority group of being blamed for things which the majority has done or suffered, and which offend its moral sense.

The moral sense develops early in social evolution. Rudiments of ' conviction of sin ' are to be observed even among our domestic-ated animals—e.g., the awareness of wrongdoing, the feeling of guilt towards its master, of a dog or horse. Among primitive peoples communal guilt or sin is regarded almost as a physical stain which conscience demands shall be removed. Prayers and sacrifices to the gods are not restricted to the desire for fertile crops or successful wars, but are also offered for ' purification ' from sin and forgiveness for wrongdoing. Among the ancient Jews arose the practice of removing the sins of the community by the high priestly transfer of them to the head of a scapegoat which was then led away into the wilderness, to be released there in an appropriate domain of evil spirits. The goat bore the stains formerly carried by the human community ; the fault or blame was laid on it.

In the course of the development of society throughout the world ' sin ' came also to be transferred by being projected on to a minority human group ; on whom, in a rather different sense and manner, the blame was laid for the misfortunes, failures or defects of the larger community, and for the famine, pestilence, political unrest, etc., with which the majority were supposed to be divinely visited. In early days the Christians suffered from this same ' projection ' in the Roman Empire. In a famous passage the Church Father, Tertullian, cries : ' If the Tiber overflows into the city, if the Nile does not flow into the countryside, if the heavens remain unmoved, if the earth quakes, if there is famine or pestilence, at once the cry goes up : " To the lions with the Christians ".' The minority group was held responsible. It was accordingly cruelly, even murderously, attacked ; and it came to be regarded as the majority's bitterest enemy. Hatred became an excuse for further suspicions, just as guilt became an excuse for further fears. Thus a minority group became hated not only because it was thought to display evil characteristics ; evil characteristics were further sought in it because it was hated. The most obvious example of this ' projection ' which is relevant to the thesis of this book is the common charge that ' the Jews ' have debauched public taste and entertainment. Doubtless public taste is poor, and there are some Jews among those who purvey it. But Jews can scarcely be responsible for the failure of the Churches and of public education to meet the cultural needs of today to improve our taste.

In addition to projection there is a second mechanism which the psychologists identify as *Displacement*. It affects alike individual and group relationships. In displacement we direct a pent-up emotion to a different object from its original target. We ' take it out on the dog ' usually because we fear the consequences of taking it out on its original cause—the government whose regulations irk us, the employer who refuses our request, the wife who burns the kippers. In the same way we blame a minority when things go wrong with us, if we cannot, or fear to, put them right ourselves. When these two mechanisms, projection and displacement, have come into play to embitter relations between two individuals or groups, there steps in a third to quiet our consciences on the subject—*Rationalisation*. We invent a justifiable and respectable reason for our true motives and feelings and, equally, a disreputable and discreditable reason for the activities of the minority. If a man beats us at business by being cleverer or harder working than we are, we do not like to admit this, and so first invent a discreditable reason for his success and, afterwards, feel a righteous justification for blaming him for succeeding.

All these feelings are equally applicable to individual or to group relationships because, in fact, once we are considering a minority in this light, it is treated as an individual in the very important sense that differences within the minority are not recognised. Antisemites never talk about ' Jews,' but always about ' *the* Jews.' All are treated as alike. If this is too glaringly absurd, then it will be insisted that any member of the minority who shows different characteristics is a rare exception. We all know the kind of remarks which begin with " some of my best friends are Jews but. . . ." But the picture which is drawn will not merely deal with the minority as though it were a single individual; it will also inevitably be a simplification, and so to some extent a caricature, of the supposed characteristics of the minority. It could not be otherwise, for a ' type ' cannot have too subtle and complicated characteristics, or it would cease to be useful as a type. We are in fact only doing with the minority the same thing that we constantly do with other things. If we mention a lawyer, a parson, a chorus girl, or even a house or a chair, it conveys a definite ' image ' of what we mean, based on a few clear-cut characteristics, even though they are almost certainly inaccurate about the particular specimen of the type we are referring to.

In actual fact in all human groups the variations within the group are bigger than its divergencies from other groups. It is a commonplace that ' Norwegians are tall', but statistically the variations in height among Norwegians themselves are greater than the difference between the average height of a Norwegian and that of any other normal human group. The same is true of the mental and moral characteristics of any minority. In fact they vary enormously. But once they become the subject of ' projection ' or ' displacement ' or ' rationalisation ' all members of the minority are assumed to have similar recognisable characteristics.

When the minority is actually not too dissimilar from the majority, and especially if it is not living a separate life segregated from the rest of the population, this already simplified picture will receive a further and serious distortion. *The virtues of the minority and its estimable members will be taken from it and attributed to the majority.* It is a natural human characteristic to identify ourselves with that which we admire. If we admire courage, and we are English, we like to hear stories of courageous Englishmen and, if we hear of a gallant incident, we are sure the hero of it is English. If we know he isn't we say: ' he might almost be an Englishman.' If we are good local patriots, we take pride in the famous men from our town or village. We feel they belong to us, and we share in their reflected glory. It is extraordinary to what lengths people will sometimes go to find a link between themselves and something or someone they admire. Relics with ' historical associations ' are eagerly sought after—the bed in which Queen Elizabeth slept, the table at which Queen Victoria had tea—and the man whose brother had once been gardener at a house in which the aunt of the popular idol of the moment had stayed for a night would probably find the relationship good enough to justify him in relating the entire incident at length to any audience rash enough to give him an opening.

In the same way when a member of a minority performs some action or exhibits some characteristic we admire, we think not of his membership of the minority, but of something else in him whereby we can link him to ourselves. His son was at the same school as our nephew; he was born in the same town as we were; and in any case he is at once 'English.' The period of the last war provided innumerable experiences of this phenomenon in the case of Jews. The press constantly published details of black-marketeers when the names were foreign or Jewish, because the ordinary reader could then feel that none of the shame of the offence fell on him. But if a Jew performed a meritorious action, or won a decoration, it was the rarest thing for the press to draw attention to his Jewishness. And if his name happened to be English he was never associated with the idea ' Jew ' at all. There was a Major Wigram, the inventor of battle drill, who was killed with guerillas in Italy; there was Harry Errington, a winner of the George Cross—but the press did not associate either of these two Jews with 'the Jews'. They were English heroes and all could be proud of them. In other words, when the minority cannot be automatically distinguished by the fact that it leads a completely segregated life, or is totally dissimilar physically from the majority, the picture drawn of its character and activities will be based wholly on those traits in the minority from which the majority wishes to dissociate itself, and will completely ignore all qualities of the opposite character.

This is the normal situation which any group has to face which wishes to retain its identity as a minority within a larger society. This does not, of course, mean that all the various psychological mechanisms described will continually be brought into play against it all the time. It will not be constantly punished by the ' projections' of the majority, traduced by their 'transferences', or ravaged by their 'rationalisations'. This is equally true of a group and of individual relations. But in both cases, when a situation arises in which it is comforting or convenient to call these psychological mechanisms into play, it will be on an identifiable ' stranger ' or minority that they will be most likely to be discharged.

What has been so far described is independent of the actual character and activities of the minority itself. Individual reactions to a ' stranger ' are based simply on his strangeness, and are un-affected by his virtues or vices. But this cannot be the whole story in anything as complex as the relations of two historical human groups. They do have actual group characteristics and, quite factually, these group characteristics may provoke pleasure or displeasure on the part of others with whom they come into contact. Those who remember the war will remember the trouble between the country folk and the ' Londoners ' in the period of mass evacuation. American troops in Britain, British troops abroad, will provide other examples. Today in many British cities the coloured immigrants from the Commonwealth are the most obvious illustration. Much rumour, exaggeration and invention can be built up on an actual substratum of real differences. And the same will be found to be true when we come to deal with the Jews as a minority.

There is yet one final factor to be considered. Where a majority-minority relationship is permanent, neither the majority nor the minority remain exactly as they were before. Both are affected by the strains and consequences of this specially charged relationship. The minority is, of course, the more deeply affected. So far as the majority is concerned, its attitude to a minority will be only one of the matters engaging its interests, and determining its character. But the behaviour to it of the majority has such a profound and all-embracing effect on the life of the minority, that it will be much more strongly affected by the nature of the minority-majority relationship. How completely a minority may change its previous character under this new influence is shown, for example, in the physical and mental deterioration of certain of the Red Indian tribes on the American and Canadian Reserves. So extreme a deterioration is, however, only likely to occur when the minority has abandoned every hope of ever recovering its former freedom or status, and has no inner resources wherewith to meet its new position. The negro slave must have felt as hopeless as the American Indian, but he saved himself from the latter's deterioration, long before the hope of emancipation appeared over the horizon, by the development of new qualities—gentleness, religious escapism, personal loyalty to his master—which he can scarcely have shown in his native Africa.

A minority which has not abandoned hope will make every effort to keep alive and to strengthen those elements on which its hope is based. It will develop pride in its own traditions; and this will often be offset by contempt for the culture of the majority which possesses the physical power over it ; it will concentrate on the field in which it feels itself superior, and develop a philosophy to support that superiority. At the same time, while this is fermenting in its inner life, it will tend to conceal it from members of the majority, and develop an attitude of compliance and submissiveness towards them. It will therefore scarcely escape from the charge of insincerity and obliquity ; and the majority will still feel the fear based on insecurity in its dealings with it, for it will feel that there is something there which it does not understand. So, in a typically vicious circle, the feelings on either side will be deepened and intensified. It is an example of what can be generally recognised in any sphere—school, home or factory—that excessive power on one side and excessive dependence on the other cause various kinds of deterioration to both parties.

In the case of the Jews it will easily be seen how completely they fill the rôle of a ' minority,' and how they have this characteristic, peculiar to themselves, that, outside Israel, they are everywhere a minority. Everywhere therefore they are subjected to the same possibilities of psychological reaction on the part of the majorities; and in consequence the typical picture of a Jewish minority drawn by the majority in one country is ' confirmed ' by the discovery that the picture in another country appears exactly the same. Of course there are common features in the Jewish character and tradition everywhere, but this confirmation of a caricature which inherently is based, not on Jewish characteristics, but on the way in which a majority draws a minority, makes it peculiarly difficult for the public in any country to see what really is the nature of its Jewish minority, and what actual problems, if any, are involved in its presence.

On the basis of the general examination in the previous pages of minorities as such, it is also possible to see why antisemitism can spread so suddenly, and why Hitler's technique was so successful. Hitler created a world-wide feeling of insecurity, and all the feelings associated with insecurity came into play. In such times the sense of danger causes a group to coalesce and close its ranks; and its fears make it look with suspicion on the outsider. In the times of prosperity and stability before 1914 the civilised world had shown a wide measure of toleration and capacity to absorb new elements. It had relatively easily digested the several million Jews who fled from Tsarist Russia between 1881 and 1914. Between 1933 and 1939 the situation had so changed that it could not digest the few hundred thousand Jews and others who sought refuge from Nazi persecution; and the old established minorities, not merely Jews, who had previously felt perfectly secure, suddenly found themselves isolated and mistrusted.

This, however, is not the whole story. Although the political antisemitic movement only dates from 1879, and its modern form from 1933, the problem of Jewish relations with the majorities among which they lived goes much farther back than that ; and the success with which modern antisemites have done their work would have been impossible without that long inheritance behind them.

When in times of prosperity conflicts such as those between a majority and a minority tend to disappear from the surface, they are not thereby dissolved or eliminated from the body politic, any more than the complex of an individual is rendered harmless by disappearing underground into his subconscious. Old pictures of Jewish behaviour, some religious, some social, some economic, still lingered in the memories of the peoples. Nor was it these pictures alone which aided the task of the antisemites. It has already been said that the dominance-submission relationship in individuals or groups alters their previous character on each side, usually for the worse. So past *attitudes* remained as much as past pictures, waiting to be resurrected at a touch.

These pictures and attitudes as between Jew and non-Jew are not only worldwide in extent, since the Jews are dispersed throughout the world, they are also profoundly ingrained into the mentalities of Jew and non-Jew since they may have arisen at any point in the almost forty generations of the dispersed life of Jewry as a group of scattered minorities. It is therefore quite Utopian to expect that they can be effectively dealt with in a few years simply by legislation or by uninformed goodwill. They will take time and patience to eradicate ; and this is all the more true because we have thus far been discussing prejudices which, except in extreme cases, can be identified, admitted and overcome by reasonable people. For it is absurd to pretend that ' people like ourselves ' are, on the one hand, immune from prejudice or, on the other, incapable of correcting it. But this is never the whole story when group attitudes and political activities are involved. There exists the type that is immune from argument : the prejudiced personality who has no intention of altering his views, or indeed capacity either to do so or even explain them reasonably. So far as this type is concerned the problem is not how to cure him, but how to render him innocuous.

It is rare that such a type comes to a position of national leadership, though the career of Hitler himself warns us that it is not impossible ; for Hitler was the typical irrational antisemite, who had made a conscious failure of his own life, and avoided facing the fact by blaming it all on 'the Jews,' a practice which we shall see later[1] he learned in pre-1914 Vienna. But the type who has been a failure in life, and who in consequence has a deep-seated and irrational hatred of the society in which he has failed, provides the majority of the rank and file as well as the lesser leadership of most antisemitic movements. American psychiatric studies in this field provide astonishing evidence of the total irrationality of men or women who become hate-filled bigots. There is no coherence or consistency in the views they profess of the objects of their hatred ; and it is more or less a matter of chance which minorities they select as the cause of their failure. It is only certain that it will be a minority, some group, or a member of some group, which can be regarded as weaker than themselves, though that fact they will not usually admit. They can get immense satisfaction out of inventing immeasurable power in the objects of their hatred, and so endowing themselves with tremendous courage in daring to express their

[1] Page 33.

hostility towards them. It may be negroes, it may be Roman
Catholics, it may be Jews. And, just as it may be one of many
different groups, so the reasons will be given in relation to the
prejudiced persons themselves, and not on the basis of any evidence
about the individuals or group selected. Their real qualities and
characteristics do not matter at all. If it is Jews, then for one of such
bigots, Jews are all capitalists. For another they are all Communists. For a third they are the secret controllers of the political
and economic life of his particular society or of the whole world. If
it is negroes on whom he fixes his hate, then it will most likely be for
a different set of reasons. They are lazy; they are biologically
inferior ; they are sexually uncontrolled and dangerous for any white
woman. They are determined to destroy the ' pure ' white by rape
and miscegenation. He will see another set of vices and dangers in
Roman Catholics, and one can be sure that somewhere in the list
of their vices will be the popular stereotype of ' the Jesuit,' or the
immense secret power of the Vatican and of the confessional.

It is a waste of time to argue with such characters. They alone
can cure themselves, or they must be cured by psychiatry rather
than argument. They provide a problem just because they provide
followers for the professional rabble-rouser, and because the
advertisement of their being given legal punishment and public
prohibition feeds their ego rather than deflates it. In a study of forty
such bigots who had selected Jews as the cause of their failure and
the object of their hatred, two American psychologists analyse the
world out of which their patients had come.[1] Its keynote is
insecurity. Even if the patient appears to have won considerable
success, and achieved a secure position for him or herself, closer
examination reveals a basic feeling of insecurity, a basic inability
to find any fixed moral standards in contemporary society, any
genuine religious beliefs, any inner peace. The authors admit that
these conclusions constitute a serious condemnation of American
competitive society, though they rightly remind the reader that this
is only one side of the picture. Its importance in the present context
is that it is a reminder that antisemitism, like other social maladies,

---

[1] *Antisemitism and Emotional Disorder* by N. W. Ackerman and M. Jahoda.
Harpers 1950. This is one of the studies sponsored by the American Jewish
Committee. Two other valuable American studies are : *Why Men Hate*, by
S. Tennenbaum, Jewish Book Guild of America, 1947, and *Christians and Jews :
A Psychoanalytic Study* by R. M. Loewenstein, International Universities Press,
1951.

cannot be cured in isolation from the society in which it manifests itself. It is not in the United States alone that these group prejudices are signs of social insecurity. The whole world feels insecure. On the other hand, it is foolish to say that we must wait until we have dealt with the fundamental disorder of our society before we tackle its specific diseases. The two go together, and must be tackled side by side. Every victory over prejudice is a step towards racial security and well-being ; every step towards a more stable and balanced society reduces the influence which a rabble-rouser can exercise over unstable personalities.

The foregoing is a reasonable generalisation. But, as we go on, we shall encounter situations in which there is a definite priority on one side or the other. In South Africa, for example, it is obvious that no minority, such as the Jews, can by its own action escape from a situation in which it could only further endanger the position of the coloured population by openly espousing their cause. If it did so in present circumstances it would merely provide the supporter of *Apartheid* with a glib argument that the opponents of this racial doctrine were tarred with whatever brush South African anti-semitism was currently using to attack the Jews. Probably Jews would be identified with Communists. In any case, the Jews would be endangered and the Africans would not benefit.

The same difficulties frustrate the goodwill of people in the Western world, Jews and others, who seek to remedy the sur-viving antisemitism in the Soviet Union which is described in Chapter XI. Their protests are to a large extent unavailing, because they are regarded by the Communists as merely a part of anti-Communist western propaganda. On the other hand, in any country which allows variety of political opinion and activity, the fact that antisemitic opinion is allowed expression is the authority for a direct counter-attack upon it. There may be argument as to the wisest policy to pursue in the counter-attack; but there is no reason to argue for delay until all other social evils are remedied.

III

JEWS AS POLITICAL SCAPEGOATS
(1879-1914)

THE POLITICAL CONFLICTS and opportunities of the 19th century
are responsible for the particular form which antisemitism takes
today. A large part of the political history of that century is made
up of the struggle, first of the middle class, then of the working class,
to secure parliamentary votes ; and of the parallel struggle of the
representatives whom they elected to secure effective control of the
government. In Britain the latter struggle had been won during the
previous century. The House of Commons had become master of
the political life of the country well before 1800, but only a very
small number of people were qualified to elect it, especially before
the great Reform Bill of 1832 abolished the ' Rotten Boroughs ' and
created an intelligible franchise. Previously they were selected by
the hazards of history, not by any special fitness to vote. Fifty
constituencies returned members though they had no electors at all,
and their owner simply nominated whom he would. One con-
stituency had actually disappeared under the sea ; another was a
ruined wall, survival of a medieval borough. Many had only a few
electors whose votes were at the disposal of the highest bidder. In
Europe the franchise, where it existed at all, was as narrow and as
uncertain ; and it was only towards the middle of the century that
real representation, regularly constituted, began to come into
existence. And even then the battle to secure control of the Government had still to be fought, and in nearly all of Asia and Africa, in
much of Latin America, as well as in central and eastern Europe,
had not been won before the Second World War, after which the
division of the world into rival blocs created a new picture.

The fact that European parliaments came into existence without
their being intended actually to control governments probably
explains why outside the United States and Great Britain the two

party system never took root. It was a natural development when an executive government had to be found from the elected representatives. But so long as the functions of a parliament were limited to those of a ' talking shop ' and stopped short of executive responsibility, it was more natural for men to fall into the many different groupings which corresponded more exactly to their individual interests.

The emergence of the middle class into the political arena was primarily due to the industrial revolution and to the creation of a new source of wealth and power in the products of industry. It was inevitable that the holders of this wealth should challenge the political authority of the older class whose wealth depended on the possession of land. For, owing to their different needs, industrialists made different demands on governments. The conflict over the Corn Laws in England was a good case of this. The landowners wanted high prices for their corn ; the industrialists wanted to keep costs down by cheap bread for their workers. On the European continent, where landowners were often semi-independent rulers, they were quite prepared to keep a multiplicity of small states, where each could charge tolls on goods transported across his frontiers. But industrialists wanted large areas with uniform laws and freedom of passage, to enable them to sell their goods as advantageously as possible.

The middle class was not only an industrial class ; in Europe at any rate it was also the class of the intellectuals. And if in England it was largely the industrial interests which compelled the Reform Bill of 1832, in Europe it was largely the intellectuals who caused the series of revolutions which marked the year 1848 in France, Germany, Austria and Hungary. Though these revolutions were all unsuccessful, yet from then onwards the democratic slogans which had first been heard in the French Revolution became part of the political life of Europe, and ideal conceptions of human equality, abstract questions of moral justice, and a general assault on privilege, jostled the increasingly complex demands of industry for the attention of governments and of parliaments.

During this period the electorate was growing in numbers. But it was not necessarily growing equally in education ; and political questions were becoming more and more complicated. These complications inevitably involved long and bitter conflict between rival groups with different interests ; and in consequence new techniques had to be evolved for securing the favour and votes of the electorate. Governments likewise needed new techniques for winning popular support. For even if a Sovereign, a Chancellor, or the President of a Council of Ministers might not be constitutionally dependent on his Parliament, it was much easier for him to rule if he could carry a majority of them with him. The success of the techniques discovered was not always proportional to their honesty or their relevance. In fact forgery, deception and red-herrings were discovered to be as capable of winning enthusiastic support, and to have as great vote-catching value, as honest expositions of policy or the intellectual enlightenment of electors.

Even in France, the oldest representative democracy in Europe, the electors could be so completely misled that in 1851 they voted enthusiastically for the abolition of their own hard won rights. In that year Louis Napoleon, nephew of the great Emperor, secured from the eight million voters of the country a majority of nearly seven million for the abolition of the Constitution, the degradation of Parliament, and the vesting of all power personally in himself. The history of political democracy is shorter, more unstable and more embarrassed than people realise.

This book is concerned with an equally striking but more comprehensive example of the capacity of European electorates to be deceived. There is no better example of this capacity than the 19th-century emergence and use of antisemitism as a political weapon. There had, of course, been feeling against the Jews among particular classes, or generally among the populace, for many centuries of European history. This will be examined in Chapter V. But it had tended to dwindle in the liberal and 'modern' atmosphere of the 19th century, with its contempt for the superstitions of the past. Where it had survived it was either among the more ignorant of the peasants, or among the more obstinate of those who stood to lose from the developments of the century—the old landowning aristocrats, and the clericals anxious to retain the privileged position of the Churches. They hated the entry of the Jews into their ' Christian ' society ; they hated the democratic, urban, commercial and secular civilisation in which the emancipated Jews found themselves at home. And they suddenly discovered that this feeling, rooted both in jealousy and in ancient prejudice, was a most convenient rallying point for those who, from the most diverse points of view, disliked the 19th century ; and that it was a most versatile and effective stick wherewith the conservatives might beat the progressives.

Political antisemitism had extremely little to do with the Jews as such, just as it had extremely little to do with the real reform of the many evils of the untrammelled industrialism of the century which the Jews were supposed to control or exemplify. It is necessary to be clear on this point. There *were* serious moral and social problems created by the rapid progress of industry and commerce; there *were* many spiritual and cultural values which were lost, or gravely compromised, by the headlong rush after wealth and material comfort which characterised the period. In addition, the sudden emancipation of the Jews in western Europe, and the situation of those Jews who still lived a medieval life in eastern Europe, *did* create real problems. But the political antisemitic movement has not to its record a single example of a serious attack upon any of these real problems ; in consequence, it has not to its credit any real analysis or understanding either of the Jewish position, or of the evils of the century. Of both it drew an imaginary picture for its own ends. In fact, just as the evils of the century were but a small part of its life, so the reference of the antisemites to actual and precise evils and their reform formed but a small part of their armoury ; and just as the Jews formed but a minute fraction of the middle classes, so actual Jewish conduct formed but a tiny part of their onslaught on ' the Jews.' The enemy was ' Liberalism,' ' industrialism,' ' secularism '—anything the reactionaries disliked ; and they found by experience that there was no better way of persuading the electors to dislike these things also than to label them ' Jewish.'

There was also a particular advantage in possessing so comprehensive a weapon in circumstances where both sides of the conflict were made up of alliances and coalitions between various groups. It provided the attackers with a cement to bind them together, in spite of great diversity of interest ; it enabled all the enemy to be lumped together under a single head, although they also, in fact, represented all sorts of groups and interests.

Finally a word should be said here about three of the four Jewries which form the background of this chapter. Russian Jewry needs special treatment, but in Germany and France were very small Jewish communities just over and just under one per cent of the general population respectively. In the old Austro-Hungarian empire the percentage was a little bigger, but the Jews were only one among many still larger minorities, Polish, Rumanian, southern Slav and so on. In France Jews had enjoyed citizenship since the French Revolution at the end of the eighteenth century. In Germany and Austria-Hungary it came later and more partially. But in all three countries the real problems, in which Jews were involved, were those of a new industrial and urban class coming into violent clash with the old landowning and peasant society which had prevailed for centuries, but which 19th-century developments shattered. In this new society Jews found every opportunity for advancement. It was urban, they were urban ; it was speculative and adventurous, so were they ; their concentration in the new fields was accentuated by the fact that many fields, open to others of a comparable standing in wealth or education, were closed to Jews in Germany and Austria-Hungary. Unless they were willing to be baptized, Jews were not welcome in the armed forces or the Civil Service. This meant that in the ' free ' professions of medicine and law, and the many branches of commerce, journalism and entertainment, Jews were numerous. But nowhere did statistics reveal that there was a special *Jewish* aspect of the problems involved in the new society thus created ; and nowhere was there an exceptional Jewish delinquency, though there was often an exceptional Jewish participation.

Much influential as well as popular journalism, for example, was in Jewish hands, and so was much popular entertainment, so that it was natural, indeed inevitable, that anyone attacking the influence of these professions in Central Europe seemed to be attacking Jews. The trouble was that he usually assumed that he was attacking *the* Jews, whereas Jews were as frequent as Christians among those who disliked the brashness, speculation and materialism of the century. For a large proportion of them remained devoutly attached to traditional orthodoxy, and saw in the new society only temptations to apostasy.

In Germany

The scene of the first successful political employment of 19th century antisemitism was the new German Empire created by Bismarck. The year was 1879. Germany had only just realised her unity. It had taken three wars—against Denmark, Austria and France—and all the skill, strategy and lack of scruple of Bismarck, to win this unity out of the kingdoms, dukedoms, principalities, free cities, and what not into which Germany was still divided even after Napoleon had unified, modernised, and co-ordinated the nine hundred odd ' states ' which existed at the beginning of the century. The conservatives in Germany were those who, in various forms and from various motives, wanted to retain many of these old, almost independent societies resting on land ownership and ancient rights ; and the progressives, of whom the most important section was the National Liberal Party, were the party of industry and the big cities, who saw no chance of development so long as the country was divided into so many separate units, each with its own legislation, its own control over expenditure, even its barriers against its neighbours. Industry required a larger field in which to manoeuvre ; raw materials and man power were not conveniently divided according to the innumerable frontiers which broke up the country. The progressives desired unity largely for the purposes of trade and business development ; but there was also a strong group of intellectuals who desired it in order that the German people might take its place among the peoples of Europe as a great cultural and political unit.

Bismarck also desired unity, but for the sake of the power of the House of Prussia. For many years the progressives and he worked amicably together. As Chancellor he was not dependent on a parliamentary majority, such as an English Prime Minister would need, for he held his power from above, from the German Emperor, not from below, from the elected representatives of the people ; and he even ruled without any parliamentary sanction for his budget for a period of four years. But it was convenient, and on a long view necessary, that his policy should command the support of a majority of the Parliament, and up to 1879 the progressive group had provided this. The weakness of this support was that his motives were not theirs. Though the success of his policy, and the resounding *éclat* of his three successive military victories had roused a great deal of patriotic fervour, their effect was bound to wear off in time. The business element among the progressives was ultimately more concerned with the development of what was known as ' Manchesterism,' the free trade, *laissez-faire* policy under which England had become astoundingly wealthy and the factory of the world. The idealist element among the progressives desired to establish in Germany the responsible, representative, parliamentary government which they admired at Westminster. But Bismarck and his

Sovereign, the aged William I, abhorred both Manchesterism and parliamentary democracy, and by 1879 the Chancellor felt strong enough to do without such dubious support. In consequence he set out to disrupt the progressives and destroy their influence.

Now that the Empire was unified and at peace, Bismarck had two immediate objectives. The first was to prevent the transfer of power from the Monarchy to the Parliament, and the second was to secure independent financial resources for the Imperial Chancery, which so far had been dependent on grants made by the separate states out of which the Empire was built up, or on allocations from the Parliament. The best source of this revenue he saw in the imposition of a tariff. In neither of these objects would the progressives help him, but both would be approved or, at least, accepted by two other groups, the various nationalist and conservative elements, and the Catholic elements grouped in the Centre Party. Unfortunately none of these were friendly to him.

Bismarck had demanded £200,000,000 from France after her defeat in 1870, and France had paid this huge indemnity—twice her total annual budget—in less than three years. This vast sum threw the German economy badly out of gear. There had been a short period of wild speculation, and then, in May 1873, an appalling crash. In this speculation many of the old landowning class had badly burnt their fingers, and naturally blamed the Government's alliance with the liberal industrialists and bankers for their own follies. And in addition they did not like the secularist, or idealist, or modernist atmosphere of the new Empire. More serious had been the conflict between Bismarck and the Catholics. In the German Empire which he had created Protestants outnumbered Catholics by about two to one. The centre of the Empire was Protestant Prussia, and the Catholic south and west were consequently inclined to foster separatist tendencies, and to regret the complete exclusion of Catholic Austria from German affairs. Fearing these inclinations, and disliking the political ferment among the Catholics which had followed the Vatican Council of 1870, Bismarck decided to call them to heel. In 1873 he launched a campaign of repressive legislation against them which had no parallel in a ' modern ' western European State. This attack—known as the *Kulturkampf*—lasted for several years, and brought the humiliating spectacle of a modern state persecuting and even imprisoning aged and respected bishops and priests for no more than loyalty to their religion. The Catholics were certainly not likely to be easily won to support the Chancellor.

Now it happened that, as one might expect since the Jews are largely occupied with commerce, there had been some spectacular Jewish bankruptcies in the crash of 1873 ; and it happened that among the prominent leaders of the National Liberal Party were two Jews, Eduard Lasker and Ludwig Bamberger ; and it happened that an important Catholic newspaper of the Rhineland was in the hands of a fanatical priest of the name of Augustus Rohling, who was convinced that the Jews were at the back of everything which at any moment he disliked.

Although there was no notorious event in 1879 to draw any special attention to the National Liberal Party, all of a sudden a nation-wide campaign of extraordinary violence swept Germany of which the burden was the identification of the Jews with the National Liberals, and the National Liberals with everything any good German would avoid.

The actual origins of the campaign have never been fully explored but there is little doubt that the mind behind it was the mind of Bismarck. It was not due to any hostility to Jews on the Chancellor's part. He had been helped in the critical years of his policy by a section of the Parliament in which there were some prominent Jews, of whom Lasker and Bamberger were fairly intimate personal friends ; and he had been able to finance the Austrian war by the aid of a Jewish banker, Bleichroder. But something had to be done to discredit the progressives and, as Bamberger himself says in his memories of Bismarck, it was typical of his method that, when a weapon came along which others had forged for him, he should not let go of it, but keep it in his arsenal to make use of at a convenient moment for the discomfiture of his enemy.'[1] Bismarck himself is reported to have said : ' I expressed my disapproval of it, but I did nothing more, as it was a most useful means of attacking the progressives', and this pleasant equivocation he communicated to those of his entourage who had relations with the press.

That the launching of an antisemitic campaign had in Bismarck's mind nothing to do with the Jews as such is shown by the facts that one of those whom he had invited to frame the imperial Constitution, which he was now determined to maintain against the progressives, was the converted Jew, Karl Rudolf Friedenthal ; that the intellectual founder of the Conservative Party to which he proposed

[1] Quoted in *Bismarck und die Juden*, Otto Johlinger, p. 61, cf. also p. 115.

to turn for support was another Jewish convert, Friedrich Julius Stahl ; and that the man whom he had chosen to be Minister of Justice in 1879 was a third, Emil von Friedberg. In fact nothing could more clearly show the nature of modern antisemitism than its first emergence. It was a political manoeuvre which found ' the Jews ' useful ammunition, but had no interest in them as Jews.

Having made this discovery, the German Conservatives proceeded to develop it vigorously. An Antisemitic League was founded, and the antisemites discovered a leader in a Lutheran Court Chaplain, Adolf Stoecker, creator of the Christian Social Workingmen's Union. It mattered nothing to the Conservatives that the reason for Stoecker's semi-socialist antisemitism was that ' the Jews ' were capitalists, for Stoecker himself sat in Parliament with the Conservatives ; and it did not disturb Stoecker that the Conservatives supported him because they felt that his tepid socialism would be an insurance against the more violent or ' Jewish ' form of the disease, represented by Marx and Lasalle. It was an adequate bond of union to regard ' Jews ' as the enemy. Antisemitism also helped to bring the second group whose support Bismarck desired to cultivate, the Roman Catholic Centre Party, into alliance with the Protestant Conservatives. For the *Kulturkampf* could now be represented as the work of Jewish-led Liberal secularists. Indeed Bismarck's lieutenant in executing his anti-Catholic decrees had been a Jewish lawyer, Heinrich von Friedberg. One could forget that he was the brother of the Minister of Justice, and that he had been converted many years previously to Christianity ; or, perhaps one remembered that he had become a Protestant and not a Roman Catholic.

It was altogether a most curious alliance, and it is not surprising that the one thing which it never seriously attempted to do was to produce a policy on the Jewish question. For on this it could never have reached agreement, since its propaganda on the subject was quite incoherent. To Stoecker and the Christian Socialists Jews were an economic class ; to Rohling and the Roman Catholics they were a religious group ; and to the great historian, Heinrich von Treitschke, and the Conservative intellectuals they were a race. Its real point of union was hostility not to Jewry but to the progressive ideas of liberalism ; it mattered little to Bismarck from which gunsite the enemy was discomfited.

If it did not produce a Jewish policy, the antisemitic movement certainly provided German politics during the fifteen years of its existence with an unexpected element of vulgarity, violence and vituperation, and in the dust storms it created the progressives disintegrated and their power disappeared. Germany had to wait until 1918 to make her first unsuccessful essays in parliamentary democracy and cabinet responsibility.

In Austria-Hungary

The same story was repeated in Austria-Hungary, with complications suited to the situation in the dual monarchy. Austria-Hungary was a ' ramshackle empire ' which included within its frontiers Germans in Austria and Bohemia (the Sudetens), Czechs in Bohemia and Moravia, Slovaks, Poles in Galicia, Hungarians, and various groups of southern Slavs. During the whole period of this story, the empire was ruled by a single Emperor, Franz Joseph, who ascended the throne in 1848 in the middle of the revolutions of that year, and died in 1916 in the middle of the war which removed ' Austria-Hungary ' from the map of Europe.

As in Germany, the developments of the middle of the 19th century brought an urban, middle-class, liberal, progressive party into prominence and power ; and it was, as in Germany, against this party that antisemitism was directed. But in much more complicated circumstances. The progressives wanted a modern, liberal, centralised state with responsible parliamentary government, an idea which cut not only across old prejudices, as in Germany, but also across the conflicting modern idea of nationalism. For the nationalities did not want a centralised state, which meant German dominance ; except, of course, the German nationality. But German conservatives did not want liberalism. Then Hungary wanted complete independence for Hungarians, but desired also to dominate her own minorities from other nationalities. So there the conservatives wanted centralisation, and the progressives federalism, or at least more generous treatment of the Slav and other minorities. And of course any of the partners might change places at any particular moment to conform to some particular figure in the dance of power. The President of the Council, like the German Chancellor, was responsible to his Emperor, not to Parliament, and the same President might, and did, secure all kinds of different groupings to support him, by adroit concessions to one side or the other.

In this conflicting medley antisemitism was a most useful card for the opponents of liberalism. They could agree to it for their own particular purposes, while interpreting it in their own particular way. And they had this additional advantage, that the share of Austrian Jews in developing modern capitalism in Austria was very substantial, and that the rapacity and speculation of early capitalist development, and its enormous profits—of which the aristocracy willingly took a large share—exposed it to legitimate attack.

The scene actually opens in France, where in 1878 a ' Christian ' financier, by name Bontoux, launched the *Union Générale* as a ' Christian ' bank designed to counter ' the international influence of the Jews'; which, in this case, meant the Rothschilds who had, in fact, passed the zenith of their political influence but were still immensely wealthy. The project was supported by many both of the highest nobility and of the Roman Catholic hierarchy. But it was not long before the shares of the Bank began to depreciate, and finally in 1882 it crashed owing to the speculations of Bontoux, and involved its exalted supporters in ruin. Although there was no evidence that it was more than the speculations of Bontoux which had caused the rapid fall in its shares and its subsequent failure, its victims were easily persuaded that it was Jewish envy and hostility which had led to the loss of their money. One of them was particularly determined to have her revenge. This was the Austrian Archduchess Maria Theresia, wife of the Comte de Chambord, pretender to the throne of France. She was already in contact with an Austrian colleague and counterpart of Bontoux, the Ritter von Zerboni di Sporetti. In 1881 she despatched him to Germany with instructions to study the technique and activities of the antisemitic movement there. He returned with a mass of literature and ideas. At the same time an Austrian prince of the Church persuaded the Imperial Government to appoint the leading, and most venomous, Roman Catholic antisemitic writer in Germany to a Regius Professorship at the University of Prague. This man was Augustus Rohling, who made a speciality of denouncing, not the political or financial activities of 19th-century Jews, but the religious pronouncements of the Talmud. He was in no way restrained by an almost total ignorance of Hebrew since, in fact, he did no more than rehash the contents of an immense anti-Jewish work of the early 18th century, the *Judaism Revealed* of Johann Andreas Eisenmenger.

The stage was thus set for an alliance between clericals and

Conservatives on the familiar model, and it was precisely the support of these groups that the President of the Council at the time desired. With memories of the project of Bontoux they proclaimed their purpose to be the rescue of the soil of Austria from Jewish financiers, and this rallying cry served also to bring in the Catholic Christian Socialists, a party very similar to the Protestant Christian Socialists who formed the backbone of the antisemitic movement in Germany. From Austria Zerboni extended his activities to Hungary, where he was already in contact with a Hungarian Member of Parliament, Geza von Onody. It was in Hungary that the first actual battle was fought, a battle which was to strike the keynote of the particular character of political antisemitism in the Austro-Hungarian Empire. The antisemites planned to do no less than revive the medieval accusation that Jews practised ritual murder in order to get Christian blood for their Passover bread. It was a curiously roundabout way of attacking a 19th-century liberal, secularist and industrialist section of the population, but it seemed at first that it was going to be successful.

On April 1, 1882, four days before the Jewish Passover, Esther Solymossi, a girl living in Tisza Eszlar, the town which Geza von Onody represented, disappeared. Onody at once proclaimed that the Jews had murdered her for ritual purposes, and had the beadle of the Jewish synagogue arrested. His two children—aged five and fourteen—were coached with a story of the guilt of their father which they told the magistrates. Unfortunately for Onody and his friends they had been careless on details. The children reported what they had seen through keyholes which could not be seen through, and so on. The trial looked like being a fiasco, especially as no evidence could be produced that Esther had been murdered at all ; she had simply disappeared. However the fates appeared to be on the side of Onody, for shortly afterwards the body of a girl was found in the river, and the matter at once came to life again—there were by this time a considerable number of Jews in prison on Onody's denunciation. Medical evidence showed that the girl was several years older than Esther, and her body also showed no signs of having been stabbed or bled to death. Nevertheless, the trial was proceeded with, and the whole country kept in a state of agitation for some months. It was more than a year before the absurdity of the whole matter was publicly exposed by the withdrawal of the Crown Prosecutor when presented with the actual evidence ; and during all that time the unfortunate Jews were in prison. The final exposure discredited antisemitism in Hungary, but in the meantime an oil painting of the ' murdered ' girl was being publicly exhibited at antisemitic meetings in Germany, and attracting much attention and sympathy.

While the affair made the antisemites ludicrous in Hungary, the behaviour of Professor Rohling was making them dangerous in Austria. The Professor was furious at the acquittal of the " murderers " of Esther Solymossi, and whenever any occasion offered he demanded to be heard on oath giving proof that the Jews committed murder for ritual purposes. Austrian magistrates, however, were largely men of enlightened minds ; and as none could be found anxious to assist the Professor to perjure himself, he was compelled to unburden himself by publishing his views in books and pamphlets, and especially by reissuing the work which had originally brought him into prominence—*The Talmud Jew*. This was a hair-raising collection of mistranslations and inventions, most of which he owed to Eisenmenger and other predecessors. (Actually when he was finally brought to book he appeared unable to translate the simplest Talmudic text himself). Rohling's *Talmud Jew* kept the ritual murder accusation alive, and the next move made by the conservatives was interesting. Out of the Tisza Eszlar affair they tried to create an antisemitic party among the Socialists in order to secure a united ' Christian ' front of all classes. Relying on the fact that Austrian workers were to a considerable extent both ignorant and devout, they employed a paid agitator in the industrial suburbs of Vienna to stir up antisemitism among the working classes, on the grounds that rich Jewish capitalists had secured the acquittal of their co-religionists from the accusation that they had murdered a poor Christian girl. For some months it looked as though they would succeed. It is the only case during the whole period in which the Socialist party of any country came near to falling into the trap of believing that ' the Jews ' were the enemy which they should be fighting. But by the courageous intervention of Dr. J. Bloch, the Jewish rabbi in the chosen suburbs, the attempt failed and was not repeated. It is worth noting that August Bebel, the great German leader of the Social-Democratic Party, once said that ' Antisemitism is the Socialism of fools.'

The Conservatives then turned to the small traders, who proved more amenable ; for the Jewish pedlar, the big Jewish shop and Jewish capitalist industry could all easily be represented as the cause of their poverty and decline. The peasant also listened, for during the 80's and 90's the price of wheat fell, and this could be placed to the debit of the Jewish corn-merchants instead of to its real—but remote—cause, the flooding of the world market with Canadian wheat. Since both classes were extremely ' religious ' a suitable mixture of ritual murder and Rohling's *Talmud Jew* fell on fruitful soil. In fact it stirred up feelings so violently that the Conservative leader, Count Belcredi, was summoned by the Vienna police for seeking to provoke a breach of the peace. Belcredi was acquitted on the evidence of Rohling—the sworn depositions of the Regius Professor of Hebrew of the University of Prague were at last heard in court.

This acquittal had an unexpected effect. The Jews of Vienna were not particularly pious ; they were essentially a middle-class, cultured and emancipated community ; and they were completely dumbfounded by the trial and the acquittal. Ignorant of the Talmud themselves, they could not believe that a Regius Professor, who was also a Canon of the Church, could have deliberately given false evidence on oath. They felt themselves compelled to believe that the Talmud *did* contain the awful sentiments and intentions which Rohling attributed to it, and they did not know how to meet the situation. The chief rabbi of Vienna issued a colourless denial, but it had little effect. The Talmud, as interpreted by Rohling, held the stage ; and this success of the religious line of attack on the secularist, liberal Jews of Vienna determined the character of Austrian antisemitism for the next ten years. It took two years to bring Rohling himself to book, but it was finally done successfully by the same Viennese rabbi, Dr. J. Bloch, who had prevented Austrian Socialists from adopting antisemitism. He published such libellous articles on Rohling that he compelled the Professor to bring him to court. But on the day previous to the trial Rohling withdrew the charge, accepted a heavy penalty for costs, and thereby admitted the falsity of his statements. But the accusation persisted, and all kinds of ritual murder accusations were made in various parts of Austria for years afterwards, in spite of the fact that, every time a case came to court, the charge was dismissed.

During the period from 1880 to 1890 the Government was supported by a majority of the conservative nationalist groups together with a large proportion of the clerical elements ; and antisemitism was mainly used as an attack on the opposition liberal papers which were largely the product of Jewish journalists. But in 1890 a new coalition including the liberals was formed, and the nationalist and clerical groups changed the nature of their antisemitic propaganda in consequence. In fact, as in Germany, a definite party using the title 'Antisemitic Party' came into being. It was made up of the more intransigent elements of the nationalists led by Georg v. Schoenerer, whose pan-Germanism anticipated that of Hitler, together with the Christian-Socialist (i.e. conservative) element of the clericals. Its leaders were Prince Lois von Liechtenstein and Dr. Karl Lueger. In 1895, on the eve of the elections, it actually secured the papal benediction on its policy and its newspapers, to the great indignation of a number of the more moderate and more far-seeing sections of the Catholic hierarchy in the country.

In the national Parliament the antisemites failed to carry a majority and they decided to try to carry the elections for the municipal council of Vienna. In this they were so successful that they won two-thirds of the seats. In spite of the indignation of the Emperor, Dr. Lueger became Burgomaster of Vienna, a post he held for fourteen years; and it was during the time of his mayoralty, and while antisemitism was one of the main planks of the Viennese elections, that the young Austrian, Adolf Hitler, came to Vienna and formed his opinion on the Jewish question. But the irony of the situation is that what was merely an election device for Lueger became a passionate conviction for his pupil. The former was perfectly prepared to befriend, and to be friendly with, Jews in private while he denounced them on every occasion in public. His antisemitism was an openly anti-liberal platform device. His pupil really set out to destroy physically those whom his master so constantly taught him to regard as the most dangerous enemies of the German people.

In France

The majority of the countries of western Europe escaped an attack of the disease of antisemitism. In Scandinavia, Spain, Portugal and Italy, Jews were so few that they would scarcely have provided the minimum peg necessary for a political campaign based on their supposed iniquities or influence. In Great Britain there was a momentary danger when many members of the Jewish community swung over to support the Conservative Party at the time when Disraeli, as Conservative Prime Minister, was preparing for the negotiations about the future of the Balkans which led up to the Treaty of Berlin in 1878. The Liberals, whom Jews usually supported, sided with Russia against Turkey ; and Russia was the great oppressor of eastern European Jewry. Disraeli supported Turkey, who had traditionally been kindly towards her Jews. Even men like Gladstone, and other Liberal leaders, spoke rashly of Jews considering their own interests rather than the interests of England. But the success of Disraeli in bringing back from Berlin ' peace with honour ' put an end to the danger, and made the emergence of antisemitism as an English political weapon inconceivable. Even apart from the general respect in which Disraeli came to be held, and which the leaders of the Jewish community already enjoyed, there is no evidence that the British at the time could have been persuaded that they were in any danger from their well-assimilated Jewish fellow-citizens. It is true that the Parliamentary battle to allow Jews to enter either House was long drawn-out. But its length was not due to popular opposition or to public feeling, but to the innate conservatism of British institutions and to the dislike which even progressive-minded Englishmen feel towards the modification of any formula which has the sanction of long tradition—in this case, the Parliamentary Oath of Allegiance taken ' on the true faith of a Christian.' It is more remarkable that antisemitism did not emerge into the political arena in either Holland or Belgium ; for in the former country especially Jews were a prosperous and prominent community, and the relatively even division of the country between Catholics and Protestants might have seemed to offer a favourable breeding ground for its use against one side or the other, especially in view of the part which the two Churches played in the movement across the Rhine in Germany.

In France, however, there was a period of violent antisemitism at a moment when the main fires in Germany and Austria were dying down.

The Third French Republic came into existence after the defeat of Napoleon by Prussia in 1870. Military defeat was followed, especially in Paris, by a period of revolutionary disorder which was suppressed with ruthless severity. The new leaders were nationalist, conservative, and not very republican ; the influence of monarchist and clerical enemies of the republican form of government was strong among these, and it was only gradually that France assumed a more liberal and bourgeois appearance. But, once the monarchist element was defeated, the real battlefield emerged as a conflict between the clericals and the secularists, especially in the field of education. Napoleon III had encouraged religious control of education, and during his rule the Church in France regained much of the ground which it had lost since the French Revolution. Many of the best schools were in the hands of the religious Orders, especially of the Jesuits. But the republican government was determined to obtain control of education and to destroy the political influence of the Church. The battle raged for many years, without a decisive victory on either side. But in 1892 a terrific financial scandal shook the stability of the republicans. The scandal was connected with the French company interested in the digging of the Panama canal ; and in the crash it was proved that many of the highest officials and most prominent politicians of the anti-clerical parties had been dangerously compromised, or even involved in extremely shady transactions.

There was at this time a highly organised and very vociferous antisemitic movement led by an able and unscrupulous demagogue, Edouard Drumont. The movement had extensive support in both military and clerical circles, but it had not yet actually launched itself into direct political action or directly challenged the republican form of government. It had confined itself to agitation by meetings, by publications, and by its newspaper *La Libre Parole*. The situation in France was more difficult for the reactionaries than in Germany and Austria-Hungary. For the political influence of the old landed aristocracy had been almost completely eliminated by the Revolution of 1789. There was no group which still commanded a semi-feudal loyalty in the minds of the masses, and neither the Bourbon nor the Napoleonic claimants to the throne provided a good rallying ground. Even the Church had not the basic authority it had in Austria. It enjoyed considerable political power, but it had had to struggle to obtain it, and knew it was insecure. But in 1894, while the republicans were still weakened by the Panama revelations, there seemed to be delivered into their hands the perfect opportunity for an onslaught on the republic, an onslaught in which the clerical and reactionary elements could make full use of the valuable weapon of antisemitism, while keeping their own monarchist and clerical pretensions in the background.

The Army General Staff had known for some time that there was a leakage of secret documents, in which some officer with access to confidential information must be involved ; and in September 1894 a note (the *bordereau*) was discovered, giving a list of further documents which would be delivered to an attaché of the German Embassy. The note was declared by the staff officer in charge of the investigation to be in the handwriting of a certain Captain Alfred Dreyfus, and Dreyfus was an Alsatian Jew. He was arrested and, in spite of his protestations of innocence, condemned in December to military degradation and life imprisonment on Devil's Island. The fact of the condemnation of an officer for treason was published, but his name was not given until it was privately communicated by an officer concerned to Edouard Drumont, who immediately published that the traitor was a Jew. Certain details of the trial then leaked out and caused some of the family of Dreyfus, as well as certain left-wing politicians, to doubt whether Dreyfus was really guilty or, at any rate, whether the trial had been fairly conducted. A certain disquiet made itself felt, and the antisemites seized their opportunity—the Jews and their allies were attacking the Army.

This was a far better cause than the Monarchy or the Church for attracting immediate public sympathy. For the Army occupied a peculiar place of affection in the hearts of all Frenchmen, who looked to it to avenge the dishonour of the disastrous defeat of 1870 and the loss of Alsace and Lorraine. The Army was supposed to be above party politics, and its integrity, and the integrity of its leaders, were supposed to be above criticism and reproach. Therefore in casting doubts on the guilt of Dreyfus or on the fairness of his trial ' the Jews and their allies ' were impugning the honour of the Army in a most tender spot, the integrity of military justice, and of the Ministry of War and the General Staff.

It is not necessary to recount in all its details the extraordinary story of the *Affaire Dreyfus*. It is a story of forgery reinforced by forgery, of suicide and attempted judicial murder, of careers made and reputations broken, of extravagant coincidence and still more extravagant accusation. For five years French politics and social life were rent from top to bottom by the bitter feud between *dreyfusard* and *anti-dreyfusard*, and it was twelve years before the complete innocence of Captain Dreyfus was publicly admitted by both Chambers of the French Parliament and the Supreme Court of Appeal. But now, after France's tragic humiliation in 1940, it is well to remember to her honour that a question of abstract justice and of the rights of a single obscure individual could so move to its depths the heart and mind of a great nation.

The clericals and anti-republicans had staked everything on the *Affaire Dreyfus* and the finally proved innocence of the Jewish victim meant their complete downfall. Hence the bitterness with which they defended his guilt, and the trickery to which they descended to confute and overthrow his defenders. In their frantic manoeuvres they compromised the Army whose reputed integrity they had expected to use to compromise the Government. So far from vindicating its honour, they caused the disgrace and resignation of some of its highest officers. They compromised the Church, for though it was only the clerical politicians who took open part in the affair, Catholic sympathy was almost wholly on the side of the *anti-dreyfusards*. Above all they compromised the cause of religious education. Their fall brought about the complete separation of Church and State, the complete control of education by the State, the exile of all the religious Orders except those which consented to public registration and confined themselves to work among the sick and poor and, finally, the confiscation of Church property. Apart from a brief period of mainly emotional influence immediately after the first war, the clericals disappeared as a political factor from the remainder of the life of the Third Republic. They only regained the influence which they lost when they decided to make use of antisemitism after the downfall of the Republic and the creation of Vichy France under Marshal Philippe Petain.

In Russia

In western and central Europe the antisemitic parties betrayed their real intentions by the fact that they had no precise programme for doing anything about the Jews. The formal cancellation of Jewish citizenship might, indeed, stand in their ' Aims ' ; but they were far more concerned with general denunciations of the progressives than with any precise actions in the field of Jewish affairs. In Russia the situation was very different. There Jews were not citizens, and they were far more numerous than anywhere west of the Russian frontier. It had been the policy of the Government for a long period to treat them with every kind of administrative hostility. In the period 1772-1815 Russia had acquired an enormous Jewish population—it finally amounted to about two-thirds of all the Jews of the world—by extending her frontiers to the west and south, and so absorbing the Jewish populations of ancient Poland and of various territories bordering on the Black Sea.[1] In inner Russia Jews had never been allowed to dwell ; and, with small exceptions, this rule held good until the end of Tsardom in 1917. In the ' Pale of Settlement,' a group of provinces stretching from the Baltic to the Black Sea, they were allowed to reside, but even there they were restricted both in their economic occupations and their geographical distribution. The Tsars made no secret of their conviction that Jews were unwanted subjects. They made efforts— sometimes exceedingly brutal efforts—to convert them ; but these were not unnaturally a failure. Jews, on their side, had no desire to assimilate, and lived a life as completely separate as economic necessity permitted. They dressed differently, were differently organised, and spoke and wrote a different language from the peasants and proletariat among whom they lived.

Outside the authorities, the Russian Orthodox Church was their bitterest enemy, and such popular hostility as they encountered was usually stirred up by the teaching, action, or direct incitement of local clergy. As for the general population, they also had no political rights, little real freedom, and were themselves too depressed and restricted to take active steps against anyone except—if occasion arose—their oppressors.

Only a very small number of Russian Jews had any chance of rising in the social or economic scale. But the 19th century had penetrated even to Russia ; and a small number of Jewish financiers and speculators were among the pioneers of railways and other commercial developments, and had permission to live in Moscow or St. Petersburg in consequence. There was also a small group of professional men who had managed to get a university education, and they also were allowed to live in cities from which the bulk of the Jewish population was excluded.

---

[1] How Jews came to find themselves in these territories is part of the record of their history in the Middle Ages. They were largely the descendants of those who fled east and north out of the line of the Crusading armies of the 12th and 13th centuries, of those who fled from other persecutions during the later Middle Ages and of those who were attracted to the Kingdom of Poland by active kings who desired to encourage trade and industry among their subjects. The peasants were serfs ; the nobility were too proud to engage in such activities. The Jews filled the gap. In the Crimea and southern Russia Jews had been settled since Roman times. Their numbers were considerable by the 18th century, but what their proportion of the total was there are no statistics to show.

In Tsarist Russia there was no Parliament and, in consequence, there were no defined progressive parties in the western European sense. But there were inevitably influential groups which had been affected by political developments in the West, and which desired to replace the imperial autocracy, resting on a vast nominated bureaucracy, by a constitutional monarchy resting on a Parliamentary régime. At the end of the 19th century some of the younger Jews were to be found among the various progressive groups, but Jews lived so isolated a life that they had played little part in their formation earlier in the century. To encourage the population to attack the Jews could, therefore, only at moments of extreme tension serve to render the general progressive movement unpopular. Such a moment occurred when Alexander II was assassinated in 1881.

At the beginning of his reign Alexander II had himself believed in a prudently progressive policy, and in 1861 he had achieved the complete emancipation of the millions of serfs who still formed the bulk of the peasants. But when it came to taking the next logical step, and to completing the value of personal liberty by the grant of political liberty, he and his Administration drew back. The era of reforms came to an abrupt end, and the Government settled down to its traditional autocratic policy. In such a situation it was inevitable that parties which in the West would be open and constitutional, should be secret and revolutionary. It was the members of one such secret group which in 1881, after several failures, succeeded in assassinating the Tsar.

His son and successor, Alexander III, hated all liberal and democratic ideas, and was determined to maintain the autocracy of his ancestors unimpaired. In this he had the full support of his bureaucracy, led by his old tutor, Constantine Petrovich Pobyedonostsev. They were determined to defend their privileges by every means in their power ; but it did not help them to have to admit that there was such widespread and profound hatred of autocracy among the Tsar's own subjects that educated men and women were prepared to organise themselves secretly to assassinate their rulers. This was a moment in which, in imitation of the example of Germany and Austria, it was most useful to find a scapegoat and blame the Jews. Accordingly rumours circulated all through the south and west of the country, where the Jews lived, that it was the will of the Tsar that the murder of his father should be avenged on the Jewish people ; and the ignorant peasants were given to understand that they had licence to work their will (which turned to loot more than to massacre) during the Easter period. There is no doubt of the official inspiration of the pogroms which followed in many cities ; the naive statements of peasants on trial betrayed it, even had other evidence been lacking ; and, for the moment, it successfully deflected public attention from the underlying causes of the assassination.

During the next twenty years the Administration continually harried its Jewish subjects, not only because it was the tradition of reactionary Administrations so to do, but because it maintained the fiction that it was the Jewish element which was primarily responsible for the spread of liberal ideas in the empire. In fact this was completely untrue ; the centres of liberal and even revolutionary activity were to be found throughout the Russian universities—to which only the tiniest percentage of Jewish students were admitted —and in all Russian intellectual and professional circles—in which there were not half-a-dozen outstanding Jewish figures. But repression inevitably sent many young Jews into the rank and file of the revolutionaries; and a small group of them, of whom the chief was Leon Trotsky, joined the extreme revolutionary party, and shared their rise to power in October 1917.

In 1894 Alexander III was succeeded by his son, the last Tsar, Nicholas II. Nicholas was, perhaps, of a mild and kindly disposition but he was weak, obstinate and as determined as his father to preserve intact the autocratic government of his empire against the demands of progress. In consequence his reign was a succession of defeats, of concessions made too meagrely and too late, culminating in 1917 in his abdication and his murder the following year. The peculiar feature of the antisemitism of the Administration during his reign is that one of its main activities was to persuade the Tsar himself that his chief enemies were his Jewish subjects, that they were leagued against his person, his religion and his empire in a secret and determined world plot, and that only the most ruthless repression of the Jews would stamp out the liberal movement in the country.

A first step in the official propagation of this idea had been taken some decades previously, and it was possibly the fact that the same tactics had been employed for the ' education ' of the bureaucracy and especially the political police, that suggested the subsequent fabrications (which became famous throughout the world as *The*

Protocols of the Elders of Zion) for the ' education ' of the Tsar.[1]

In the middle of the 1860's, Jacob Brafman, a Jewish ' convert ' to Orthodox Christianity who had turned police spy, offered ' evidence ' to the reactionary Russian Governor of Vilna, Michael Muraviev, that there existed in the *Kahal*[2] a secret Jewish organisation with widespread ramifications and despotic power over all Jewish communities. For a consideration he promised to reveal its secrets, and published a book which was based on the actual minutes of the officially recognised Jewish Kahal of Minsk fifty years previously. For a *Kahal* is no more than the name of the Committee of Elders governing a Jewish community. But, in the manner of Rohling in the West, these minutes, both innocent and dull in themselves, were embellished with faked Talmudic quotations and elaborate inventions by which the Kahal of Minsk was made to appear merely the local branch of a world Jewish organisation whose centre was the recently founded philanthropic institution the *Alliance Israélite Universelle* of Paris. Brafman, however, achieved a triumph of which even Rohling did not dream. His *Book of the Kahal* was issued at the public expense and sent to all Government officials as a guide in their relations with the Jewish population. It was particularly circulated among the political section of the police.

Fifteen years later another man of Brafman's calibre, but this time not of Jewish origin, came to add fuel to the fire. Hippolyte Lutostansky first appears as an ex-Roman Catholic priest in the middle-western province of Kovno, unfrocked by the Church authorities for a picturesque variety of offences from embezzlement to rape. He then joined the Russian Orthodox Church and became a student at a religious academy. Though entirely ignorant of Hebrew he selected as his subjects the ritual murder accusation and the Talmud. Having composed a scurrilous work on these subjects he tried to blackmail the Jewish community into paying for it not to be published. When this failed, he printed it, and had a copy accepted by the future Tsar, Alexander III, and by the Chief of the

---

[1] See Chapter IV.

[2] The word *Kahal* merely means community organisation. Jews had possessed official *Kahals* until 1844 when they had been abolished and Jewish autonomy largely liquidated. It was the claim of Brafman that the Organisation had not disbanded and had far wider influence than was known to the Russian authorities. For this he produced no evidence which stood the light of critical examination.

political section of the police. This work also was circulated by the latter, at public expense, to all officers of his section throughout Russia.

When, therefore, at the beginning of his reign it seemed necessary to strengthen the conviction of Nicholas II that his Ministers were really attacking the nerve centre of liberal and revolutionary action in attacking the Jews, it is not surprising that the minds of the authorities should turn to the production of a new and fuller version of the works of Brafman and Lutostansky. Probably owing to the stress which had been laid on the supposed authority of the *Alliance Israélite Universelle*, the commission was entrusted to the Paris office of the Russian police. And it was there that, between 1895 and 1900, the *Protocols* were fabricated. The story of their fabrication will be told in the next Chapter, as a prelude to that of their distribution throughout the world. Here the Russian end of the story will be followed through. Almost every fact concerning their first appearance in Russia about 1900 is veiled in mystery, including even the first date of their publication as a printed work. But this occurred somewhere between 1901 and 1905, a period of increasingly vehement demand for the granting of political rights.

As always happens when constitutional demands meet no response, power and influence among those seeking reform had gone more and more to the extremists, and the assassination of officials had become a daily occurrence. The Tsar's uncle, the Grand Duke Sergius, Governor of Moscow, many of the Tsar's Ministers, and thousands of the hated political police perished by the hands of revolutionaries, many of whom made no attempt to escape. Then in 1905 the Russians suffered a humiliating defeat at the hands of the Japanese, and partly as a consequence of the loss of prestige following this defeat, and partly because of the steady increase of revolutionary violence, the Tsar in October issued a Constitution and summoned a Parliament (Duma) for the following year. In the conflict between the Administration and both the revolutionaries and the elected representatives, which dragged on through the remaining years of the empire, the former brought into being a pro-autocratic—Fascist as we would now say—organisation called *The League of the Russian People*, which replied with counter-violence alike to the violence of the assassins and the speeches of the constitutionalists. The pogroms against the Jews of 1905 and the following years were largely their work. The members of this patriotic League were often recruited from the hooligans of the slums, and were known as the ' Black Hundreds'. But the Tsar himself consented to be their patron and to wear their badge.

If the Tsar was prepared to go so far as to accept such an ' honour', there was good reason to hope that the work produced by the Paris office of the Russian police would be successful, and would bring about complete conviction in his mind as to the dangerous nature of Jewry. What happened to the document between 1900 and 1905 is unknown. Possibly the authorities who received it were themselves doubtful about its value ; possibly it was mislaid, possibly— but why continue? Anything may have happened. But in 1905 it was finally issued to the public and presented to the Tsar. Strangely enough, it had very little effect on the Russian situation. The Tsar read the *Protocols* but in the end did not believe them to be genuine ; and there is no evidence that copies circulated widely among the public, in spite of the book being re-issued several times.[1] The supreme effort of Russian antisemitism apparently fell flat. But, once they were brought to western Europe, the story is very different. Since 1919 they have been issued in innumerable editions in many languages, and have been one of the main weapons of Nazi antisemitism throughout the world.

[1] It is for this reason that it is so difficult today to establish precise details of dates of publication ; there are very few copies in existence inside or outside Russia. There is no mention of *The Protocols* in the standard work by Simon Dubnow on the Jews of Russia, published in 1916.

IV

THE PROTOCOLS OF THE ELDERS OF ZION

JACOB BRAFMAN HAD pointed to the *Alliance Israélite Universelle* of Paris as the centre of international Jewry : and the suggestion must have seemed reasonable to any Russian administrator who disliked the limelight which the charitable and educational work of the *Alliance* was constantly throwing on the unhappy situation of the Jews in Russia ; for it was foremost alike in asking for an amelioration of their lot and in helping the streams of unhappy refugees who were driven to seek refuge in western Europe or America. It was therefore in Paris that the political police determined to seek for further evidence of the sinister activities of Jewry, in order to convince the Tsar of the necessity of a policy of ruthless repression against his millions of Jewish subjects.

At the instruction of General Orgeyevsky, one of their leading officials, members of that organisation in Paris (where their task was to report on the activities of Russian emigrés and travellers) set to work to procure material. They were, however, not very competent historians, for the first result of their labours, entitled *The Mystery of Jewry*, was such a farrago of nonsense that when in 1895 General Orgeyevsky forwarded it to General Cherevin, Commander of the Imperial Guards, for communication to the Tsar, Cherevin decided to do nothing more than deposit it in the archives of the political police. Here it was found and examined by the Minister of the Interior, Peter Arkadyevich Stolypin (assassinated 1911), who wrote on it ' this kind of propaganda is wholly inadmissible to the government '—which is not only a tribute to his intelligence, but evidence that the intention of its creators and inspirers was that it *should* be used by the Government, as had been the works of Brafman and Lutostansky.

The Paris Office were, then, presumably, instructed to try again, and produce more satisfactory evidence. The rest of the story, which is the story of the production of the *Protocols*, is now fairly clear, though important details are still not widely known. For they are embodied in a book, *L'Apocalypse de Notre Temps*, by Henri Rollin, which was published only in the autumn of 1939, with the result that almost all the copies of it were seized by the Germans and destroyed on their entry into Paris in 1940. As to the statements on the subject made by the various editors of *The Protocols*, it is sufficient to observe that, while naturally all of them assert their Jewish origin, their many stories are so totally inconsistent, and some of them so frankly ridiculous, that they are of no value whatever in tracing the history of the document. This, however, is not important, since we can build up the story from other sources. The successor to General Orgeyevsky was General Rachkovsky, and they were sent by him to St. Petersburg some time between 1895 and 1901. Rollin makes it clear, however, that they were not composed in his office, but stolen, together with other documents, from the villa at Territet in Switzerland of a Russian doctor and political controversialist, E. de Cyon. The villa was burgled in 1897 by the agents of Rachkovsky on the orders of the Russian Finance Minister, Count Serge Julievich Witte. De Cyon, a Jew by birth and a convert to Roman Catholicism, was an ardent and dangerous opponent of Witte's policy which he regarded as fatal to the cause of autocracy and order in Russia ; and he had already attacked him in many writings. There are most interesting parallels between *The Protocols* and the work of de Cyon. One of his attacks took the form of plagiarising a denunciation by a French author, M. Gomel, of a French Finance Minister of the 18th century, Charles Alexandre de Callone. De Cyon simply changed the names ; and this was found in 1921 to have been just the technique used by the compiler of *The Protocols*. They were plagiarised from an obscure satire on Napoleon III, as we shall see below. Moreover the charge that *The Elders* were engaged in a subversive plot against ordered society was precisely the charge that de Cyon launched against Witte, and those portions of *The Protocols* which are not based on the satire on Napoleon correspond in large measure with projects of Witte which de Cyon opposed. It is therefore a convincing suggestion that the work was that of de Cyon, originally intended to be circulated as an attack on Witte. Once in the hands of Rachkovsky, relatively few alterations and additions would be needed to turn it into an exposure of ' the Jewish world authorities ' against whom evidence was required.

At first at any rate, *The Protocols* shared the fate of their predecessor. They failed to win acceptance, and they were not published. But copies apparently circulated, for there is evidence that various officials had them in their hands. Finally through the instrumentality of a provincial ' Marshal of Nobility ' of the Province of Tver in southern Russia, they came into the hands of a somewhat unstable and excitable mystic, Sergei Nilus. Nilus translated them into Russian from their original French and published them under the melodramatic heading of *Antichrist : a Near Political Possibility*, as appendix to the second edition of a mystical work *The Great in the Little*. Exactly what story was told to Nilus of their origin is obscure, though it is evident that he believed them to be absolutely genuine. But he gives no less than three separate and contradictory accounts of how they reached Russia, and one is left to conjecture. This much, however, is certain. He received them at a time when he was the centre of a Court intrigue in which they were likely to be of considerable use to him.

The superstitious susceptibilities of the Tsar Nicholas II and the Tsarina Alexandra, which were later revealed in their domination by Rasputin, were manifested from the beginning of their reign. In their early days an extraordinary Frenchman, Dr. Encausse, known under the name of Dr. Papus, and the leading European authority on esoteric mysticism and magic, founded a Martinist Lodge in St. Petersburg, of which the Tsar was the secret head. The Martinists were an order of Christian Masons founded by Martinez de Pasquale, a fervent disciple of Swedenborg, in memory of an obscure French philosopher, Claude de St. Martin. To the influence of Papus succeeded that of one whom he claimed as a disciple, M. Philippe. All those who knew him are agreed that Philippe was no charlatan, but a man with an extraordinary gift of healing and suggestion, to whose advice the Tsar and Tsarina willingly lent themselves. The Russian Court was the centre of continual and bitter intrigue, and the Dowager Tsarina and her sister-in-law, the Grand Duchess Elizabeth, wife of Sergius, the Governor of Moscow, were determined to find a strong Orthodox character to become confessor to the Tsar and counter the influence of these foreign 'charlatans'. Their choice fell on Sergei Nilus whose mystical book had much impressed them. He was brought to Court, and instructed to prepare a new edition and present it to the Tsar. It is in this edition that *The Protocols* appear and, as on this first appearance Freemasons are named as jointly responsible with the Jews for a world plot against Christendom in general and Russia in particular, it is not too far-fetched to suppose that Nilus was provided with the document by the Dowager Tsarina, the Archduchess or someone of their entourage who detested Masons, and that he was given a confused story of how they had been 'discovered'. For it was essential that he should believe them to be true. The reference to the Freemasons in this original version was, of course, directed against Dr. Papus and M. Philippe.

The plot failed, and Nilus never became confessor to the Tsar, but the important fact is that through some connection with this plot *The Protocols* appeared. The book is not really a collection of 'protocols'[1] at all, but rather a series of lectures supposed to be given by an ' Elder of Zion ' to people to whom he could reveal with complete frankness the Jewish plot for which the Elders were responsible, and the actual stage which they had at that moment reached. The many editors of *The Protocols* are as confused as to the identity of ' the Elders of Zion ' as they are on the subject of the origin of the document. They even differ as to the language in which the lectures were given.

On the background of a highly-coloured but yet recognisable description of the troubles at the end of the 19th century, particularly in Russia—widespread unrest, a general breakdown of hitherto accepted standards of conduct, wars and acts of terrorism, growing national debts, and in the background the rising power of ' international finance '—the lecturer draws a picture of all these events as being the outcome of a deliberately conceived Jewish plot, which was manipulating national states and societies with the sole intention of securing the domination of Jewry. The industrious authors may have thought they were painting the portrait of a good revolutionary, but they certainly made him no stylist and a very poor thinker ; for the lectures are verbose to a degree, and completely confused in their order. Moreover they have created the same confusion in the development of the plan of the plotters. In fact, though they are sufficiently alarming at first reading, it might be claimed that any plotters as muddled as the Elders could really

---

[1] According to the Oxford Dictionary the nearest meaning of Protocol would be ' a formal or official statement of a transaction or proceeding.'

be a danger only to themselves. At the same time, confused though they are, the story is unfolded with a wealth of apparently convincing detail ; and it is easy to see that men might sincerely believe that ' there must be something in them ' when they found one detail after another which appeared to them to give a possible interpretation of certain activities of Jews or Jewish groups at the time. It is this fact which gave *The Protocols* their tremendous vogue when they first came to western Europe and America at the end of the First World War.

It was a time when, for a brief moment, Jews seemed to be both prominent and powerful. By the Balfour Declaration of November 1917 the Zionists had secured a National Home in Palestine from the British Government ; the first leaders of the Bolsheviks were all commonly believed to be Jews, and a certain number of them actually were ; there had been Jewish leaders in the Communist *Putsches* in Germany and Hungary. But not only were nationalist Jews and revolutionary Jews apparently powerful, but ordinary Jewish citizens seemed more prominent than would be expected. Among the many unofficial delegations representing the most varied interests at the Versailles Peace Conference were Jewish delegations from U.S.A., Britain, France and Eastern Europe. An American Jew, Bernard Baruch, was believed to share with Colonel House the position of President Wilson's most confidential adviser. And so on. Moreover men had been thrown off their balance by the strain of four years of war, and by the mass of confusing problems of which the new world seemed to be composed. There was confusion and disorder on all sides and men were prepared to believe what in more sober moments would have been rejected ; there was a widespread fear of Communism ; the antisemitic movement of the previous thirty years had left memories. This passing prominence of the Jews re-awoke them. The widespread reception of *The Protocols* as genuine is not really surprising in view of all these facts.

The *Morning Post* of London sounded the first alarm in an article of August 7, 1917, which made the extraordinary statement that ' the Jews are a great nation, emphatically a nation, and *the able statecraft of their secret rulers* has kept them a nation through forty centuries of the world's history. In their hands lies the traditional knowledge of the whole earth, and *there are no State secrets of any nation but are shared also by the secret rulers of Jewry*." (My italics.)

In the turmoil and concentration of war the passage fell absolutely flat. The *Jewish Chronicle*, in a protest against the whole article, referred indeed to ' insidious, not to say incoherent, incitements ' but showed no special interest in the words I have italicised. The amazing statements that there had been a secret government in Israel since about 2000 B.C. (that is to say, several centuries before Moses), that this government still existed, and that *there are no State secrets of any nation but are shared also by these secret rulers*, apparently aroused no comment.

In the following year (1918) the documents which were believed to prove these contentions, *The Protocols of the Elders of Zion*, were extensively hawked around the Ministries and newspaper offices of western Europe by White Russians. Extracts from them were simultaneously distributed to English and French officers serving in the White Russian armies. Among the Russians in the same armies they had had a considerable effect, and the number of Jews who fell as victims to the fury of the soldiers of the anti-bolshevik forces in southern Russia ran into tens of thousands. But western Europe still refused to take them seriously.

At the end of 1919 the situation changed. In November a complete German translation was published by Captain Mueller v. Hausen, writing under the pseudonym of Gottfried zur Beek, and presented to the Princes of Europe in a dedication which implored them to take heed while there was yet time. In a lengthy introduction and a still longer closing comment the whole history of the Jews was reviewed, and their sinister influence on European history expounded—and it was emphasised that their tool and partner in crime was unquestionably the British Empire, and the vainglorious and arrogant British people. A couple of months later an English translation appeared, which completely endorsed the German view of the sinister rôle played by the Jews in European history, but naturally discovered the tool and ally of Jewry not in England but in Germany. Almost simultaneously lengthy extracts appeared in newspapers in France and the United States, soon to be followed by complete translations of the documents. A Polish edition was in existence at the beginning of 1920, and an Italian version followed later. Today it exists also in Spanish, in Arabic, in Turkish, and even in Japanese.

In February 1920 the *Morning Post* reviewed the English edition in a tone of serious alarm, recognising that the authenticity of the documents was not yet proved, but expressing the belief that at least they corresponded to the facts. In March a question was asked in the House of Commons as to the advisability of suppressing the documents on the ground that they were a malicious attempt to stir up anti-Jewish feeling *and to injure the Entente*. In May an anonymous correspondent in *The Times* of London pointed out that no review of the documents had appeared in that paper, and asked the agonising question whether England ' by straining every fibre of our national body, had escaped a " Pax Germanica " only to fall into a " Pax Judaica ".' In July the *Morning Post* devoted seventeen special articles to the subject, and subsequently republished them anonymously in book form, with an alarmist introduction by the Editor himself, under the title of *The Cause of World Unrest*.

Finally, however, in August 1921 *The Times* correspondent at Constantinople was able to produce conclusive evidence that they were a forgery. He obtained from a Russian refugee a coverless book which was subsequently identified as the *Dialogue aux Enfers entre Montesquieu et Machiavel*, and was, in fact, a satire on the ambitions of Napoleon III written by a French Radical lawyer, Maurice Joly (who was not a Jew). All that the authors of *The Protocols* had done was to substitute the ' Elders of Zion ' for Napoleon, and remake the material to suit their new purpose. Incidentally all strictures on the style and confusion of *The Protocols* fall on their authors, not on Joly. For the original is both brilliantly written and wittily conceived. The plot described by Joly is realistically and logically planned ; it is the forgers who have hopelessly bungled the admirable original. But as proof of their dependence it may be said that, apart from hundreds of lines of adaptation and summary, over 180 passages, comprising 1,040 lines out of a total of 2,560, have been lifted bodily and without alteration, either of order or of content, from the *Dialogue*. In nine of the 24 *Protocols* more than half comes direct from Joly. Much of the addition was to dress the material for Russian consumption ; and some of it can even be traced again to previous sources. The forgers were not very original !

What is interesting is to find that passages which do seem accurately to describe particular *Jewish* situations were taken bodily from Joly and actually describe the policy of Napoleon III, or what Joly thought the Emperor would like to do if he could.

Jews, for example, did own a good deal of the Central European Press. Jewish journalists wrote a considerable proportion of its

cultural and political articles ; and the international news agencies
of Reuter and Wolf were founded by Jews. It might then be thought
to be established that, in view of acknowledged Jewish prominence
in journalism, *The Protocols* had a genuine Jewish origin when we
find in *Protocols* V and XII that[1] :

> ' The principal object of our directorate is this : to debilitate
> the public mind by criticism ; to lead it away from serious
> reflections calculated to arouse resistance ; to distract the
> forces of the mind towards a sham fight of empty eloquence
> . . . In order to put public opinion in our own hands we must
> bring it into a state of bewilderment, by giving expression
> from all sides to so many contradictory opinions and for such
> length of time as will suffice to make the Goyim lose their
> heads in the labyrinth.'

or again that :

> ' Not a single announcement will reach the public without our
> control. Even now this is already being attained by us inasmuch
> as all news items are received by a few agencies, in whose
> offices they are focussed from all parts of the world. These
> agencies will then be already entirely ours and will give
> publicity only to what we dictate to them.'

But in fact these passages are taken straight from the designs
attributed to Napoleon III ; that is, they are the opinions of
Machiavelli in the *Dialogue*. In the seventh dialogue Machiavelli
says[2] :

> ' The principal secret of government consists in enfeebling the
> public spirit to the point of disinteresting it entirely in the ideas
> and the principles with which revolutions are made nowadays.
> In all times people, like individuals, have been paid in words
> . . . We must benumb (public opinion), strike it with uncert-
> ainty by astounding contradictions, work on it with incessant
> diversions, dazzle it with all sorts of different actions, mislead
> it imperceptibly in its pathways.'

And in the eleventh he says :

> ' How does foreign news arrive? By a few agencies which
> centralise the news which is transmitted to them from the four

---

[1] The quotations from *The Protocols* are from the edition of The Britons Publishing
Society, 1936.

[2] *Dialogue* pp. 72f. and 134 in the original, and from pp. 116 and 150 in the
translation in *The Truth about the Protocols*, H. Bernstein, on which the above
text is based.

quarters of the globe. Well, I suppose these agencies could be paid, and then they will give out no news except by order of the government.'

Moreover the relation of these passages to each other is exactly similar in both works. References which editors of *The Protocols* have found to ' international finance ', to the Bolshevik Revolution, and to other ' Jewish ' activities, will similarly be found in almost identical language, and in the same sequence, in the *Dialogue*, and there applied to Napoleon III.

There is then no doubt that the content of *The Protocols* came from Joly. But the form was borrowed from a story which had already been printed on various occasions in Russia. The idea of ' Elders of Zion ' meeting secretly is found in a work of a German novelist, Hermann Goedsche, who wrote thrillers in the 1860's and '70's under the romantic pseudonym of Sir John Retcliffe. In one of these, *To Sedan*, there is a chapter describing, with all the proper effects of a good thriller, a secret meeting in the ancient Jewish cemetery of Prague which is overheard by two strangers. Once every century the Elders of all the Tribes of Israel (Goedsche is a little shaky on his tribes) meet to plan their conquests for the succeeding century. The President is, of course, the Devil who appears and disappears with blue flames and in the form of a monstrous golden calf.

When doubts were first cast on the authenticity of *The Protocols* antisemitic parties responded by producing a number of other documents which, according to them, confirmed the reality of a Jewish plot. With all of them we cannot deal, but this fiction of a secret meeting of the Elders in Prague is the basis of one of the most frequently quoted. It is, therefore, interesting to trace the record of this ' evidence ' of an ' event ' which first appeared as a piece of straight sensational fiction—and as fiction it is fairly good, and worthy of a place in ' A Century of Ghost Stories '.

Not only is it pretended that the two people in the novel who secretly overheard the meeting are real people who are pursued by the infuriated Elders (and are given various names), but Sir John Retcliffe, the *nom-de-plume* of Goedsche, passes through various transformations until he finally becomes John Readcliffe, chief rabbi of London! In 1872 this particular chapter of the novel was republished in Russia as a novelette. It was still presented as fiction, but the sinister words were added that *it was not wholly the invention*

of Sir John. In 1886 the story reappeared in France as the speech of
a Grand Rabbi, made in 1880 and ' extracted from an advance copy
of the forthcoming work of the distinguished English diplomat,
Sir John Readcliffe, entitled *Annals of the politico-historical Events of
the last ten Years*. It was next published in a Russian newspaper in
Odessa as the speech of a rabbi made to the secret Sanhedrin of
1869 (apparently a reference to the First Congress of Reform
Judaism which was held in that year at Leipzig). The Russian was
translated from the French translation of the English translation of
the original Hebrew, and its authenticity was fully vouched for by
the fact that it was published by Sir John Readclif, an aristocrat of
the notoriously Judeophil country, England !

When the non-existent Readclif, or Retcliffe, had finally fallen
a victim to the Elders, as several authors assure us was the case, the
speech continued to be reported. The antisemitic *Deutsch-soziale
Blätter* reported an unnamed rabbi as having made it in 1893. It
was next reported as having been made at a non-existent Zionist
Congress at Lemberg in 1912, and by this time the orator is called
either Reichorn or Eichorn. Finally, in 1921, after the exposure of
the forgery of the Protocols, it was brought out again, on the basis
of the Odessa text.

In one form or another it is to be found in almost any antisemitic collection of documents ; and, having acquired a good deal
of variety in its migrations, different texts are then used to bolster up
each other's authenticity. But in fact they betray themselves in an
odd and unexpected fashion. In his account of the original meeting
of the Elders at Prague Goedsche gives a list of all the Stock
Exchanges which are supposed to be in the hands of the Jews, and
this list occurs *in exactly the same order* in all the versions. But ' Paris,
London, Vienna, Berlin, Amsterdam, Hamburg, Rome and Naples '
is not an inevitable or official order, and its constant repetition
quite clearly proves one common source for all the speeches. Moreover, while the Stock Exchange of Naples may have had some
importance before the unification of Italy in 1870, it had little
afterwards, and yet it is still quoted in versions of the speech
supposed to have been given long after that date.

The supposed *Protocols*, and the fictional speech in the cemetery
of Prague, are the main documents quoted in antisemitic sources to
prove the Jewish plot. But there have been numbers of others which
equally fail to stand up to any critical examination. The most

amusing is a letter supposedly written to the Jews of Constantinople
by the Jewish community of Arles under the threat of compulsory
baptism, and the advice of the Jews of Constantinople in reply. The
way in which their ' authenticity ' is guaranteed is a fair specimen
of the sort of proof advanced, a trick which unhappily antisemites
did not invent, but which bad scholars made use of centuries before
them. It is to quote, in support of a statement, some document which
the reader is unlikely to be able to consult. In this case it is claimed
that the letters are ' proved ' to be genuine by the fact that they are
quoted in the *Revue des Études Juives* which was financed by James de
Rothschild. This is factually true, *but* they are quoted in volumes 1,
15 and 19 of the *Revue* as a witty and widely disseminated satire on
the many thousands of Spanish Jews who had been compulsorily
baptised by the policy of Ferdinand and Isabella in 1492 and were
now scattered all through the Spanish population.

Another document is attributed to the great American patriot,
Benjamin Franklin. Yet another is a ' Manifesto ' to ' the Jews of
the Universe' by the French Jewish statesman, Adolphe Crémieux,
at the founding of the *Alliance Israélite Universelle*. Then there is one
which is supposed to have been taken from the dead body of a
Russian Jewish sergeant called Zundar in 1919, and to be an address
to Jewish revolutionaries all through the world. Here again one may
expose something of the absurdity of these documents. It is addressed
to Jewish revolutionaries, of whom there were, indeed, quite a
number in 1919 ; but it addresses them in *Hebrew*, a language
understood only by the orthodox or Zionist sections of the population, both of whom were completely opposed to the Jewish revolutionaries ; and it promises the restoration of Judaism to that
element in Jewry, firmly atheist, which would have been quite
uninterested.

It would be tedious to recount all the other documents used by
antisemitic parties. They are alike in their inability to stand the
test of critical examination. And most of them, by their naïveté,
betray the class of the community to which they expect to make an
appeal. One antisemitic writer, whose pseudonym is Ernest Sincere,
reaches the height of absurdity when he states that this supposed
Jewish plot was started in 929 B.C. by King Solomon, and is carried
on by the Elders of Zion with the assistance of exactly one million
nine hundred and twenty-one thousand, six hundred and one
fellow plotters. We are thus presented with a secret shared by

1,921,601 people which has been in existence more than 2,890 years, and is still not susceptible to any external confirmation or proof. Really, if 1,921,601 people can keep a secret for nearly three thousand years they deserve to succeed!

The defeat of the Nazis, the utter impotence of the Jewish people to prevent the murder of nearly two-fifths of their number, and the wide circulation of the proofs that they are a forgery, have not prevented *The Protocols* from remaining an effective weapon of antisemitism. The most persistent one-man organisation in this field is, I suppose, that of the Swede, Einar Åberg. He read *The Protocols* in 1922 and has deluged the world with correspondence ever since affirming their authenticity, and using them as support for the widest variety of antisemitic charges. Now in his seventies, condemned again and again by Swedish courts, the subject of a special law, known by his name and outlawing group libel, he continues to affirm their authenticity for the benefit of Arabs, Nazis, and the rabble-rousers of every country. The law forbids ' any one threatening, slandering or defaming a population group of a certain race or religious belief.' We shall return to it in the final chapter.

The late Arnold Leese was another fervent believer in them, and continued to publish them after 1945. Also, the book has been published in the past fifteen years in Britain, Australia, Canada, New Zealand, Eire, Turkey, Greece, the United States, Mexico (whence it is circulated to all Latin America), the United Arab Republic, the Lebanon and Morocco. In Germany they have begun to publish again also the supporting pieces ; and the speech of Rabbi Reichorn or Eichorn, which is itself a repeat of the meeting in the cemetery in Prague described by ' Sir John Retcliffe,' is now issued as the speech of Rabbi Rabinovich, and is said to have been made in Hungary as a witness to Jewish co-operation with the Communists.

V

THE CHRISTIAN ROOTS OF ANTISEMITISM

IT IS TIME to go back to the little man in the Nazi meeting who heard Hitler blaming all the troubles of Germany on the Jews, and who called out ' and the bicyclists.' (p. 5.) In the anecdote Hitler turned to him and asked : ' Why the bicyclists? ' and he rightly replied : ' Well, why the Jews?' Earlier chapters dealt with the psychological character of group prejudice and the causes of its prevalence. Its manifestations in nineteenth century European politics, where it was always the Jews who were selected as the scapegoat, were then passed in review. In the nineteenth century Jews fitted well into the needs of unscrupulous politicians, because they were a universal minority, identifiable and, if one chose particular professions and occupations, prominent. Now it is time to ask : why was this so? Was it due to an inherent ' racial ' characteristic? Were Jews actually a menace to the non-Jewish world? Or rather, were ' *the* Jews ' such a menace? For, of course, there were individual Jews, like individual Englishmen, Frenchmen, Americans or Italians, who were criminals, and there were other individual Jews whose activities, lawful in themselves, were disapproved of by others—other Jews as well as others who were not Jews.

It is equally important to ask why ancient and largely forgotten accusations, often proved false in their day, were revived in the nineteenth century. Why the revival of false quotations from the Talmud? Why new accusations of ritual murder? Why the widely held belief in the improbable story that there was a dangerous Jewish world plot against the vast and infinitely more powerful ' Christian world? ' We know the answer to these questions, because there is nothing obscure about the history of the Jews. No other people's story is so well and objectively documented over so long a period of time. On the other hand, we cannot assume or predict

57

the conduct of Jews of one century by accounts of their conduct one or two millenia previously. The temptation to prove Jewish brutality and vengefulness in modern times by reference to the prophet Samuel who, before 1000 B.C., hewed Agag in pieces as a religious act—the frequent repetition in sermons that Jews adopt the policy of ' an eye for an eye ' in contrast to the Christian doctrine of love towards enemies and so on—these are as false and illogical evidence about the nineteenth century as would be the basing of an estimate of the present or future policy of the Scandinavian states, the most obviously peaceful states in the world, on the conduct of their ancestors in the 10th and 11th centuries when the Norsemen were the scourge of the whole European continent, viewed with utter terror because of their ruthless and pitiless raids on peaceful towns, villages and religious centres. Peoples *do* change their characters.

The history of the Jews in ancient Palestine itself has very little bearing on the problem of Jewish—non-Jewish relations. It is the fact that the majority of the identifiable Jewish people have lived in scattered communities in the non-Jewish world for well over two thousand years (i.e. from some centuries before the time of Christ and the birth of Christianity) that is significant. We can study them in an almost infinite variety of situations, and in contact with the civilisations, cultures, and religions of half the world. From this immense perspective we can draw a simple and sufficient generalisation : *Jewish history is unique : the reaction of Jews and their neighbours to that history is the reaction of ordinary human beings.*

In the ancient world there is evidence of both good and bad relations between Jews and their neighbours. What is both interesting (and normal) is that the same quality provoked contrary reactions in different people on different occasions. The Jews were the first consistently and continuously monotheistic people, and their monotheism involved either special privileges or special isolation. It could not be otherwise. Jews had to be excused from offices and practices which involved idolatry ; and Jewish families had to be careful to keep their young of both sexes uncontaminated, for example, by the temple prostitution of both boys and girls practised by many of the peoples among whom they lived in the pagan world. But naturally this separatism could cause irritation.

One of the earliest records of such irritation is given us by the anonymous author of the *Book of Esther*, written towards the end of the second century B.C. In it Haman, the Vizir of the Persian king, tells his master that ' there is a certain people scattered abroad and dispersed among the people in all the provinces of thy kingdom ; and their laws are diverse from all people ; neither keep they the king's laws : therefore it is not for the king's profit to suffer them.' (Esther 3 : 8.) They found the clannishness of Jews insulting, and their indignation was shared by Roman satirists and other writers who attributed it to hatred of other mortals. It is well to remember that in the first Christian century the Roman writer Tacitus interpreted Christian separateness in exactly the same way. He found it due to " hatred of the human race."

Some pagans particularly disliked the secrecy surrounding the Temple worship at Jerusalem, where even of the Jews only the High Priest could enter the Holy of Holies, and that only once a year. They therefore invented stories that the Temple contained the head of an ass which the Jews secretly worshipped, or even a young man, being fattened up for subsequent sacrifice. Again it is salutary to remember that these same pagans circulated the story that at the Eucharist (from which all but members of the Church were excluded) Christians began by eating babies, and went on to every form of sexual excess.

But the opposite reaction is equally genuine. It was Jewish ethical monotheism which drew a thoroughly healthy element in the Hellenistic world to the worship of the synagogue. The Gentile Christian Church was founded on such men and women. In what contrast the ethics which they had learned in Jewish teaching and worship stood to the ordinary morals of the time one can discover by studying what happened when St. Paul conducted a mission far from the synagogue in the pagan slums of Corinth. As his letters show, the manners and morals of these converts shocked him to the very depth of his Jewish soul : ' Now therefore there is utterly a fault among you, because ye go to law one with another. Why do ye not rather take wrong? Why do ye not rather suffer yourselves to be defrauded? Nay, ye do wrong, and defraud and that your brethren. Know ye not that the unrighteous shall not inherit the kingdom of God? Be not deceived: neither fornicators, nor idolators, nor adulterers, nor effeminate, nor abusers of themselves with mankind, nor thieves, nor covetous, nor drunkards, nor revilers, nor extortioners, shall inherit the kingdom of God. And such were some of you.' (I. Corinthians 6 : 7-11.)

Such was the general situation : ethical monotheism instilled a high standard of ethical living, and this meant a certain separation from the life around. But there were also local situations. The great Jewish community of Alexandria celebrated the Passover annually, and the Passover contains many references to the Egyptians which are not at all flattering to Egyptian pride. So a rival Egyptian story was circulated. The foreign dregs of the population (i.e. the children of Israel) were driven out of the country because they were completely ridden by such loathsome diseases that the Egyptians could only purify the land by expelling them. The Egyptian story is just what one would expect. But the Passover, outside Egypt, continued to attract ordinary Christians by its Biblical origin and the beauty of its celebration for many centuries after the separation of Christianity from Judaism. The evidence for this comes from countries as far apart as Syrian Antioch and Spain, and continues right down to the Dark Ages.

One could go on with such instances, showing how completely Jewish-Gentile relations followed the normal pattern of relations between neighbours, now good, now bad, now roused to active enmity by some special irritation, now moved to approval and imitation by something which was admirable. But it would bring us no nearer the understanding of antisemitism. For antisemitism is a unique expression of group prejudice, and arises out of a unique cause.

That which changed the normal pattern of Jewish—Gentile relations was the action of the Christian Church. The statement is tragic but the evidence is inescapable. What is still more tragic is that there is no break in the line which leads from the beginning of the denigration of Judaism in the formative period of Christian history, from the exclusion of Jews from civic equality in the period of the Church's first triumph in the fourth century, through the horrors of the Middle Ages, to the Death Camps of Hitler in our own day. Other causes indeed came in during the passage through the centuries ; the motives and climate of the Nazi period owed nothing to Christian teaching ; individual Christians risked and forfeited their lives in rescuing his victims. But so far as the Churches are concerned the line is still unbroken by any adequate recognition of the sin, by any corporate act of amendment or repentance.

It is useless to say that the Christian denunciation of Judaism was the inevitable consequence of the intolerance of monotheism ; and to defend or justify the action of the leading writers and preachers of the early Church on that score. Islam is just as intolerant as Christianity, perhaps more so; and Islam has had intimate contact with Jews and Judaism during the whole of its existence. In fact from its foundation up to the twelfth century the more populous and important Jewish communities were in Islamic not in Christian territory. But there is no trace in Muslim writing or tradition of the appalling travesty of Jewish history which we encounter in the Church Fathers; there are none of the vile inventions of medieval superstition, ritual murder, the poisoning of wells, the spreading of plague, the invention of world plots, such as proliferate among the more ignorant sections of the Christian population of Europe right into the twentieth century. The story of Jewish communities under Islam has been an increasingly miserable one for well over half a millenium, but the record of the Muslim peasant and proletariat is not much better. Both have been victims of a culture which became stagnant; but neither the Jewish nor the Christian minority was further denigrated and humiliated, persecuted, expelled or murdered, on such baseless charges as caused the deaths of tens of thousands of Jews in medieval Christendom. Under Islam they were treated with galling arrogance, harshness and contempt but, provided they recognised their inferior status, their religion was tolerated, their lives and property were safe. On the other hand, it may be readily admitted that the Church did not deliberately set out to create this evil thing. It was a by-product, but a by-product of a basic falsity in Christian thinking. The manner of its growing was thuswise.

In the first decades of the life of the Church there was continuous argument with Jews as to whether Jesus of Nazareth was, or was not, the Messiah. This was not an academic question. The whole attitude of the apostolic leaders towards the admission of Gentiles to the synagogue (for the Church was at that time officially a Jewish sect) was founded on the Christian belief that the Age of the Messiah had begun, and that a new policy towards the Gentile world, foretold by the prophets, was its natural consequence. Moreover the Christians could not avoid the argument with Jews because it was as a *Jewish* sect that the first churches were protected from Roman scrutiny, since Judaism was the only licensed mono-theism. We might today conduct the discussion on the basis of the character or teaching of Jesus of Nazareth. It was inevitable at that

time that it should be conducted quite differently, on the correspondence of his life and death with the predictions of messianic
prophecy. St. Matthew's Gospel is full of statements that this or
that happened in order that a prophecy might be fulfilled. St. Paul,
in his argument on the truth of his preaching, insists that it is
'according to the Scriptures' (cf. I. Cor. 15 : 3f). This first conflict
between Jews and Christians was, thus, a conflict about interpretation. Both sides admitted the authority of the same Scriptures, but
Jews interpreted them differently. In any case it was an argument
conducted with great violence on both sides, and it was not a debate
in which Jews or Christians today can take pride. But it was not the
cause of antisemitism. When the two religions separated that
particular controversy died down.

The disastrous action came later, when the Church was faced,
not with Jews, but with the educated, sophisticated and sceptical
Hellenistic world. It was in the line it chose for its approach to this
world that the terrible seeds of all subsequent antisemitism lay
buried. For that which differentiates antisemitism from other group
prejudices, whether suffered by Jews or any other people, is that
group prejudice is normally related to something contemporary,
something which actually happened, even if it be wrongly or
distortedly interpreted ; whereas antisemitism has almost no
relationship to the actual world, and rests on a figment of the
imagination perpetually bolstered up by other figments.

In its apologetic to the pagan world around it, the Church was
not concerned to argue that Jesus of Nazareth was the Jewish
Messiah, an argument which would have left the Hellenistic world
completely indifferent. It was arguing that Christianity was the
true, original, universal religion of humanity, that it predated and
outshone all that the poets, philosophers and lawgivers of Greece
and the East could offer. It could make such a claim only on the
basis of the possession, as exclusively part of its own history, of the
story of Israel as revealed in the Old Testament. We accept today
that the Old Testament reveals the early history both of Judaism
and of Christianity, but it would have been strange to either Jew or
Christian in the Roman empire to agree to such a statement.
Moreover though Judaism may not accept the validity of the
Christian claim today, its denial of it is confined to its own members,
and to scholarly or semi-scholarly work. But in the early days of the
Church, the Jewish community was as large, as widely scattered

and, until the fourth century, more powerful than the Christian. Jews were open opponents of the Christian claim to be proclaiming the true religion. Neither Christian nor Jew of that day would have been willing to admit that they *shared* the great collection of Scriptures which were sacred in the minds and hearts of both of them. To either side, possession of it by themselves was a denial of it to the other.

Perhaps it would not have mattered if the Church had claimed the *whole* of the Old Testament—if it had seen in its very objective pictures of human failings a record of its own ancestors, if it had taken to its own bosom and laid on its own conscience the denunciations of the prophets ; if it had read into its own history the record of betrayal and evil-doing of the monarchs and wealthy men of Israel and Judah. But the spokesmen of the Church did not do so. They claimed only all the heroes and virtuous characters of the Scriptures ; they allocated to themselves only the promises and the praise of the Scriptures. And to the Jews they allotted only all the villains and idolators, only all the threats and denunciations. Moreover this was done by men who believed that every word had divine authority, so that this description of villains and idolators, perpetually false to every hope, perpetually revelling in every vice, perpetually betraying the truth, perpetually seeking falsehood, was God's own description of the Jewish people. And they preached this sedulously in every writing and from every pulpit throughout the breadth of Christendom Sunday by Sunday, century by century, whenever there was reference to the Jews. It is no wonder that ordinary Christians came at last to believe that Jews were children of the Devil vowed to their destruction, and to act on that belief. The greatest tribute to the complete falsity of this picture, which the theologians had preached from the second century onwards, was that it took eight hundred years to be believed. The first general massacre of Jewish communities took place in Northern France and the Rhineland during the religious excitement of the First Crusade in 1096.

This terrible misrepresentation of Jewish history could be illustrated from almost any page of early Christian literature. It will be enough to quote four of the most eminent writers of the fourth century, chosen from East and West : Hilary, Bishop of Poitiers, Ambrose, Archbishop of Milan, Eusebius, Bishop of Caesarea, and John Chrysostom of Antioch, Archbishop of Constantinople. Hilary, commenting on Psalm 52, says that the tyrant who boasts of his wickedness represents the Jewish people who ' had always persisted in iniquity and out of its abundance of evil gloried in wickedness.' The key incident in the attitude of Ambrose arose out of the burning of a synagogue by a mob, led by the bishop, at Callinicum in the eastern provinces of the empire. The emperor had rightly punished the bishop for this violation of public order. Ambrose publicly refused the sacrament to the emperor until he had rescinded his sentence against the bishop, asking contemptuously who minded if the synagogue (which he described as a miserable hovel, a home of insanity and unbelief which God himself had condemned) was destroyed : ' God whom they have insulted or Christ whom they have crucified ?'

Eusebius, the greatest apologist to the pagan world in the century of the victory of the Church, composed a whole elaborate work to demonstrate the antiquity of Christianity. It is ' the most ancient organisation of holiness, the most venerable philosophy of mankind.' It pre-dates the appearance of Judaism, which was a temporary discipline introduced to control those who had been corrupted by the life of Egypt, and not intended to be permanent. But Jews never observed even that, and so were perpetually under a curse, and perpetually doomed to final and complete ruin. Even the remnant, described as faithful by the prophets, did not refer to Jews. It referred to Christians who lived side by side with Jews during the period of the Law. In this way all the virtuous characters of the Old Testament were taken over by the Church, even during the period of the Mosaic dispensation.

Finally, Chrysostom. He preached a series of sermons at Antioch in 387 in which there is no abuse too obscene for him to hurl at the Jews of that city, with whom the Christians were, in his opinion, holding much too friendly intercourse. He tells these Christians that their Jewish neighbours 'sacrifice their sons and their daughters to devils ; outrage nature ; overthrow from their foundations the laws of relationship ; are become worse than wild beasts ; and, for no reason at all, murder their own offspring to worship the avenging devils who are attempting to destroy Christianity.' These words occur in the first of the series, and it looks as though some of his congregation felt that he was going too far, for in a later one he suddenly interjected that, even if they no longer murder their own children, they murdered the Christ, which is worse.

In a word, generation after generation of Christians were taught that in early Christian history (that is, in the pre-Incarnation period related in the Old Testament) there were no scoundrels, and that in the whole of Jewish history there was nothing else. For, of course, from the birth of Christianity onwards, there was no question of their criminality. The Jews were a deicide people wholly and eternally under a curse though, according to some theologians, some would be converted and saved at the second coming of Jesus Christ. Here are the roots of the abnormality and uniqueness of antisemitism.

Here again it is particularly instructive to consider the different story of Jews and Judaism under the intolerant monotheism of Islam. Islam claimed the great prophets of the Old Testament as the precursors of Muhammad, but they did not deny that they were Jews—though they changed the land promised to Abraham from Palestine to Mecca—and they did not attempt to incorporate the whole of the Jewish Scriptures into the sacred writings of Islam. The Quran was not a 'New' Testament to be added to an accepted 'Old' Testament, but an entirely fresh, total, and final revelation, which surpassed and superseded the Scriptures—true in their day—of Jew and Christian alike. Hence there is none of the deformation of 'Jewish' history which is so conspicuous a part of the Christian tradition. As has already been said, both Jews and Christians, as minorities, came to suffer greatly under Islamic domination. But their sufferings were not accompanied by intolerable denigration and falsehood, and no part of the history of either minority in Islamic countries contains the appalling pages represented by the constant massacres of Jews in the Middle Ages or the horrors of the Nazi period in our own day. The Arab who protests that Christendom should have solved its own problem at its own expense may have failed to see the Jewish link with Palestine, but he has been given a good deal of justification by Christian actions in the past and Christian evasion of responsibility in the present.

The Christian writers who have been quoted all lived in the century in which the empire made peace with the Church, and in which consequently Christian influence could be brought to bear on imperial legislation. The leaders of the Church were neither slow nor squeamish in exercising this power. Christianity had been a licensed religion of the empire for less than three years when a law was passed making it a capital offence for any Jew to make a convert and imposing a like penalty on the convert. This was the first, and unbelievably abominable, action wherein Christian leadership proclaimed its second equally disastrous decision : to implement in imperial legislation its theological view of the criminality of the Jewish people and its abhorrence of Judaism, which it described in the majestic books of Roman Law by vulgar terms of army slang.

It was reasonable that the special privileges to protect their monotheism from contamination by idolatry should be cancelled when the empire became wholly monotheist, but Christian legislators did not stop at that point. They soon passed over to the offensive, and set out to destroy that equality before the law which Jews, in common with all other citizens of the empire, had enjoyed since the beginning of the third century. Jews were excluded from one profession after another. They might receive no civic or imperial honours. When an onerous duty was accompanied by an appropriate title of dignity, they were to perform the duty, but not enjoy the dignity. Their religious autonomy was undermined ; even their domestic relations were regulated ; their testamentary rights were limited ; and their worship was submitted to censorship. Death sentences and confiscation followed even minor transgressions. Having done all they could to undermine any Jewish loyalty to Roman and Byzantine rule, Christians then turned on Jews in anger and indignation in the seventh century when they naturally preferred the domination of the Muslim invaders in Egypt, Palestine and Spain.

The Church saw to it that the Jews entered medieval Christendom rightless ; and they were rightless entirely for religious reasons. There was no economic reason, let alone justification, for their inferior status. This is most strikingly illustrated by the terrible massacres of 1096 all through the cities of the Rhineland while forces were being collected by Peter the Hermit for the First Crusade. Their neighbours in the cities tried to protect them from the crusading mobs, which killed and looted to the cry that it was absurd to cross half the world to rescue the tomb of Christ when his murderers were living at ease among them. The civic authorities, bishop or count, were willing to offer their Jews shelter in whatever castle the city possessed. Nowhere did they take part in the massacres, though they were apt to withdraw their protection if it endangered themselves. To underline the religious nature of the attack, some Jews were offered their lives by the mobs in return for immediate baptism.

The consequences of rightlessness soon added to the causes of hostility. Jews could get permission to settle in any place only by becoming the private property of the ruler who gave them a written licence. He naturally wanted a *quid pro quo*, and the price demanded arose out of the nature of medieval economy—not out of any existing Jewish capacity. Jews were an urban community, with a high proportion engaged in trade. Traders were one of the few classes who handled money (the others were the collectors of customs, the possessors of shrines visited by pilgrims, and the papacy, not as head of the Church but as heir to the mercantile Roman empire). Therefore as Europe passed in the twelfth century from a subsistence economy to a more prosperous phase, money came to be an important factor, and coin was perpetually short. Those who had it lent it profitably. Jews had it ; and as they belonged to the princes, the profits nicely accrued to the princely coffers.

Jews were never the only moneylenders in the Middle Ages, and were very rarely the most important. But they handled much of the petty lending on agricultural crops and small enterprises ; and they were given a licence to do so because the profits passed so conveniently to the ruler, while the odium which indebtedness brings in its train passed to the Jew, not to the prince behind him. It was thus that a second, *economic*, cause for prejudice was added to a religious one. Mobs became accustomed to looking for the IOU's and burning them as an accompaniment to their attacks upon Jewish communities. As a matter of fact, as moneylenders Jews ranked favourably, for Christian moneylenders, being often unlicensed and unsupervised, were usually far more exacting and unscrupulous than Jews. But no medieval moneylender could be anything but a burden, for the interest charged was by modern standards preposterously uneconomic.

It was, however, still the basic medieval conviction that Jews were literally children and emissaries of the devil, vowed to the destruction of Christendom ; and it was this which caused the terrible record of medieval treatment, and which is not atoned for by individual protests and appeals coming occasionally from the papacy or some leading Christian. To medieval man the Jews were less than human ; they waited for the coming of the anti-Christ ;

and in the meanwhile the devil employed them to do all they could to harm the Christian cause and Christian nations. They mixed magic potions to poison them—so the Middle Ages explained the Black Death which destroyed a third of the population of Europe in 1348 and the following years ; and their practice of medicine only covered their designs on Christian lives ; they insulted the Christian religion, spitting on and defiling its sacred statues and objects of cult, mocking it and blaspheming against it in their evil books ; dark stories circulated that they conspired with its enemies—human ás well as satanic—to blot it out ; above all, medieval man believed that they used Christian blood for their nefarious practices, and to cure themselves of the revolting smell and disgusting diseases which were the penalty of their unbelief ; and that they constantly murdered children to secure the needed blood.

It is easy to see that, to the religious and economic arguments for hostility, a third soon came to be added : the strangeness of Jewish life and customs. It is dangerous to call this 'foreign-ness,' for medieval man had little feeling of nationality, and foreigner to us denotes the holder of the passport of another sovereign state. But, while the Mediterranean world was accustomed to a rich cosmopolitan variety in its city life, northern Europe was not ; and as the northern European became conscious of Jews, he became conscious that they were mysteriously different. Language, religion, writing—all could be endowed with the terror of the unknown, once there were other reasons for hating and fearing those who exhibited them. It is not surprising that Jews resisted with all their power the compulsion to wear a distinguishing mark on their dress, a mark which prevented them from passing unnoticed through the streets or on their travels.

As Europe began to be conscious of national differences, this consciousness began to be doubly marked in the case of the Jews in their midst, because the 17th and 18th centuries are in some senses the ' dark ages ' of European Jewish history. Broken and embittered by centuries of persecution, poverty-stricken and dealing only in the smallest and most ignoble trades, the appearance of the majority of the Jews in the 17th and 18th centuries was more distinctly and visibly ' foreign,' even if they rarely wore a badge, than it was in the Middle Ages.

To the third fact of social *foreign-ness* was quickly added a fourth. With the French Revolution and the 19th century Jews began to become citizens of various countries of western Europe. In England, though legally and politically their rights were restricted until 1858, they enjoyed complete social freedom, and their communities were to be found in most of the cities, especially the seaports, of the country.

The fourth fact was the combination : *foreign-ness* plus *citizenship*. On this, with a suitable *réchauffé* of all the previous fables, the immense structure of modern antisemitism was reared. This is not to say that there were not actual problems, both internal to the Jewish community and arising out of Jewish-Gentile relationships, during the period. There were such problems, and some of them presented very real difficulties, but the antisemites required a larger canvas for their fantasies, and it is rare to find any serious study of actualities in antisemitic literature.

In the early period of emancipation two main problems confronted the Jewries of western Europe, the acquisition and the exercise of the rights of citizenship, and the absorption of the new knowledge and culture which their re-entry into European society made accessible to them. It was a dual problem of assimilation. The most devastating blow struck at Jewry by the Christian Church had been the deprivation of citizenship. In some spheres, both intellectual and economic, Jews had still been eminent in the 12th century. It would be difficult to find a sphere in which they were eminent in the 17th. There was a millenium of lost ground to make up, once citizenship was recovered ; and Jews spared no pains to recover it. This brought them into the political struggles of the period on the side of the liberal and progressive forces, from whom alone they could hope for their emancipation. But there was no country in which these liberal and progressive forces owed their existence exclusively to Jews, even when individual Jews were prominent among their leaders. The winds of the French Revolution blew in other quarters besides the ghettoes of Europe ; and the problems of the new industrialism affected others more than Jews.

More profound and far-reaching than the actual struggle for citizenship was the plunge into the new cultural, social and economic life which the removal of medieval restrictions brought in its train. And this involved a sharp conflict within Jewry. It is doubtful whether any rabbi, however orthodox, would have been prepared actually to fight for the restrictions of the ghetto against the obvious human claim to equality. But many viewed with fear and distaste

the breakdown of the old ways of life which they foresaw would
follow the opening of every avenue to Jewish talents. The Talmud
had come to be almost the whole of their intellectual world ; and
they regarded access to the literature, the science, and the arts of
the Gentile as access to forbidden things, a temptation to be
steadfastly resisted. But it is not surprising that many of the younger
generation refused to follow them, and eagerly absorbed all that
they could discover of the strange life around them.

There was, in those days, little ' liberal Judaism ' to provide
them with a spiritual home and background from which they
could safely adventure into the new waters. Until a new ' conservative ' Judaism developed which made some concessions to
novelty, the synagogue remained rigidly orthodox ; so that those
who accepted western European ways of thought were, at first,
almost completely cut off from their own community. At the same
time, many found it difficult to win wholehearted acceptance in
Gentile society.

This brought a new intensity to a very old problem in relations
between a Jewish community and the majority among whom it
lived. In Palestine and in the greatest community of the Diaspora,
that in ancient Mesopotamia which Jews always called ' Babylon,'
Jews had lived a more or less self-contained life. They filled a
whole region, and their relations with their Gentile neighbours
were not matters of every day intercourse. But in medieval European
Jewries and in the emancipated communities which followed them,
Jews were not self-contained communities. Their daily buying and
selling, their renting of houses and purchase of goods, even questions
of staff and domestic service, brought them into daily and continuous dependence on non-Jewish neighbours. Now these neighbours were not anxious to see Jews as competitors. If they belonged
to trade guilds and associations, they refused access to Jewish
newcomers ; if there was no formal exclusion, then there was still
the immense power of social pressure. The good and stable jobs
they kept to themselves.

The result was natural and inevitable. While the majority of a
Jewish community lived by the ordinary routine of everyday
occupations, the most active and imaginative members were driven
to finding *new* ways of earning a living. Because pioneering brings
both bankruptcies and fortunes, some Jews went bankrupt—and
this was quickly forgotten—and some individuals made fortunes—

which was remembered with envy and jealousy against ' the Jews.' All through European history down to today, this natural characteristic of a new community, denied complete acceptance by an established society, shows itself in the economic history of the Jews. They pioneered in the short-term agricultural loan in the Middle Ages ; they pioneered in many fields of industry and commerce in central and eastern Europe in succeeding centuries. In Rumania and elsewhere they pioneered in the creation of market towns. And when the nineteenth century came the opportunities of pioneering were almost unlimited.

At the same time, pioneering in a new environment has its dangers and temptations. Coming at a time when an old order was being shaken and old values discarded, the pioneers were very apt to become *deracinés*, men without roots, always a class creative of social difficulties. The whole period, however, was so full of change that they were by no means the only men in such a condition. A new bourgeoisie was growing out of the wealth produced by industry, successful men of business, unwillingly accepted into the older society of 'gentry,' but very conscious of the gulf between themselves and the rest of the class from which they had sprung. But this social tension was not accompanied, as it was in the case of the Jews, by religious or national isolation. Nor were these newly-rich among the British and other western European peoples as distant from the old ways as were inevitably the newly emancipated Jews. They still had some regard for tradition, for ceremony, for the panoply of the dying feudal and ecclesiastical society. So while the Jewish group was, as it were, one hundred per cent nineteenth century and saw that century as a wholly new world, their fellow radicals among the new middle-class had more limited and practical objectives in their political radicalism, and a more moderate, even half-hearted, hostility to the old order.

It is, therefore, not difficult to understand how those who hated the new society saw ' Jews ' everywhere where the new order fought the old ; nor, on the other hand, how the emancipated Jews threw themselves sometimes with more enthusiasm than discretion into the battle, just because their boats were burnt behind them, and they could not possibly return to, or be incorporated into, the old world of the ghetto and the orthodox Synagogue. The world of Jewry was thus even more divided than the rest of western Europe.

The general battle against the supposed influence of the Jews was waged around certain identifiable storm-centres. Of these the first, and throughout the early period the greatest, was the House of Rothschild. The amazing financial success of the five brothers born in the ghetto of pre-emancipation Frankfurt, and received in all the courts of Europe, was inevitably a subject of legend. Their financial power was, in actual fact, great ; their political power was much less than their critics and opponents credited them with. For the British end of the House inevitably adopted a British attitude, and the Austrian an Austrian attitude, and so on ; and these attitudes were often at variance with each other, and cancelled out the political activities of the House. The frantic speculation which inevitably accompanied the uncontrolled expansion of early capitalism led to many horrid manipulations among the financiers, and many disastrous losses among the speculating public. On both sides of the picture there were, of course, Jews. But only when they were among the first group were they remembered ; and their rôle was so exaggerated that *all* financial scandals were assumed to be Jewish, and to be part of a vast web, with the Rothschilds in the centre, for the exploitation and impoverishment of Christian Europe. This was the thesis of one of the first books which prepared the way for 19th-century antisemitism, *Les Juifs, Rois de l'Epoque*, by Toussenel.

Another storm centre was the press and the world of literature. Jews took readily to journalism, and became prominent to some extent in every country, but particularly in Austria-Hungary. The liberal press was the centre of the day-to-day attack on tradition, privilege, and reaction. The attacks were often violent, sometimes unfair. But they were too frequently unanswerable, and thereby only increased the bitterness with which they were resented. It was in this field, perhaps, that Jews, as the most complete and uncompromising representatives of the new trends of the 19th century, earned the bitterest enmity. Was the Church attacked? It was not surprising if sometimes the most scathing denunciations came from Jewish writers. For what did the Church represent to them, but the body which had persecuted their people for centuries? Was it the feudal nobility? Again it represented the power which had locked their ancestors into ghettoes. Was it the old learning, and the unreformed universities? They were the bodies which had denied them learning and those intellectual pursuits always dear to the Jewish people. In a second foundation work of modern antisemitism, *Le Juif, le Judaisme et la Judaisation des Peuples Chrétiens*, by Gougenot des Mousseaux, this aspect of the question plays a very prominent rôle. Nor would des Mousseaux have found comfort, but the reverse, in the fact that Jewish orthodoxy could be pilloried with the same vigour as non-Jewish tradition by these Jewish journalists and writers.

While the battle was fought with fierceness by the combatants actually engaged, it must not be thought that it occupied the attention of anything but a small minority either of the Jewish or the non-Jewish population. The immense majority, Jewish and other, was occupied with the opportunities of the rapidly expanding economy of the age. A period of expansion is a period of ready tolerance in matters which the business man regards as non-essentials. Political, national and religious questions would all come into such a category. Consequently the majority of western Jews assimilated themselves very successfully into the new environment of their emancipation ; developed their businesses, acquired the social outlook of their neighbours, and ignored all wider questions. And the majority of their neighbours, having themselves ample elbow-room for expansion, did the same and regarded Jews with tolerance and indifference. The question of religious distinctions appeared to them an entirely private affair ; and the origins of their Jewish neighbours interested them as little as did their own.

Such was the situation up to the year 1881. The appearance of the new political antisemitism a year or two earlier was indeed a danger signal, but its importance was pooh-poohed in sound business circles. The antisemitism of the Russian government was regrettable, but it appeared at first a matter for charitable action and cautious diplomatic intervention. In reality the period of ease and security was over, and European Jewry had entered on the fateful road which led ultimately to the horrors of the Nazi extermination camps of 1942–1944.

VI

THE JEWISH WORLD SINCE 1881

IN THEIR LONG and troubled history Jews have never passed through a period of less than a century which contained so much tragedy, so much elation, as that which began with the flight from Russia from 1881 onwards. Its external aspects are not difficult to tell. Its effects, the Jewish people and their many neighbours are still experiencing.

Of those who managed to escape from Tsarist Russia, the majority sought to reach the United States, whose community increased by leaps and bounds until New York became the city with the largest Jewish population of the world. Next came England. In these two countries the Jewish population in 1880 stood approximately at 230,000 and 60,000. By 1914 the former figure had passed a million and three quarters, and the latter a quarter of a million. Smaller numbers settled in the British Dominions and on the continent of Europe. But there the increases were not striking. In Germany, for example, they rose from just under 450,000 in 1880 to just over 500,000 in 1910—an increase of 10 per cent as against the American 700 per cent.

The migration of these substantial numbers was financed entirely from western Jewish sources. The western communities also spent a great deal of time and money in helping Russian Jews to understand and adapt themselves to their new environment. By 1914 the immigrants were beginning to ask for a share in communal leadership and in shaping Jewish policy! They sent delegations of their own to present the Jewish case at Versailles, because they did not trust or agree with the old-established and assimilationist proposals of the dominant oligarchies in the western communities.

In Russia itself the government of Alexander III and Nicholas II callously announced that it intended to harry its Jewish subjects

74

until one third died, one third emigrated and one third accepted
the charms of Orthodox Christianity. Administrative brutality was
continuous. From 1905 onwards it was punctuated by periodic
outbreaks of violence, known as *pogroms*, whose official inspiration
was scarcely concealed. The other eastern European country with
a substantial Jewish population was Rumania. There the situation
was better than in Russia, but still Jews were denied any of the
privileges of citizenship and exposed to a good deal of economic
discrimination and administrative hostility. By 1914 the political
antisemitism of France and Germany was dormant and of the
Austro-Hungarian empire was waning except in Vienna—the city
where unfortunately the young Adolf Hitler eked out a miserable
existence.

Though it was not much noticed by the bulk of Jewry, one of
the most important things which was happening between 1879
and 1914 was the beginning of Jewish agricultural settlement in
Palestine. It is a mistake to speak of a ' return of the Jewish people'
as though they had all deliberately left the country close on two
millenia earlier ; and much misunderstanding and disapproval
might have been avoided if it had been realised that a Jewish
population, as large as the ever-dwindling resources of the land
and the hostility and ignorance of the fellaheen and bedouin would
allow, had remained all through the centuries. Jewish villages had
dwindled to one ; Jewish bedouin had finally disappeared early
in the 19th century ; only town life remained possible. But the
largest element in Jerusalem itself was already Jewish well before
any Jews began to come back under Zionist inspiration. *As a
people*, as a single corporate entity, Jews had never physically or
spiritually abandoned the belief that the land of Israel was their
' home ' even when they regarded a physical return as postponed
to a distant future or the coming of the Messiah. But in *numbers*
the Jewish inhabitants, living in the four holy cities of Jerusalem,
Hebron, Safed, and Tiberias, had been reduced to some tens of
thousands. The new settlers, however, introduced a new factor
only in their determination to cultivate the soil, and restore the
fabled prosperity of a ' land flowing with milk and honey'. Agricultural villages of several different types accounted for some
tens of thousands of new Jewish immigrants by 1914.

This was the basis on which the British Government in November
1917 issued the Balfour Declaration, favouring the establishment of

a National Home for the Jewish people in Palestine, and subsequently accepted a Mandate of the League of Nations to implement
it. There followed thirty years of stormy history, until in 1948 the
British Foreign Office under Ernest Bevin admitted a complete
and ignominious failure in their administration and withdrew under
conditions which humiliated the many British administrators who,
in increasing difficulties, had sought to be loyal to Jews, Arabs,
and the British Administration at the same time. The reasons for
this *impasse* will naturally come into discussion in the consideration
of the Arab-Israel conflict in Chapter Eight. But in the picture of
the development of the Jewish people since 1881 the experience
and activities of those who settled in Palestine occupy a noble
and important place.

Some of the British difficulties stemmed from the basic intention
to favour the creation of a *national* home. However that vague
word be defined, it was clearly a loyal interpretation of it that the
responsibility for growth should, to the maximum extent possible,
be left in Jewish hands. The British should not create it for them.
From the beginning, therefore, the Administration was faced with
that most difficult situation of an *imperium in imperio*, an authority
within its authority, which meant that it had only indirect access
to an increasingly numerous and important section of—one cannot
say ' its subjects ' for neither they nor the Arabs were its subjects—
the people living in the area which it administered. As the simultaneous administration of the Arab inhabitants was a normal and
enlightened colonial administration, it is not in the least surprising
that the British—who were chosen from the Colonial service, not
from the eastern European Consular service (where they might
have become familiar with the Jewish situation)—found it easiest
to get on with the Arabs.

Nevertheless a strong Jewish democracy with a modern economy
and agriculture were created under a Jewish administration, the
Jewish Agency, supported by and containing representatives of
Jewish communities outside Palestine. The agriculture rested on
a series of villages experimenting with different varieties of co-
operative, which attracted considerable attention in the rest of
the world. The *Kibbutz* showed the co-operative in its purest form,
and was undoubtedly the most effective and economical instrument
of agricultural pioneering in the modern world. Its members,
human in their differences of temperament, interest and mutual

tensions, were united in service to the ideal of the restoration of
the Jewish people to its homeland, and performed prodigies of
production and development. Industry also developed, but at a
more normal pace and under the great burden of lack of any important raw materials except the potash of the Dead Sea. The
economic life of the country was largely integrated into the remarkable general trade union movement of the Histadruth, uniting
both manual and intellectual workers. Both Mr. Ben Gurion and
Mrs. Golda Meir began their career in the service of the Histadruth.
In relation both to it and to the Kibbutz movement, Israel is now
faced with the ancient problem that it is not normal human experience that one can transmit the idealism and pioneering of
one generation to one's successors living under different conditions.

The whole upbuilding of the country has, of course, demanded
and still demands great contributions from outside. But this is
more normal and reasonable than critics sometimes assume. I
would quote an analogy I used in another of my books, *End of an
Exile*, which seems to me to be a fair comparison : I live in an
eight-room house on two acres—eight dunams by Israel measures
—of land. I have a two-storey barn as large as the house and a
smaller barn which is now a pleasant annexe used by scholars who
come to study in the library, and members of staff working elsewhere. My land is surrounded by a wall. Before my gate runs a
first-class road, and the public mains for electric light, water and
telephone. The whole property cost me just over a thousand
pounds. The house was built between four and five hundred years
ago, the barns are nearly as old, and the land has been cultivated
in all probability for a thousand years. By today's prices the money
I spent on the whole would not replace the barn. But whether the
man who built the house made a profit or loss on it is no longer
any concern of mine, what wages were paid to bring my land into
cultivation does not affect me. To bring in the electric light, water
and telephone cost me very little. The upkeep of the road, the
school, and all the other communal services make a sizeable
charge on the rates, but a mere trifle compared with the cost of
making the road, building the school, and so on. To create a similar
property today, and to pay my share of linking it by road to the
towns and villages north, south, east and west of Barley, and of
installing all the services I enjoy, would certainly cost me between
ten and twenty times what I originally paid. And this would be a

sum I could not possibly meet out of the profits of two acres of land. So Israel, which has to pay all the costs in contemporary money, needs outside help to be viable.

Up to 1948 the Jewish community had grown to something over half a million, forming about a third of the total population. It had been proposed in 1937 by a Royal Commission that, as Jews and Arabs could not co-operate, the land should be divided. Jews accepted it then, but the Arabs refused, and the British could not make up their minds to a viable frontier. During the war the Arabs were largely neutral, feeling that it was no war of theirs ; Jews volunteered in larger numbers than the British could absorb. After the war the British first sought to associate the Americans in finding a solution, but refused to accept the unanimous decisions of the Anglo-American Committee which they jointly set up. They then handed the whole matter over to the United Nations, but refused to take any constructive part in implementing peacefully the partition which the United Nations accepted as inevitable. The Jewish community, however, was prepared to take responsibility, and the State of Israel was declared to exist, with an improvised government under David Ben Gurion, as soon as the last British High Commissioner left the territory.

The other settlement of the status and place of the Jewish people which was attempted in the Peace settlement of 1919 was the protection by a series of Minority Treaties of Jewish rights and interests in the area of central and eastern Europe west of the Soviet frontier. The Jewish communities affected extended from the Baltic to the Black Sea. Apart from the Balkans, antisemitism was endemic in the whole area. It stemmed largely from the period when these countries were part of the Russian empire, but in Rumania and Hungary it had its own roots. At the same time it was in this area, of which the centre had once been the Russian Pale of Settlement, that Jewish life still maintained most of its traditional features. In the little market towns of Poland, Rumania, Slovakia and elsewhere modern ideas were penetrating only slowly. Traditional scholarship was still venerated, the mystical movement of Chassidism, product of the sadness and restrictions of ghetto life, was still powerful. Assimilated western communities which sought rabbis of unimpeachable orthodoxy still looked for them in eastern Europe.

In Czechoslovakia, where the genius of Thomas Masaryk and

ancient European traditions of membership of the Holy Roman Empire had produced a genuine educated democracy, Jewish conditions were tolerable, indeed prosperous. But in none of the other countries involved did Jews succeed in finding a creative relationship with their Christian majorities, not because they lacked the will or energy to do so, but because the majorities were too inexperienced in democratic government, and in the complex social regulation of a modern state, to be able to absorb their Jewish minorities. Everywhere the Jewish communities were larger, both actually and proportionally, than the well-assimilated Jewries of western Europe. They had their own language, their own dress, and their own traditional customs, all of which they wished to maintain. They sought recognition as national minorities, and they would have put forward the demand, had it had the slightest chance of acceptance, of being regarded as all constituting parts of one national unit, the Jewish people.

It was not the fault of the majorities that they could not absorb their Jewish fellow-citizens. They had inherited from Russia a problem it would at best have taken several generations to solve, for they had inherited huge Jewish communities quite un-jewishly impoverished in technical skills, in self-supporting independent enterprises, in professional abilities, in strong communal organisa-tions. All these things are normal parts of organised Jewish life. All had existed in the eastern European Jewries during the time the majority were subjects of the kings of Poland ; but a century of Tsarist oppression, the anti-judaism of the Orthodox Church, and the ignorant hostility of the Russian bureaucracy, had combined to undermine their vitality and destroy their communal and economic autonomy. Only their Jewish self-respect was left to them. This is not a hypothetical statement. Those who succeeded in fleeing to the West, and in building up free lives in the United States and the western democracies, showed, as did their children with them, that their basic Jewish qualities were unimpaired. They showed it by the industries which they created, the contribution which they made to professional and scientific life, the social and charitable organisations which they maintained, and the speed with which they were absorbed into the life of the nation which had received them.

As to those who were still in eastern Europe after the First World War, they were victims of the fact that the majorities themselves

in Poland, in the Baltic States, in Rumania, had likewise been
stultified by foreign oppression, and faced immense problems in
beginning or modernising their own industries, in developing their
educational systems, in setting up their own instruments of central
and local government ; and were quite unable at the same time
to blend into their heterogeneous states substantial minorities—of
whom Jews were only one—which demanded both the advantages
of full citizenship, and recognition of their separate corporate
entity. Whether another generation would have seen a beginning
of a creative solution it is now academic to debate. These are the
Jewish communities which provided the majority of Hitler's victims,
and only fragments remain, and remain behind the Iron Curtain
where conditions are determined largely by Moscow.

West of these communities which sought independent recognition
as national minorities was the great German Jewish community.
It could trace a history going back to the coming of contingents
of the Roman armies of Titus to Cologne after the destruction of
Jerusalem in A.D. 70. It was deeply integrated into German
economy and culture. In the war of 1914–1918 it had fought
loyally beside other Germans ; and it saw in the Weimar Republic
of 1919 the disappearance of the last barriers to complete equality
which had prevented Jews in Imperial Germany from becoming
officers in the army, judges, or university professors, except through
baptism, or of attaining the highest ranks in the civil service.
The antisemitism of the 19th century had practically disappeared ;
and few noticed the dangerous fact that many of the highest judges
and the university professors of history had been trained by the
generation in which antisemitism had deeply penetrated into
German academic life. This was to mean later that undue sympathy
was shown to the early manifestations of nationalist extremism
and vulgar antisemitism when the Hitler movement first came into
conflict with the Republic. The Weimar Republic was often betrayed
by its own judges and professors. But we shall return to the German
situation in the next chapter.

In all Jewish communities of the world outside the Soviet Union,
(of which the Jewish community and its treatment is the subject of
Ch. XI), the years between the wars saw a great increase in international organisation. There never was a secret ' Jewish World
Government ' or any approach to it ; for in their international
relations Jews showed the same characteristics as were to be seen

in the Jewish communities of different countries—an immense variety of opinions and a general unwillingness to give way and join up with those from whom one differed. To this there was only one exception, an exception which is thoroughly to the credit of the Jewish tradition. Jews of the most varied opinions would combine to help other Jewish communities in economic distress or victimised by political oppression. The story of the American Jewish Joint Distribution Committee, a body created during the First World War, is a record of fantastic ingenuity and variety, of raising and distributing sums which put any non-Jewish charity to shame, and of perseverance against such odds that the roll of martyrs of this one organisation equals that of many Churches.

The two main international Jewish organisations are the World Zionist Organisation and the World Jewish Congress. The former was founded at the end of the 19th century : the latter was largely the result of inter-war antisemitism and the rise of Hitler. In ideology they are very similar ; both see the Jewish people primarily as a people, not as a religion, though both have religious groupings in their membership. Their tasks are sufficiently easily distinguished for their co-operation to be easy. The Zionist Organisation was naturally focused on Palestine and now on the State of Israel ; the World Jewish Congress is concerned with the Jews of the Diaspora, that is, the Dispersion. There they seek to keep the Jewish spirit alive by sponsoring educational courses, the teaching of Hebrew, and the establishment of schools ; and spend a great deal of their strength in combating antisemitism and discrimination in all the continents of the world. Their identity of outlook is manifested in, and emphasised by, the fact that the same distinguished Jewish statesman, Nahum Goldmann, is President of both.

The decimation of European Jewry by the Nazis left the Jewish community of the United States bearing the main responsibility for the maintenance of Jewish life and tradition. They had been growing in importance in world Jewish councils all through the interwar period. European communities had, in their many difficulties, been upheld by the Joint Distribution Committee. The World Jewish Congress was largely their inspiration. In the battles of the Zionists with the British Administration American support, though not always intelligently directed or aware of the real difficulties involved, had been constant.

It must not be assumed from this that American Jewry had become a united community in which all Jews thought alike. The point is different : American Jews had become completely American. Like other Americans they were divided into many groupings, like other Americans they were strongly moved by sentiment, indeed by sentimentality ; like other Americans they were becoming mainly ' other-directed ' persons, rather than the rugged pioneers who were still the American father-figures. Between the wars they, like other Americans, had become increasingly disinterested in religion ; after the second war they had had just the same type of revival of adherence to a religious centre as had moved Protestants of many denominations and Roman Catholics. The revival with them, as with others, has not been theological, but has created a sense of ' belonging.' Perhaps they will even develop their own forms of the fringe emotionalism which periodically sweeps the American continent, though they have not yet produced a Billy Graham or a Jewish Pentecostalism. To one who is neither Jewish nor American, the overwhelming impression which they leave is the generosity of their giving to relieve Jewish distress, and to build up Jewish communal life, in less fortunate countries. Their gifts to non-Jewish causes are also considerable.

Like other minorities and business interests in the United States, American Jews are ready to exercise pressure on the President and Administration when Jewish interests are involved, though they do not, like others, maintain a permanent ' pressure group ' in Washington. But it is an exaggeration to say that there is a ' Jewish vote ' which exercises a determining influence in any vital political decision. Outside questions of the basic rights of oppressed Jewish communities elsewhere, or flat discrimination against Jews, American Jews are divided, and this is so even on support of the State of Israel. The sense of responsibility which weighs down American Jewry is not unnatural, for the outside observer cannot help noticing that (at any rate so long as the numerically great Soviet Jewry is a cipher in world Jewish affairs) the Jewish future hangs on the twin poles of New York and Jerusalem ; and Jewish spiritual health depends on each being an autonomous creative centre of its own and at the same time a centre which enjoys—in the full sense of the word—creative rivalry and competition with the other centre. For two thousand years the Jewish people has consisted of centre and Diaspora, and it is too late to change the basic image now. Something new might emerge from the total collapse of one pole or the other, but it would not be a recognisable bearer of the millenial tradition of Jewry.

Demographically the Jewish world, once it had absorbed the fleeing millions from Tsarist persecution between 1881 and 1914, remained relatively stable until the tragedies of the Second World War. The refugees from Hitler's Europe were but a tithe of those who fled from the Tsar's Russia ; though, in spite of their high social and intellectual average, they proved more difficult to absorb. For they came at a time of economic depression and contraction, and into a class of which the world, indeed, had inexhaustible need, but which it could not easily pay for in a declining economy. Nevertheless their contribution to scientific work and discovery during the second war was no negligible factor in the Allied victory, if only from the fact that Hitler had deprived his own economy of their services. They served also in the armies of all the Allies. In the first war they had had the pain of seeing Jew fight Jew in the armies of both sides. In the second they were at least united on a single side. Completely Jewish units took part in the battles of North Africa and Italy. Many Jews were engaged in secret activities behind the Nazi fronts, and in guerilla movements in occupied Europe ; and Jewish soldiers took a prominent part in the rescue of the survivors of the Concentration Camps, and the passage, by open or secret means, of many of them from life in a Europe which had become repellent to the National Home in Palestine.

It was said earlier that Jews had a unique history, but that they had normal human reactions. It is inevitable therefore that to have passed through the experiences described in this chapter and the next should have left traces on the survivors—for it must be remembered that nearly two-fifths of the whole people perished between 1940 and 1945, victims in many different ways of Hitler's antisemitism. But what is interesting is that this normal human reaction shows itself today only in a very understandable sensitivity, and has no special economic or social features. It is only seventeen years since my previous book on antisemitism appeared. But in that time all the special problems which troubled the ordinary man, and seemed to him to explain and even excuse hostility to Jews, have in fact disappeared.

Writing in 1944 one was writing with the flight from Russia as an *immediate* background. Men were still living among the leaders of western Jewish communities who would describe the tense moments in their childhood when, concealed in a wagon-load of hay, or stepping fearfully by forest paths at night, they had passed across the Russian frontier into freedom. Today the flight from Russia, and its economic consequences, are part of past history. The same in fact is true of the second flight from Nazi violence. The refugees from Germany were too few and too dispersed to make anywhere a particular social or economic pattern which could last for seventeen years. But in 1944 one could often associate the word 'Jew' with foreign-ness. Since 1945 the world has been divided into the two camps dominated by the U.S.A. and the U.S.S.R., and this has been a more prominent and determining factor of our problem than the position of any ethnic minority.

Yet it is too early for those of us who are not Jews to forget entirely the strains upon the Jewish community which lie behind the present situation. It has been a period of Jewish history full of movement, mostly involuntary ; and such a period is bound to create problems of adjustment. The world absorbed the refugees from Russia into the expanding economy of the 19th century more easily than it did the much smaller number from Nazi Germany during the depression of the '30's ; and this, of course, is what the Nazis intended. Refugees, apparently prosperous or arriving without money, could be pilloried by the national pro-Nazi party in the country concerned, and pointed to as foreigners coming to take what jobs there were, as part of the world-wide Jewish plot against the Gentile.

The whole work of providing for the refugees had to be conducted under the intolerable searchlight of constant Nazi propaganda, echoed by their jackals in all other countries. There is no people in the world which could have escaped such an ordeal unscathed. None of us are perfect, and our faults differ, so that it is possible for each and all of us to ' thank God we are not as other men ' at our neighbour's expense. The uncivilised behaviour of many white Americans to negroes, the arrogant attitude of many English-men to ' niggers ' and ' dagos,' the *petites économies* of the French which seem to many other people meanness, all are characteristics at which their neighbours can justifiably point a finger of contempt or hostility. And it is easy to imagine to what a state the world would be reduced if there was an internationally organised, heavily

financed body which, in the press, in meetings, in whispering
campaigns, set itself steadily to emphasise these characteristics to
the exclusion of all else, whenever our relations with each other,
and our needs of each other, were delicate or difficult. The same
would befall us as has befallen Jewry. Each individual among us—
especially those we would least like to be thought representative
of our way of life—would be a trustee for all of us. For his failings
would be imputed to all of us, and our disclaimer would be rejected.
Men would go about saying ' some of my best friends are Englishmen ' to show their objectivity in relating the latest item of the
whispering campaign. And we should be powerless to stop it, for
it *is* true that there are Englishmen whose only classification of
foreigners is ' niggers ' or 'dagos'; just as there *are* scandals between
black and white in America ; and the French *do* love their little
economies.

Of course there are Jewish knaves ; of course Jewish leaders
have committed mistakes ; some of the actions of individuals
were unwise ; and immigration amounting to tens of thousands
was bound to include some downright criminals ; often Jews have
protested too violently and too loudly. But there is no rational
explanation of how such little and individual affairs could become
a menace not only to the Jewish community itself, but to the whole
nation in which they constituted scarcely one per cent of the
population ; no rational explanation of why Jewish defence which,
in the main, was both accurate and reasonable, met with no success
comparable to the effort put forth.

Sympathetic and well-intentioned Gentiles frequently asked why
' the Jews did not do something ' about some particular scandal.
Sometimes there was a real core of fact in the complaint, for any
refugee body will cause a certain amount of social friction ; more
often the scandal was invented and circulated by members of the
British Union, or multiplied from a single incident. Few people
who expected the Chief Rabbi or the President of the Board of
Deputies of British Jews to be able at once to suppress anti-social
conduct on the part of Jews, would ever have dreamed of expecting
the Archbishops of Canterbury or Westminster to accept responsibility for a nominal member of the Anglican or Roman Catholic
communions. Jewish leaders and Committees worked incessantly
for the good name of their community. Every complaint—even
the most fatuous—was examined. They had, of course, no legal

power ; often they could only regret that some things were inevitable so long as men remained imperfect. But all was of little avail. Anti-Jewish feeling had gone beyond the rational stage, even among those who, did they know the actual facts, would have reacted reasonably. But the facts were lost in a cloud of rumour. It is this which is the background of contemporary Jewish sensitivity.

VII

THE NAZI PERIOD OF AUTHORITY (1933-1945)

THE REPUBLIC, BORN at Weimar after the defeat of imperial
Germany in 1918, was never the complete master of its subjects,
and it did not always command even a tenuous loyalty from some
of those whom it set in authority.

It was at one time fashionable in Britain and elsewhere to
ascribe almost all the evil elements in the Germany of 1919–1939
to the effects of the hostility of the victorious allies and the severity
of the treaty of Versailles. This was never true, though it would
appear that there was a period in the middle twenties when a
different policy and a determined effort at reconciliation might
have proved successful. But even at this period there would have
been no universal abandonment of the dream of revenge, or
universal acceptance even of a share of the guilt of the war. From
the beginning there were strong groups in Germany which regretted
not the war, but only the defeat, and desired to regain the lost
influence of Germany as a great power only that she might become
powerful enough to seek revenge. As the years went on the weaknesses
and mistakes of successive republican governments steadily increased
the influence of these groups, and it was among them that Hitler
found his followers, and out of their feelings that he built up his
political propaganda.

Everything which Germans resented or regretted was most
skilfully attributed by him to the Republic, always called by the
Nazis ' the System ', a vague, all-embracing word, covering social
and moral issues as well as political. However, a more concrete
enemy was also necessary, and it had not only to be concrete but
also to be safe. Germany was far too weak in the early days of
the Nazi movement for public attention to be directed against
the real enemies, France, or the Allied Powers in general ; and

87

the Nazi party within Germany was also too weak to risk carrying
its attack against the Weimar Republic to the point of compelling
its Government to take really vigorous action. Nor could even
' the System ' be usefully made the sole menace, so long as there
was little hope of destroying it by frontal attack. What was wanted
was an enemy sufficiently concrete to be usable in the most vulgar
propaganda addressed to the most ignorant sections of the populace,
and sufficiently weak to give the Nazis a cheap victory, both
psychological and physical. The Jews of Germany exactly supplied
the need.

The extent to which they did so, and the appalling consequences
of the choice, are both due to the beliefs and convictions of Hitler
himself. Taught by Lueger, he believed passionately in the truth
that ' the Jews ' were an evil and dangerous menace. But he was
also shrewd enough to know that antisemitism was a most valuable
political weapon. Hermann Rauschning, a late recruit to National
Socialism who then repented of having joined it, has left us invaluable information from the actual ' table talk ' of Hitler himself.
On one occasion Hitler said to him[1] :

> ' My Jews are a valuable hostage given to me by the
> democracies. Antisemitic propaganda in all countries is an
> almost indispensable medium for the extension of our political
> campaign. You will see how little time we shall need in order
> to upset the ideas and criteria of the whole world, simply
> and purely by attacking Judaism. It is beyond question the
> most important weapon in my propaganda arsenal.'

Here are the two elements which can be traced all through his
career. His hatred and fear of the Jews he conveyed to the whole
German public by the hypnotic effect of his speeches ; the shrewdly
calculated spread of an essential anti-democratic weapon he
ensured by every institution of the Party, and, later, of the
government.

Jews were only one per cent of the German population ; and
the relics of the antisemitism of the 19th century, together with
the effects of the constant insistence on *The Protocols* and the
' Jewish Bolshevik menace,' ensured that they would find no very
valiant defenders. The republicans, already on the defensive
themselves, were not likely to endanger their popularity still

---

[1] *Hitler Speaks.* Herman Rauschning. Thornton Butterworth 1939, p. 223. A series
of political conversations with Adolf Hitler on his real aims.

further by defending the Jews. There was also this extra advantage. As in other countries, so in Germany, their history has caused the Jews to be concentrated both geographically and occupationally. They could easily be made to appear much more prominent (and therefore, from the standpoint of Hitler's propaganda, much more dangerous) than they really were. With such skill and with such constant reiteration were the different misrepresentations driven home that they came to be widely believed to be true, not only in Germany itself, but wherever Nazi influence penetrated in other countries. Many people in many parts of the world still believe that before 1933 Germany was 'dominated by the Jews', so assiduously was this ' fact ', supported with well-selected statistics, pumped into every visitor to the Reich and disseminated from every Nazi agency abroad.

Jews were certainly prominent in the cultural and professional life of Berlin, and in certain sections of its business life. Berlin statistics would therefore be given as though they covered the whole country ; similarly the statistics of the particular aspect of a trade or profession in which Jews were numerous were given as though they represented the Jewish proportion in the whole trade or profession. In the legal profession solicitors would be chosen, because Jews could rarely become judges ; in medicine, G.P.'s because Jews were mostly excluded from hospitals and universities. And the word ' dominant ' was so constantly used as a complete synonym for ' prominent ' that men actually came to believe that it was only necessary to show that ten per cent of an occupation was in Jewish hands, for this profession to be ' dominated ' by the Jews. And, to the Nazis of course, the corollary followed, that if it was ' dominated ' by Jews, the results were bad for Germany. To them, the Weimar Republic and the Weimar parliament were both entirely ' controlled ' by the Jews. How, they did not trouble to state.

A second story which was widely circulated was that Germany had been inundated with ' foreign Jews ' during the period of inflation. Germany has long had excellent official statistics, and in actual fact this ' flood ' amounted to less than one for every thousand of the population, and the majority of these were poor Jews who had fled from the unsettled conditions of Poland and eastern Europe. But a third story attributed to this element all the scandals of the inflation period, and asserted that they had made great fortunes out of the German people, and then flaunted them in the face of the national poverty. It was certainly true of some individuals, and one or two of the bad scandals of this period did involve individuals among these 'foreign' Jews. But the real profiteers of the inflation were the great industrialists and the landowners. Some were able to pay off their debts and mortgages, contracted in pre-1914 marks when they stood at 20 to the £ sterling, when the mark had fallen to one thousand millionth of its value. Others, especially Hugo Stinnes (who was not a Jew), by an ingenious system of borrowing from the State Bank and repaying the loan when the mark had fallen heavily, were able to buy up industries in every field and make enormous profits.

Different arguments against the Jews were addressed to different classes of the population among whom Hitler hoped from the first to win supporters. By pretending that he would cleanse the professional life of the country from Jewish elements, he held out the possibility of work to the large number of graduates of the universities, technical and secondary schools who were unemployed ; and these unemployed youths formed a considerable proportion of his early storm troopers. By 'fighting against the influence of foreign elements', he appealed to the Nationalists ; and by concentrating exclusive attention on Jews as the profiteers from the inflation, he provided a comfortable smoke-screen for the industrialists and landowners, while at the same time continuing to pose as a friend of the German working man. The effectiveness of this policy was shown by the enormous contributions heavy industry, and capitalists generally, made to his funds.

But the Jews were used not merely for these concrete purposes ; they had to be found a place in the inevitable background of any political movement in Germany—its *Weltanschauung*, or philosophy of life. Race and soil were the foundation ideas of Hitler's *Weltanschauung*, and the Jews were to him the racial poison of the world, just as the Aryan was the racial hero. Racial antisemitism had made its first appearance in the middle of the 19th century. A French political philosopher, De Gobineau, had introduced it, and a much greater French scholar, Ernest Renan, had, in his earlier years especially, written much against the 'semitic spirit'. But the full antithesis Aryan-Semite was finally brought out by a curiously fascinating writer, a German citizen of English birth, Houston Stewart Chamberlain. In a work filled with perverted erudition, entitled *The Foundations of the* 19*th Century* and published in 1899, he traced the conflict of the Aryan and the Semitic spirit all through history. In fact, of course, both words describe languages and not peoples, and the whole idea of ' race ' as used by these writers is fictional.

Chamberlain's method of deciding what was Aryan was simple. Everything which in his judgement was noble in history was Aryan, and no further proof was needed than that he was an Aryan himself and felt the kinship in his blood. As he was one among many who were fascinated by the racial idea, and as it was not to be expected that the likes and dislikes of all members of that school would be identical, the results of this simple method of proving what was Aryan were often amusing. Thus to Chamberlain himself Goethe was so perfect an example of the purest Aryan that he quoted him in his *Foundations* no less than 127 times (according to the index). But another writer of the same school, Lenz, calls Goethe a ' Teutonic-Western-Asiatic crossbreed', and proves it by an examination of the poet's mentality ; while yet a third, Otto Hauser, proves his mongrel nature by the fact that in *Faust* there are ' hundreds of quite pitifully bad verses'. Later, in Nazi days, the same division arose about Christianity and Christ himself ; to the German Christians, Christ was an Aryan, and I remember a Nazi theological student being very surprised that I, as a theologian, had not been taught that Jesus was a German, son of a German soldier and a Persian (i.e. Aryan) woman. He appeared, quite sincerely, to believe that this was an accepted conclusion of scholarship. But to the neo-pagan of the Rosenberg school, Christianity was the typical Semitic, un-aryan teaching which could only undermine the proud Aryan spirit by its inculcation of a slave mentality. Hitler himself accepted the views of Chamberlain with avidity, and found in him authority for his own dreams. They gave the apparatus of ' scholarly ' profundity to the prejudices which he had adopted from his teacher and idol, Lueger, the antisemitic Mayor of Vienna. When, therefore, the National Socialist German Workers' Party came into existence, it was laid down that only those of German blood could be German citizens.

When the Nazis came into power in 1933, antisemitism was systematically infiltrated into every department of life from mathematics and religion to children's books and pornography ; and broadcast, as an integral part of the Nazi way of life, from every diplomatic and consular office abroad. The German mind desires things to be both orderly and solid—*grundlich*. The statements made in the propaganda of the previous ten years had to be seriously embodied in every aspect of public, national life. Scientists, historians, philosophers, jurists were all set to the task of proving in their respective subjects that it was incontrovertibly true that the Jews were such as Hitler and his henchmen described them, and that there could be no doubt about it.

The main difficulty was, of course, to say who *was* a Jew, and fantastic as it may seem when one regards the immense superstructure built upon the thesis of the danger of the ' Jewish poison', this was the one problem which always defied solution. At one time it was proudly announced that a scientist had elaborated an instrument—apparently rather like a metronome—whose pendulum revolved in dignified and rhythmic ellipses when in the proximity of Aryan blood, but in short and erratic jerks at the proximity of a Jew ; and at another time some particular physical feature or organ was proclaimed to yield decisive and objective evidence to scientific examination. I am told that wounded Nazis sometimes preferred death to a blood transfusion from blood which was, or might be, Jewish, in the firm belief that ' Jewish blood ' would poison them. But all efforts were in vain. It was never possible to go beyond the statement originally made that a Jew was a person whose grandparents were of the Jewish religion. Nor is this surprising. For scientists know that there is no such thing as a pure race. The word ' Aryan ' denotes only a family of languages spoken by the most diverse peoples.

Germans, Jews, British, are all the product of racial mixture ; just as their civilisations also are the product of the interrelationships of peoples. There are only a few distinguishable racial stocks in the world, and no people exhibits any of them in complete purity. Why so many Jews appear to be easily identifiable as Jews in western Europe or America is because the exact mixture of ethnic stocks from which they come is only rarely found in these regions except among members of the group who profess the Jewish religion. But from southern Germany and Austria to the Mediterranean region, in south eastern Europe, and in Turkey and the surrounding countries, there will be found many possessing what the western or northern European calls ' Jewish ' characteristics, but who profess Christianity or Islam, and whose ancestors have never professed Judaism. There is no reputable scientist in any country whose researches support the Nazi theory of a Jewish race, or indeed the Nazi theory of superior and inferior races. And since the Nazis themselves failed to produce any objective scientific evidence for their theories, they had to remain content with the ludicrous definition that a Jew was one whose grandparents professed Judaism. Certain classes, Nazi officials, and those entitled to a hereditary peasant holding, had to go beyond their grandparents, and produce ' Aryan ' ancestry back to the year 1800 ; but even then, if a doubtful ancestor occurred, the only test could be ; were his or her grandparents Jews? The result was an army of officials to search and check registers, frenzied questions addressed to sources of information of all types in all parts of the world, and, no doubt, a good deal of graft to provide satisfactory pedigrees. But it remained obstinately true that it was impossible scientifically to establish what exactly it was to be a Jew.

This, however, was almost the only flaw in a system which was monumentally complete in its perversity. An Institute in Berlin and another in Munich produced ponderous and apparently scholarly tomes on the place of the Jews in German history. They were written by men familiar with the technique of research and, with their mass of references, quotations, and footnotes, were quite capable of passing as genuine and objective historical studies. In every university, and in every faculty, were appointed professors who—in spite of the basic difficulty of deciding what or who was a Jew—were quite capable of delivering lectures to distinguish the German and the Jewish spirit in law, in medicine, in philosophy, in art, in psychology and even in mathematics. Naturally the outside world perceived a considerable falling off in the merits of German scholarship, but this did not influence the Nazis, who only saw in the contempt of scholars abroad further evidence of the power and pernicious influence of Jews throughout the world. A new Protestant Church came into existence which would not accept Jewish converts, and which stripped the Christian religion and the Christian scriptures of their ' Jewish perversions '. The Nazis did not stop at educating the new generation, vitally important though this was to their success. By lectures, by the use of all the professional and scientific publications with which Germany abounded, and by the strictest and most careful control of all professional, commercial and other associations, the Nazi view

on race was inculcated into the whole middle class with a thoroughness, and an apparent irrefutability, which had—and still has in
many cases—a profound effect on the actual thinking and beliefs
of those indoctrinated. Apparently sober and factual statements,
balanced by statistics, were handed out to visitors. In consequence
many who visited Germany in the years between 1933 and 1939,
and who had known the previous situation, reported that so far
as the Jewish question was concerned, the Nazi view was extremely
widely accepted.

With the general German public other methods were used, and
every kind of violence and vulgarity was not only permitted but
definitely encouraged. The bullying of Jews, adults or children,
was considered to be of great value in teaching German youth to
despise sentimental pacifism, internationalism, and Christian
morality. A picture book which was issued by *Der Stürmer* for
children, and which was written and illustrated by a girl in her
'teens, begins with the good medieval statement that the father of
the Jews is the devil, and continues, with illustrations which would
give an English child nightmares if its foolish parents allowed it
to read it, to present the Jews as obscene and disgusting polluters
of German blood and life. Throughout it seeks to inculcate into
the youngest the idea that it is noble to fight against the Jewish
people including, of course, their children. Schoolmasters reinforced
the lesson by publicly insulting Jewish children in their classes,
and repressing all signs of tenderness or sympathy on the part of
other children. Even those whose chosen reading was pornography
were given a satisfying weekly diet of rapes, assaults and whatnot
in *Der Stürmer* which was edited by Julius Streicher, one of Hitler's
most assiduous followers.

Antisemitism was thus woven into every strand of the thought
and activity of Hitler's Germany ; it was also interwoven into
the whole of her economic life. The capital stolen from her half
million Jews was extremely useful to the Treasury ; the threat of
confiscation, delation or violence provided endless opportunities of
blackmail not only to individual Nazi officials but even to the
German government in its foreign commercial relations. And, of
course, dispossessing Jews provided a quantity of houses, profitable
businesses, furniture, jewellery, *objets d'art* and jobs to Hitler's
followers. Not even in Tsarist Russia had the whole population
been given so direct and individual a stake in the persecution and

despoiling of its Jewish neighbours. The tragic evidence is that, though a minority was horrified and ashamed, antisemitic prejudice had so hypnotized the bulk of the German people that they accepted, against the evidence often of their own eyes, the pseudo-scientific and statistical expositions of their government, and of every Nazi speaker on the subject. They consented, with no more than a shrug of their shoulders, to the legalised or illegal violence, the indecencies, murders and suicides which resulted. They had really come to imagine that Jewry was a vast and hostile world force, destroying and polluting all that the Germans held sacred, an enemy so powerful that all means were justified in the defence of ' Aryan ' culture and values.

Describing the situation in 1937, an Australian Professor, Stephen Roberts, wrote[1] :

' Worst of all, worse even than the individual suffering of today amongst the Jews, is the creation of a national mentality bred on such hate as that which the German feels for the Jew. " The other nations are not yet awake," a university professor said to me, " and the time will come when the world will be grateful to us for upholding civilization against the Jews". I showed him my Australian passport with the name of a Jewish governor-general on the front cover, Isaac Isaacs, and told him of that other Jewish commander-in-chief, Monash, who first broke through the Hindenburg Line ; and his only retort was that such a degradation of a fine community only proved the truth of his contention!

' The most tragic thought of all is that Germany is behind Hitler in his campaign against *Rassenschande* or race-defilement. I spoke about it to peasants and great industrialists, army officers, and factory labourers ; and all approved of it, although a few regretted the tone of *Der Stürmer*. (That there is some opposition, however, is evident from the numerous attacks in Party papers on " Jew-lackeys", that is, Aryans who disapprove of brutality towards Jews.) When a nation can willingly concur in a pogrom against half a million Jews—when it sees nothing tragic in the starving of little children and the holding of them up to execration in kindergartens—when it sees nothing funny in the official decree of the town of Königsdorf that " cows purchased either directly or in-

[1] *The House that Hitler Built*. S. H. Roberts. Methuen, 1937, p. 266.

directly from Jews are not allowed to be served by the communal bull", then it reaches the point where its institutions are utterly incomprehensible to us.'

It was not enough that antisemitism was thus constantly propagated and that individual Nazis and the Nazi state enjoyed the material profits of a general denunciation, looting and persecution. Every charge that had been made against German Jews was taken to be so substantiated that it needed to be embodied in precise laws and enforced with the utmost rigour. Hitler became Chancellor in January 1933 at a time when he commanded only one third of the votes ; but he manoeuvred to obtain a new election in which, by unscrupulous means, he obtained a ' legal ' majority for his government. This was at once followed by ' spontaneous ' outbreaks all over the country against Jews in every walk of life. Jewish judges and lawyers were attacked and denounced in the law courts ; Jewish teachers in schools and universities, Jewish doctors in hospitals and their practices, Jewish shops and businesses, all were objects of hostility ; and everywhere the Brownshirts, the private army of the Nazis, were prominent in the demonstrations.

The violence of the outbreaks shocked foreign visitors and journalists, and there was an outcry in the press of the world, where, apparently, it had thus far been thought that Nazi antisemitism was just a propaganda weapon used to get Hitler into power. This was, after all, the use to which it had been put by Bismarck and the antisemitic parties of the 19th century. None of them had actually legislated against Jews. Hitler soon showed that this was not to be the case again. The foreign press reaction was followed by a boycott of German Jews, so that 'they might teach the Jewish press all over the world to report German news more objectively'. Then in April began concrete anti-Jewish legislation, dividing civic rights into two categories, and creating a second class citizenship for Jews and those with Jewish blood, or married to Jewish wives.

The first laws regulated the Civil Service, the vast army of ' officials ' (*Beamten*) which in Germany included all state, provincial and municipal officials, all staffs of semi-public bodies, all teachers in schools and universities, all doctors and employees in state hospitals, all judges, and court officers, as well as such people as mayors, postmasters, railway engineers and so on. All this vast mass of Germans had to produce evidence of the religion of their parents and grand-parents to prove their 'Aryan' status. If they could not prove this, they were to be retired. At first they were to be allowed a small pension, and any Jew or non-Aryan (i.e. a converted Jew, a half-Jew, or one with a Jewish wife) who had served in the first world war, or who had lost father or son in the first World War, or who had been an official before the first World War, was allowed to retain his post. To the astonishment of the Nazi Party, which had been ceaselessly proclaiming that under the Weimar Republic all the apparatus of the state had been in the hands of 'foreign' Jews, it became apparent that the law affected very few people. To begin with only 25,000 Jewish families were affected out of at least a million families of officials; and then it became evident that of these a very large proportion was entitled to exemption. In May a new law dealt with all public employees who were not already covered ; and in June new regulations made most of the previous exemptions meaningless.

In 1934 the same treatment was meted out to any Jew who had chosen the army as career, and it was laid down that, in case of war, Jews were not to be allowed the 'honour' of fighting for Germany, but were to be conscripted as a labour force. All Jewish names were, shortly after, expunged from the war memorials of the first World War. The legal profession required more complex legislation. Judges and officers of the courts were covered by the Civil Service law, but the practice of law was a 'free profession', and for some years boycott and extra-legal action had to be made use of, because it was impossible to meet the legal needs of the country if all Jewish and non-Aryan lawyers were to be denied the right to practise. But gradually they were excluded from one after another particular aspect of their profession. Moreover the employment of a Jew by a non-Jewish client became less and less common—for a client was not likely to choose to be represented by a lawyer who was looked on with hostility by all official bodies —until it became possible in 1938 to forbid any Jew from employing an 'Aryan' lawyer and any 'Aryan' from employing a Jewish lawyer.

The treatment of doctors followed the same general lines. It had always been a profession which attracted Jews, and some 10 per cent of doctors in Germany in 1933 were Jews, and in addition about 4 per cent were 'non-Aryan'. It was impossible to dismiss all these doctors immediately, or epidemics would have followed, apart from the fact that Jewish doctors were both popular and efficient. The immense majority were general practitioners or specialists in private practice ; and these were left alone, while those in the hospitals or teaching in the universities were attacked first. The next victims were those who drew a main part of their income from the public purse for medical attention to the poorer classes. In both cases the exceptions in the Civil Service law were considered applicable—at first. In 1934 these exceptions were decreed not to apply to any new applicant who was not an ' Aryan'. But the main attack came a year later. It excluded any but Aryans from the study of medicine in the universities, and then expelled all but Aryan doctors from the public service, and the many medical Insurance Companies. In 1938 all still existing exemptions were cancelled, and the expulsion from the profession was complete. Jewish doctors might still serve Jews ; in fact no other doctor could ; but this could provide a livelihood to only a small proportion of the Jewish doctors who had not succeeded in leaving the country.

In September 1935 there were passed at the Nuremberg Rally, the annual self-exhibition of the Nazi Party, two short laws. One stated that ' Only a German subject of German or related blood who proves by his attitude that he is willing and fit to serve faithfully the German nation and Reich is a citizen . . . Only a citizen is vested with full political rights'. The second law dealt with the 'protection of German blood and honour', and forbade all marriages between Aryans and non-Aryans, all service of Aryan domestics below a certain age in a non-Aryan household. A mass of lesser laws of the same and the subsequent period rammed into those Jews left in the Reich their inferior status, and regulated with increasingly deliberate offensiveness and arrogance every detail of their lives.

Meanwhile, however, the large majority of German Jews had always earned their living in every form of industry and commerce, and were more difficult to attack directly. The picketing of Jewish owned shops became a commonplace sight in German towns ; Jewish businesses were compelled to take Aryan partners, and then the Aryan partner ousted the Jew. Jews found it increasingly difficult to obtain fresh supplies, to get licences, to get repairs when mobs attacked their premises, or to meet the needs of non-Jewish customers, who thereupon deserted them for other suppliers. In every way which would not inconvenience themselves by creating shortages, the Nazis tried, nationally and locally, to make life increasingly impossible for Jewish traders. Moreover all the time there was spasmodic violence, which was always explained as the right and inevitable reaction of German Aryans to any insult on their honour ; and this violence culminated in the pogrom of the ' Crystal Night ' in 1938 when Jews were beaten up, synagogues were burned, and shops were destroyed, all over the Reich.

The event which led up to it was an attack upon the Jews of eastern European origin, who were always proclaimed by the Nazis to have crowded into the Reich during the years of post-war poverty. That this was quite untrue has already been shown. Facts, however, made little difference to the Nazis, and it was suddenly decreed that all such Jews were to be rounded up and expelled. Some thousands were forced across the frontier with the utmost brutality at Zbonszyn, a frontier post on the line from Berlin to Warsaw. But the Poles refused to allow them to enter Poland, and they were left to die of cold or starvation in a northern November. One elderly couple of the name of Grünspan had a son who, outraged beyond endurance by this treatment of his parents, entered the German embassy in Paris and shot and killed an embassy official, Ernst vom Rath. The whole of the surviving Jewry of Germany was adjudged guilty of the crime. A fine of many millions of marks extracted what was left of their property, and the carefully organised' spontaneous' anger of the people was allowed a night of pillage and licence. That is the story of the ' Crystal Night'.

When Hitler entered Austria in the spring of 1938, the position of the Jews of Germany was thus described by Professor Roberts[1] :

> ' At present, the German Jew has no civil rights. He is not a citizen ; he cannot vote or attend any political meeting ; he has no liberty of speech and cannot defend himself in print ; he cannot become a civil servant or a judge ; he cannot be a writer or a publisher or a journalist ; he cannot speak over the radio ; he cannot become a screen actor or an actor before Aryan audiences ; he cannot teach in any educational institution ; he cannot enter the service of the railway, the Reichsbank, and many other banks ; he cannot exhibit paintings or give concerts ; he cannot work in any public hospital ; he cannot enter the Labour Front or any of the professional

[1] *The House that Hitler Built.* p. 263.

organisations, although membership of many callings is restricted to members of these groups ; he cannot even sell books or antiques. If he is starving he can receive no aid from the *Winterhilfe* organization, and if he dies in battle his name will be on no war memorial (for has he not seen the erasing of the names of his forebears from such memorials by order of Goebbels and Frick?). In addition to these, there are many other restrictions applying in certain localities. The upshot of them all is that the Jew is deprived of all opportunity for advancement and is lucky if he contrives to scrape a bare living unmolested by Black Guards or *Gestapo*. It is a campaign of annihilation—a pogrom of the crudest form, supported by every State instrument.'

The same treatment was now meted out to the Jews of Austria, and, later in the year, to those of Czechoslovakia.

Such treatment inevitably produced a continuous flight among those Jews who could escape or, at least, send their children to an atmosphere where they would not be subjected to daily fear and humiliation. The world found it difficult to absorb these refugees, for their flight took place in conditions of world-wide depression. So thorough was Nazi antisemitism that, as we shall see in the next chapter, even the fugitives from Hitler's cruelty were made to serve his propaganda and his world plots.

The outbreak of war in 1939, and the overrunning of almost all Europe in 1940, put some nine million Jews in the hands of the Nazis, and of these two-thirds perished. Death came in every possible form, from starvation and exhaustion to suffocation in the appalling trains in which the victims were transported across Europe, from poison and torture in ' medical ' experiments, to the bullets and gas of the extermination camps. Over all this horror presided Adolf Eichmann, who was found in Argentina in 1960, tried and convicted in Israel in 1961, and executed after his appeal had failed, in the following year.

The world has never known such systematized and grandiose organisation of mass murder, for which the word ' genocide ' was coined. For Jews were not the only victims. Hermann Rauschning, whose report of Hitler's conversation on antisemitism has already been quoted, records that Hitler once said to him :

' To preserve the German people we must depopulate. . . . The French complained after the war that there were twenty million Germans too many. We accept the criticism, but our friends will have to excuse us if we subtract the twenty million elsewhere.'[1]

We do not know how near the Nazis came to this figure, for in many places whole communities, together with all their records, were exterminated, and nobody was left to tell the number of the victims. But it is much more probable that the total exceeded the twenty millions than that it fell short. Exact civilian losses in the Soviet Union have never been published, but a careful estimate is that they amounted to between twelve and fifteen million. Normal warfare could not explain one half, perhaps even one quarter, of these casualties, and by far the greater number must have perished by cold-blooded murder. Exclusive of the Jewish victims, some three million Poles, one million four hundred thousand Yugoslavs, six hundred thousand Frenchmen, half a million Greeks, and Czech, Dutch and Belgian victims to the number of another half million, all perished by Hitler's command. Thus the five to six million Jews formed considerably less than half the total holocaust, though no other people lost so high a proportion of its numbers—nearly two-fifths of the Jews of the world. It is unfortunate that the figure of six million has been fixed in the world's memory as though it were the total of all Hitler's civilian victims. It was the estimate at the Nuremberg trials of the Jewish victims alone, and later information has only modified that figure to the extent of substituting ' between five and six million', as pockets of Jewish survivors were discovered in various parts of the world.

Had all Hitler's plans been carried out there would have been even more 'victims. Special punishments which would have led to millions of deaths were planned in both Holland and France, and only averted at the last minute.[2] Moreover, in addition to the live humans whom he killed, the population of Europe was intended to be reduced by the keeping of some eleven million men in work camps for from two to five years, with no contact with their wives. Truly Hitler's Germany required a wide *Lebensraum*.

Anti-democratic organisations in Germany and elsewhere have seized upon the figure of six million, and its subsequent very modest revision, as though the whole story of ' genocide ' was a Jewish invention. The plans for the murder of millions of Dutchmen and

[1] *Hitler Speaks*, p. 140.
[2] *The Magic Touch.* Joseph Kessel. R. Hart-Davis, 1961. Ch. 6 and passim.

Frenchmen, the actual slaughter of millions of Russians, Ukrainians, Yugoslavs, Greeks, as well as Germans and others, are conveniently forgotten.

Those who have had the task of tracing and examining the men who were actually responsible for the killing have discovered no signs of grief or repentance among most of them. They were men of low mental calibre, often men who had been in trouble ever since adolescence, men with an inferiority complex, men who had been failures in life. They would talk endlessly and with pride about the techniques by which they could increase the number of human beings they could kill in a single day or a single action ; but they appeared incapable even of any interest in the moral implications of their activity.

Only in one particular characteristic was the murder of Jews by the Nazis different from their murder of other peoples. In the case of the Jews it had been preceded by up to six years of spoliation of whatever Jewish population was accessible, first in Germany, then in Austria, then in Czechoslovakia, and then, with the outbreak of war in 1939, in most of the rest of Europe. So far as the government of the German Federal Republic (i.e. West Germany) is concerned, there has been no attempt to mitigate the ghastly nature of the crime. No restitution can be made to the dead. But the German government has made all the restitution in its power where property, pensions, or estates are concerned, and it has recognised in the State of Israel the heir to whole communities which have been exterminated. It has slowly, and not always effectively, tried to purge its official classes of those concerned with the mass murders of civilians. It is equally trying to ensure the proper treatment of this terrible period of German history in the schools and literature of Germany.

The Government, however, cannot control everything. In spite of its obvious absurdity, the story is again being circulated by pro-Nazi organisations that Germany was destroyed by ' a stab in the back ' in 1945, just as the previous generation of Germans was told by Hitler himself that imperial Germany was so destroyed in 1918. In one form or another Nazi groups have inevitably survived in the country. Men who had, from 1933 to 1945, taken some part in the vast machine of a modern state were equally inevitably still needed nationally and communally to contribute to the administration of the successors of the Nazis. Doubtless there are many cases where more proceedings should have been taken against ex-Nazis or Nazi collaborators ; doubtless not all repentances are sincere. It is not humanly possible completely to wash the slate clean from so gigantic a crime and offence as was Nazi Germany ; and there are many psychological and private activities of which it is true to say that ' you cannot make men good by Act of Parliament'.

Openly pro-Nazi and antisemitic parties still pullulate in the shadows of Bonn and the Länder, but their voting support is small. In the main they profit from the struggle between East and West rather than from Hitler's antisemitism. Forgetting the cynical Hitler-Stalin Pact at the outbreak of war, they proclaim that ' Hitler was right ' in seeing Communism as the greatest menace to European civilisation, and their arguments gain force from the conflict in Berlin, and the nature of the East German government. But the argument passes easily from anti-communism to anti-semitism. Yet it was a shock to the general German public when the daubing of swastikas on the new synagogue of Cologne in December 1959 triggered off a wave of similar actions in forty different countries. It was not an action without precedent in post-war Germany; for on a number of occasions Jewish cemeteries had been desecrated and tombstones broken or overthrown. But it was a reminder that, in Germany as elsewhere, the price of freedom is perpetual vigilance.

VIII

NAZI INFLUENCE FROM
1933 TO THE PRESENT

'ANTISEMITIC PROPAGANDA IN all countries' said Hitler to Hermann
Rauschning 'is an almost indispensable medium for our political
campaign. You will see how little time we shall need to upset the
ideas and criteria of the whole world, simply and purely by
attacking Judaism.'[1] Fortunately for the world there was sufficient
strength in its other 'ideas and criteria' for it to be ultimately
successful in its resistance to Hitler between 1939 and 1945. But the
cost has been exorbitant, and we are still paying it. What is, however, true is that antisemitism was the unifying cement of the Fascist
and National-Socialist anti-democratic parties which Hitler encouraged all through the world from 1933 onwards, and that it was
their antisemitism which attracted a great deal of their general
support.

It was Germany's most valuable *exportartikel*. The world will never
know how many millions of pounds were spent by Nazi Germany in
financing antisemitic propaganda in the anti-democratic movements, which were Hitler's best hope of allies in England, in
France, in Belgium and Holland, in Hungary, Poland and Rumania,
in South Africa, in Canada, in the United States and in the whole
of Latin America. The same technique was applied as at home.
There would be more or less restrained and apparently quite
objective statistics ; organisations would be fostered which
apparently only desired closer friendship in the interests of peace ;
antisemitic propaganda would be presented in a reasonable, almost
regretful, tone. It would be suggested that of course these measures
in Germany had been necessary only because the German situation
was *different* ; Germany had a different type of Jew ; and so on and
so on. And Fascists in other countries assisted Nazi propaganda by

[1] For full quotation, see p. 88.

pretending that the views they expressed were based only on their own ' national ' estimate of their own situation.

An excellent example of this stage was provided in England by the attitude of the British Union of Fascists. Its leader, Sir Oswald Mosley, protested most vigorously in 1933 that the Union was in no sense antisemitic. 'Attacks on Jews in any shape or form were strictly forbidden within a month after the movement was launched. This order has been loyally obeyed by all the members. The few who did not agree to do so were excluded from the movement. Fascism stands for religious and racial tolerance.'[1] But the programme of the Union seemed to make little impact on the British voter at that time, and the organisation remained obscure and unnoticed. Then its leaders visited Nazi Germany, and returned with the full armoury of Nazi antisemitism. In a short time they had attracted the attention of the national press by the violence which accompanied their meetings and marches. For they had made antisemitism a major plank in their platform, and had concentrated their meetings in the poorer quarters of London's East End where thousands of Jews lived, and where the falsehoods and vituperations of the Fascists were naturally most resented.

Mosley and other leaders were rendered innocuous during the war, but after the war Mosley's name occurs in various gatherings of the shabby relics of pre-war antisemitic parties in various countries. Coming out into the open again in Britain, he repeated his previous declaration that his new movement was in no sense anti-semitic. In the summer of 1962 he chose a strange way of proving his point. He requested permission for a meeting in Ridley Road, an obscure street in North East London, the scene of bloody riots during his antisemitic phase of 1934-1936, and which had no other significance than that it had been a quarter largely inhabited by the poorer Jews of the East End.

From 1933 to 1939 several Institutes, lavishly provided with funds, were churning out continuously, and in many languages, all the usual Nazi material on the Jews. The same stock quotations, or misquotations, occur in apparently quite independent publications in Montreal or Buenos Aires, in Brussels or Bucharest. And in every language editions of *The Protocols* were printed and distributed. That they could be shown to be forgeries made no difference to the

---

[1] Quoted from a signed statement contributed by Mosley to *The Economic Jewish Forum* for July 28, 1933.

Nazi antisemitic campaign. If a line of attack was blocked in one place, it was easy to open it in another. If one quotation was discredited another could easily be substituted. But usually they did not trouble. In the world-wide discontent and frustration of the thirties, they had no need to worry about their failures.

Much of this material was printed in Germany and distributed to the German communities living abroad. These, in their turn, formed valuable centres for the dissemination of antisemitism and other pro-Nazi propaganda throughout the countries where they lived. In England it was discreetly done at private meetings and dinner parties, and it was largely the ' upper ' classes which were thus infected. In South Africa the activities of the German community in the previously German colony of South-West Africa compelled the South African Government to take serious steps against them. In Latin America, and to a lesser degree in the U.S.A., the local German Nazis, supported by German diplomatic and consular representatives, largely succeeded in terrorising the non-Nazi German settlers in those countries into acquiescence and even support of their activities.

In many countries it was possible to go still further. In some, as in England, there already existed obscure Fascist bodies ; in others, such as Poland and Rumania, full-blown antisemitic organisations had already been in existence for some time. In both cases these parties were closely linked with Germany. Their leaders were invited to Berlin, and there flattered and advised how to extend their influence ; it was after one such visit that the British Union suddenly changed over from its previous attitude and flung itself into the vulgarest antisemitism on the straight Nazi model. These apparently patriotic parties and organisations were used to forward definite German ambitions, and to demand the orientation of national policy in a pro-German sense, often with complete disregard for the real national interests of the countries in which they existed. This was conspicuous in Poland in the period before 1939 in which her government was quitting the orbit of French influence and entering into close friendship with Germany. In Hungary and Rumania German policy was equally indifferent to the needs of the countries themselves. In every case there was one common feature. Germany would not negotiate with, or support, a group which did not adopt her antisemitic policy.

In 1933, when Hitler had only just come to power and Mussolini was definitely the senior partner of the Fascist firm, Mosley could write : ' Antisemitism was never known in Fascist Italy, and Mussolini has often expressed himself in this sense.' And this is borne out by many statements Mussolini made at that period. But gradually the balance of power shifted. As Hitler consolidated his government, the greater wealth and population of Germany, together with the drain caused by the Abyssinian adventure of Mussolini, enabled Hitler to demand that his partner should also toe the line. Mussolini was compelled to eat his words and make the discovery that the Jews were a sinister force ; he was obliged to forget that there were Jews among his oldest collaborators and, much more important, that there were distinguished Jews in all the professions and public services of Italy who had never known the slightest distinction between themselves and other Italians. In fact neither they themselves, nor the rest of the Italian population, were easily able to discover who were members of the Jewish community and who were not, so completely had their small numbers been integrated into Italian life. But the familiar rhythm was forced into operation. First it was the ' foreign ' Jews—many of them exiles from Germany who had come to Italy by invitation—who were found to be a menace ; then the attack was made on Italian-born Jews, on the German model. All that can be said in Italy's favour is that it was not made with quite the German brutality. But from that time on the words ' Nazi ' and ' Fascist ' have identical connotations so far as Jews are concerned, and the two words are used as synonyms in this book in speaking of present anti-democratic organisations or movements.

In several countries of eastern Europe the policy of the Nazis was necessarily somewhat different. Polish, Rumanian, or Hungarian antisemites did not need literary assistance, or instruction about ' the menace of the Jews'. In fact there were, as was said in a previous chapter, real problems, such as had never existed in Germany, connected with the Jewish position in these countries. Here Nazi policy was to support the antisemitic group openly against their governments ; to publicise as ' martyrdom ' any measures which governments might take against them ; and so to ensure that they should naturally look to Germany for support, if and when there was a chance of their attaining power.

Before 1939 and the outbreak of the second World War Nazi Germany did not reveal the full import of her contacts with these national organisations in which she had planted and tended so assiduously the seeds of antisemitism. Their full scope the world only discovered in 1940. Quisling in Norway, Mussert in Holland, Degrelle in Belgium, the Cagoulards and similar groups in France— all had been the spearheads of the antisemitic movements in their countries ; all of them were distinguished from other extreme Nationalist movements—such as the Flemish movement in Belgium —by the fact that when war came they willingly acted as traitors in the German interest.

In the pre-war years Germany had yet one further poisoned shaft for spreading the virus of her antisemitism—her own Jewish citizens. From 1933 onwards, but particularly in the year or two immediately preceding the war, Jewish refugees from Germany were unscrupulously exploited, even after they had been robbed of both property and home. In this exploitation the national fascist parties such as Mosley's British Union of Fascists and the fascist organisations in the United States, took a prominent part. The background was the immense depression of the early thirties. As in every country the working and professional classes were, by and large, convinced that the admission of immigrants meant the reduction of the number of jobs available for natives, there was no great difficulty in stirring up opinion against any additions to the population.

It was a deliberate part of Nazi antisemitic propaganda to ensure that the refugees arrived in a penniless condition. The confiscation of their property was also part of the ' export propaganda', for it made it easy game for their allies to proclaim that the refugees had clearly come to take away their jobs from Englishmen, Frenchmen, Belgians, Americans, Canadians—whatever it might be. In some cases, however, refugees arrived looking prosperous, for the reason that, since they were allowed to take so little cash or capital out of Germany, it was sensible to try and buy as many clothes, as much furniture, as possible. It not only avoided further purchases, but these could be sold if need arose. But this also was provided for. The antisemitic parties were there to shout that ' the so-called refugees ' showed no signs of ill-usage or of misery, and that many native workers would be glad to be as well clad as they. All round the world the same technique, the identical methods of attack, betrayed the same master hand, the same centre of instructions.

Finally there was the Arab world. This was selected for special care and attention. Prominent Nazi leaders took ' holidays ' in

Arab countries. Considerable numbers of Arab students were given scholarships to study in Germany, or at least free travel to visit Nazi conferences and meetings. While Mussolini poured out from his radio station at Bari anti-British, anti-Jewish broadcasts, the Nazis, with great thoroughness, fished in the troubled waters of the Middle East, harping always on the two themes of the perfidy and imperialism of the British and the iniquity of the Jews. There is nothing surprising in the Mufti of Jerusalem finding a war-time home in Berlin ; or in the pro-German rising of Rashid Ali in Iraq in 1941. Both were the result of years of careful German preparation.

An *anti*-Jewish world plot existed openly in the years from 1933 to 1945. It was backed by the whole network of Nazi diplomatic agencies throughout the world. It took little note of customary diplomatic behaviour ; it had no scruples about interfering in the life and internal affairs of other countries. It included blackmail and assassination in its armoury. It was possessed of limitless funds. It deluged every continent with such masses of propaganda, such skilfully falsified statistics, such cunningly perverted regrets and explanations, that it is not surprising that much of it found a home in the most innocent minds, and has left a heritage which still bears evil fruit.

The world rashly assumed that all this passed in 1945 with the defeat of the Nazis, and the disappearance of the immense funds which they had expended on the propagation of antisemitism. The truth was very different, but the world was too preoccupied to notice. As in Germany, so in general, public opinion was first roused when the new synagogue in Cologne was daubed with swastikas during the Christmas period of 1959, and when an epidemic of the same kind of outrage followed in some forty countries in every continent. Where the perpetrators were discovered they proved usually to be adolescents moved by no particular political philosophy, but it is very difficult to believe that a simultaneous outbreak of identical mischief occurred all over the world entirely without some central source, if not encouragement. In any case it was a reminder of the vulnerability of civilised society so long as the poison of antisemitism remains active.

In fact the swastika daubing was not needed to prove the survival of the evil injected into the world's body politic by twelve years of Hitler. Fascist societies of various kinds existed again openly in a good many countries. So far as Europe is concerned, the Nazi policy of recruiting brigades of SS from non-Germans provided a nucleus of indoctrinated antisemites. Such units had been created in Scandinavia, Holland, Belgium, and Spain. During the Nazi occupation of the Baltic and Balkan lands and a good deal of the Soviet Union, SS units were created there also. There was a Muslim SS drawn from Nazi sympathisers in Yugoslavia. In addition to these foreign groups, there were also known Nazi survivors in Eire, Spain, the Middle East and Latin America. There is plenty of material from which new anti-democratic movements could be recruited.

Two characteristics distinguish post- from pre-war anti-democratic movements. The first is that, in so far as they make use of antisemitism, they can rely on various kinds of Arab support. The second is that the European movements have a tendency to substitute the conception *Europe* for the domination of any particular country.

In Chapter Ten there is a full discussion of the real issues between the Arab world and the State of Israel, which are quite different from the imaginary ' menace ' of Jewish communities in Europe or America, and (especially as the Arabs are themselves Semites) cannot technically be characterised as ' antisemitism.' But it would be academic to expect that Arabs should reject the support offered them in their propaganda by European and American anti-democratic organisations, and be unwilling to contribute to their expenses. Moreover Cairo has been a centre which has attracted fugitives from Nazi Germany, and a good deal of the propaganda put out by Arab Information Offices is compiled by the well-known Nazi propagandist J. von Leers, working under the innocent sounding name of Omar Amin. He has changed his name but found little need to change his material.

Arab Information Offices are scattered throughout the world for the purpose of presenting the Arab case against Israel. They are nominally private organisations, but are often headed by persons with diplomatic or semi-diplomatic status, so that their activities are difficult to control. Behind them is the Arab League, and allied with them are the Arab Boycott Offices, run from Damascus, but linked with Arab embassies, legations and consular offices in all the countries which have substantial trading relations with the Middle East. Among their most effective propagandists are the many thousands of Arab students scattered in the European and American universities. The whole complex constitutes a widespread network of anti-Jewish activities with a great deal of money and very few scruples.

The second characteristic is the tendency to use the word ' European ' in the title. Post-war fascist and National Socialist groups argue that the failure of their predecessors lay in the attempt to build the fascist world on the foundation of one country only, whether Italy, Germany or any other country. The dominance of a *White Europe* has to be substituted for any exclusive national ambition ; and their common allegiance to the idea has to be expressed in some form of ' internationalism of nationalists'. A coherent expression of the paradox has not been easy to maintain, for so much of the appeal of this type of propaganda is to national vanity and selfishness. Post-war Fascism has resembled the chameleon in its changing colours, and the amoeba in its parturition by schism. All movements could agree on being anti-communist ; some were anti-American ; some were openly antisemitic, some too prudent to avow it, but very willing to make use of help from the Arab Offices. Moreover they disagreed in their attitude to the non-European world. Some still thought of the African continent as a field for ' white ' European exploitation, and were pro-South Africa. Others saw in the Arabs a main ally, because of the hostility of the latter to Israel—and because of their possession of oil. So far as national policy is concerned, all are opposed to parliamentary democracy, to any doctrine of human equality, especially of the equality of the coloured races, and to what they call ' international finance', a meaningless phrase which can cover an attack on anything or anybody.

A list of the organisations thus created would cover several pages. They include The European Social Movement, The European Liaison Office, The European People's Movement, The European New Order, The Social Organic Movement of Europe and The European Workers' League. Malmö in Sweden has been an important centre for conferences, and it is from Sweden that the ' one man organisation ' of Einar Åberg operates. Mosley or Jordan have represented English Fascists at several of the gatherings. Jordan, however, is particularly associated with a somewhat separate grouping, laying still more stress on the myth of racialism, and entitled The Nordic International. These different bodies have set up offices in various countries, at Malmö, Strasbourg, Vienna, Lausanne and elsewhere ; and they claim branches in a large number of countries, inside and outside Europe. Generally they tend to spread towards either the Latin American or the Arab countries ; but they have also gathered in exiled groups from Ukraine, Rumania, and Hungary. The last have been particularly active in spreading antisemitic propaganda as far afield as Australia.

The three countries in which groups seem to be most effectively and continuously organised, are Germany, Italy and Sweden. In western Germany and Austria cells of ex-nazis have been brought together under various innocent labels, especially as welfare bodies to assist ex-SS men and so on ; but in the former country they are also politically organised as the *Deutsche Reichspartei*, though at the moment of writing it has no electoral success to record. In Italy a neo-fascist organisation, the *Movimento Soziale Italiano* has been in existence since 1946, and has had considerable success in the elections. These two groups are closely linked with the Belgian *Mouvement d'Action Civique*, and also keep close contact with Mosley in England, and with the Swedish office at Malmö. Their most important periodical is the German language journal *Nation Europa*.

It may well be, however, that there is less danger in these older leaders, and in the shifting organisations which proclaim their adherence to the pre-war philosophies of Nazism and Fascism, than in the post-war generation and its disillusion with the whole of the contemporary world. Frenchmen dispossessed from North Africa, Belgians from the Congo, Dutchmen from the East Indies, Englishmen from Kenya and East Africa or the Middle East may find themselves allied with the schoolboys and students who placed plastic bombs for the French Secret Army, the OAS. The dissatisfaction expressed from a literary point of view in the Belgian Review, *Jeune Europe*, of the Youth Section of the M.A.C., tends to look with complaisance and even pride on the utterly ruthless technical skill of the paratroopers and others who form the military arm of the OAS, and who already have an organised force of ' three thousand outlaws, army deserters, and terrorists, with nothing to lose and ample funds ' to cover their activities.[1] The

---

[1] From a leading article by Ronald Payne in *The Daily Telegraph* of September 20, 1962.

dashing paratrooper may take the place of the jack-booted storm-trooper as the new fascist model. At present such groups despise antisemitism as *vieux jeu*, but that is no guarantee for the future.

In the United States any estimate of the real menace of anti-semitic propaganda is obscured by what appears to an outsider as the pathological fear of so many otherwise reasonable Americans at the mention of communism. While Europe is increasingly seeing in the conflict between the USA and the USSR the contemporary form of the rivalry between two power blocs to which they have long been accustomed, Americans and Soviet leaders alike seem still unaware that the United States and the Soviet Union are more and more approximating to each other, as the one becomes less individualistic and the other more affluent. The idea that either is bound to conduct an ideological campaign against the other on the grounds of two abstracts entitled ' communism ' and ' capitalism ' seems to those who are neither American nor Soviet citizens increasingly, though not less dangerously, out-dated. To this general American situation has to be added the particular fears of America's Jewish community, whose more volatile members scent fascism as readily as other Americans scent communism.

It is against this background that one needs to estimate the dangers of the many brands of ' rabble-rousers ' or ' trouble-makers ' who infest the American scene. When it comes to a show-down, men like Lincoln Rockwell are seen to have a following that would not be large enough to overthrow a parish council—or its American equivalent. It is the fears of others which have given him a publicity to which he is not of himself entitled. One can speak in almost equally contemptuous vein of antisemitic and pro-Nazi leaders like Gerald L. K. Smith, who is certainly more prosperous than Rockwell, but who has been agitating for at least thirty years with-out obtaining such a substantial following that of itself it constituted a national or even local threat. But there are two very valid reasons why it is foolish to treat these fanatics of ' the lunatic fringe ' with the contempt they deserve.

The first is the immense power in a country the size of the United States of the ' smear ' against the individual political figure. It was a technique of which the late Senator McCarthy was a master ; but it is also a technique by which a very small group can poison a very extensive atmosphere. A historic example of it was the campaign in 1950 to destroy Mrs. Anna M. Rosenberg on her appointment by General Marshall, Secretary of Defence, as Assistant Secretary in charge of man-power. Anna M. Rosenberg was a brilliant executive, who had already held many important offices, and was recognised as the leading authority on the particular problems with which General Marshall wished her to deal. *But* she was born in a foreign country which had become communist (Hungary), she was a friend of the late President Roosevelt, and she was a Jewess. Nearly every ' hate organisation ' in the country combined to destroy her by a completely unscrupulous smear campaign. The humiliations and distress to which she was subjected have been exhaustively described and documented by Arnold Foster and Benjamin Epstein,[1] so that one can see day by day the successive stages and shifts of the campaign. She was fortunate in that she could nail the various lies told about her, and secure the complete vindication of her character. But other equally innocent persons are less fortunate. In a smaller country, where personal contact is more possible, the smear campaign is more difficult to conduct successfully. But it can never be ignored, for it remains a dangerous weapon in the hands of the unscrupulous and the extremist.

The second reason for treating these fanatics seriously lies in the prevalence on the American scene of reactionary, often religious, groups brought together by the fear of communism. These groups, whether Roman Catholic, Protestant or neutral in religious matters, do not necessarily start as antisemitic, but they are anti-rational, anti-democratic, and above all anti-communist. This makes them natural bed-fellows of openly antisemitic groups. Indeed one usually finds among their members or publications openly antisemitic material, and in their attacks on various forms of democracy and international co-operation, they and the overtly antisemitic organisations usually follow identical lines. Of these right wing organisations, the John Birch Society is probably the best known. Its membership and income are not published, but it clearly enjoys a much wider and more respectable support than antisemitic organisations such as that of Rockwell or Gerald L. K. Smith. It is this wider support which makes such organisations more dangerous

---

[1] *The Trouble Makers*. Doubleday, 1952. pp. 25-61. In the succeeding pages an equally disgusting smear campaign against a Director in the Georgia Welfare Department engineered by anti-segregationists is equally graphically described. It is not only Jews who are thus attacked.

than those which openly or exclusively peddle antisemitism. Reasonable men join them, and feel that their influence will ' keep them on the right lines.' Many Germans felt that about Hitler. But then some change in the international, political, social or economic climate occurs, and it throws the power into the hands of the extremists, who find, as always, that Jews are the easiest scapegoat.

More serious than the situation in North America is that in the South and Central American republics. In none of them can it be said that the tradition of responsible democracy is stable or accepted by a wide electorate. It is an area of the world bristling with unsolved social problems ; an area in which there is still a great deal of foreign, mostly North American, financial influence ; and therefore an area in which the scapegoat can be a most useful political manoeuvre. For it is an area of very great wealth, and the eyes of the envious, whether individuals or nations, are fixed upon its

Few were so determinedly envious as Nazi Germany. In Latin America they did not limit themselves to securing political allies like Degrelle or Quisling ; it appears that they planned to create in that continent a substitute for the agricultural colonies their predecessors had failed to obtain in Africa during the colonial scramble before the first world war. There were at least 900,000 German settler. already in the continent, and they were to a considerable extent conveniently grouped to assist Nazi plans. They were therefore subjected to intense propaganda, and it became extremely difficult for any German, however long his residence and however determined his loyalty to his new country, to resist entanglement in the Nazi net. The plan was to create two new states, which were to be definitely part of the Nazi empire. One was to have the rich area of the River Plate as its backbone, and comprise the southern part of Brazil, the northern parts of Argentina, and the whole of Uruguay. The other covered the whole of the southern part of the continent from the Atlantic to the Pacific down to Cape Horn, and included the very thinly populated southern provinces of Argentina on the east and of Chile on the west. Intensive subversion in Colombia, the northern Republic overlooking the Panama Isthmus and Canal, completed the ambitious designs of Nazi imperialism.

In their propaganda they made their ' public enemy No. 1 ' the political and commercial interests of the United States. The Jews only came second. But the two could be judiciously combined, especially as all through the continent the Roman Catholic Church dominated social life, and in almost all republics the standard of education was fairly low. Thus North Americans, when not attackable as ' Jews,' could be identified as ' Protestants.' The Arab Information Offices which entered the continent after 1945 found the ground well prepared for them by Nazi activities from 1933 to 1940. Moreover there was a substantial group of surviving Nazi leaders in Argentina and elsewhere. It is interesting, in tracing the kaleidoscopic branch offices, or travels of personnel, of the post-war Nazi international, that if one finds that they have interests in Cairo, they will also have interests in Latin America. The web stretches further. When a synagogue was bombed in 1961 in South Africa, the group which did it left behind pamphlets which had been printed in Buenos Aires. In the Eichmann affair the combinations were extraordinary. In spite of the usual relations between Cairo and Amman, a pamphlet by a Cairo disciple of Åberg, Antoine Albina, on the innocence of Eichmann was produced in Arab Jerusalem, and copied by the Ku-Klux-Klan in Atlanta, Georgia ; while one produced in Cairo, describing Eichmann as an ideal citizen, was republished by the National Renaissance Party in New York.

As to the Jews in Latin America, they are considerably fewer than the Germans, but of their 630,000 over 600,000 live in the four Republics in which the Nazis were particularly interested. In the rest of the continent the numbers are negligible. But in Argentina, Brazil, Uruguay and Chile antisemitism was and is clearly one of the weapons which the Nazis could use with effect, especially as Jews are an almost exclusively urban population—only a few tens of thousands still practise agriculture in the ICA colonies of Argentina—and live largely in the capital cities. The most common occupations are the retail trades, and the people so occupied are less affected by the economic stresses and inflation to which the continent has been spasmodically subject since the war, in spite of rising production and the immense wealth of resources which it possesses.

While occasional antisemitic incidents of varying gravity have occurred in almost every South American country since the war, and while one can trace the Arab Offices or the Nazi residents, or both, in most of them, it was the secret seizure of Eichmann in Argentina which triggered off a violence which at the time of writing, was not yet allayed. Latin American countries are very conscious of their dignity and sovereignty, and the audacious seizure and removal of one of their residents produced a general feeling of outrage, quite independently of the character of his crimes.

The result was that anti-democratic elements, which had occasionally been active already under Peron (though Peron himself was not antisemitic), were allowed a licence to commit outrages against Jewish persons and property which had not shown signs of abating by the autumn of 1962. The centre of the violence is Tacuara, a reactionary and wealthy student organisation, in which a priest, Father Meinville, seems to be a leader. As against the participation of a number of priests in antisemitic agitation, the higher ecclesiastical authorities have been sympathetic and co-operative. But the national situation is too unstable for it to be easy to protect a group against whom prejudice can be easily aroused. Arrests of rioters take place rarely ; physical violence, especially such disgusting acts as branding a young girl student with swastikas on her breast, is too lightly condoned ; and the Argentinian situation reflects in a frightening way the danger run by any identifiable minority in a total situation of instability. It contains elements, especially in the involvement of lower ranks of the clergy, which recall the period of Drumont and Dreyfus in France.

The Arab Offices in Europe and America are not the only centres of Arab anti-Jewish propaganda. Cairo is also the centre of a quite different activity in the new countries of Africa, especially those which have a substantial Muslim population. The main objective in this field is to prevent Israel from finding friends and influence in Africa, and so getting support at the United Nations. Formally Cairo succeeded in obtaining the condemnation of the existence of Israel at the Bandung Conference of African and Asian countries, and it has had similar success with some, but not all, purely African gatherings. In practice its success is less visible. That the assistance of Israel is eagerly sought by a number of the new countries is natural. For Israel has been a pioneer in many fields in which they are now entering, and the assistance of Israeli experts does not factually tie an African country to either of the great power blocs centring in the U.S.A. or the U.S.S.R. Moreover Israel is very willing to communicate her techniques, and has sent many missions to Africa and received many African statesmen and students in Jerusalem. To counter the attraction of Israel, Cairo denounces the Israelis as ' colonialists ' or ' imperialist stooges,' two charges of singular unfairness to the Africans, particularly as the Arab world has nothing equivalent to offer them. It is itself struggling to create a modern economy and a stable political society, and has little yet to teach others.

There is no more difficult field in which to present a fair picture of an actual problem than the Arab political world. More even than the Russians, Arabs have mastered the technique of the ' big lie.' In no area whatever is an Arab politician or publicist likely to be realistic about himself or telling the truth about his neighbours. And yet, in so far as the subject of this book is concerned, the chapter which deals with the relations between the Arab states and Israel is the only chapter which deals with a real problem in which real Jewish action is necessary, and in which real facts of Jewish history are involved. The antisemite's Jew is a figment of his imagination. But, in spite of all the exaggerations and downright untruths of present Arab statements about Israel, a real problem exists between Israel and the Arabs, and a real solution must ultimately be found.

It is because it is a real problem that its consideration is preceded by a description of the real Jewish community.

IX

THE SURVIVING JEWISH COMMUNITY

THE TERRIBLE YEARS of Nazi oppression have left a permanent and ineradicable mark on Jewish history. More than one third of the whole people perished. This meant that whole communities with their records were completely destroyed, communities which had been of central significance in the last four centuries of Jewish life ; but it also meant that there is scarcely a Jewish family in the world which is not personally linked to the tragedy by the loss of relatives in the prisons, torture chambers and death camps of the Nazis. It needs an effort of imagination for those who are not Jews to enter into the significance of this experience. During the two world wars British and French and Germans had also the experience of a personal encounter with death. But it had not the utter meaninglessness and horror of the Nazi murders. It was death on the battle field, or death at the hands of our national enemies. It was death, suffering and sorrow which our friends and neighbours did all in their power to alleviate. There were the stretcher-bearers and the ambulances for the front and for the air raid. There were money and food to help those in need at home. There was whatever comfort men can render to their fellows in distress, comfort given without measure and without stint, with heroism and with infinite sympathy and patience. But it was not so for Hitler's Jewish victims. Few of us who are not Jews knew the knock on the door in the early hours before the dawn. We did not fear to be stopped—or even killed— when we went out into the streets ; we did not know the pitiful flight or arrest, seen by neighbours whom we thought of as friends, and who looked on in silence or shut their doors against us. If those dearest to us were among the killed, we did not have to think that men—and perhaps women—had inflicted every humiliation and bitterness on them before they died, and that death itself had been delayed by hours, weeks, months maybe, of utter loneliness, help-lessness and physical suffering. I am not writing these things to be sentimental. I am writing them because it is right that we who are not Jews—and especially we who *are* Christians—should know and remember these things that happened in our own day. It is only when we do remember them that Jews will be able to forget them.

We must remember also, especially when we come to consider the final chapter on the sterilisation of prejudice, that Jewish communities watched the growth of National Socialism and comparable movements from their very beginnings. They drew non-Jewish attention to them when they were—apparently—unimportant groups from the lunatic fringe which any large and complex community will throw up. They drew attention to them when a resolute effort would have eliminated the possibility of their becoming a political danger. This will explain why they are naturally nervous and even alarmed at any survivals of Nazi ideology and at the new manifestations described in the previous chapter. The old slogan of 'it can't happen here' has ceased to have any meaning for those who feel themselves responsible for the safety of Jewish lives.

Yet remembering this, we shall do well to remember two other points also. This natural sensitivity is today the only 'abnormal' quality of Jewish communities in the free world, for Jews are by nature optimists, more concerned with the future than with the past ; and, secondly, Jews are only one of the many identifiable minorities with which the whole world is filled. It is not only Jews who are endangered by anti-democratic movements. For man is a mobile creature and exact frontiers cannot be drawn to isolate him from his kind in watertight compartments. Jews have a particular history, and that has developed particular qualities, but that is the normal consequence of being an identifiable group ; it does not mean that they are the only identifiable group and it is equally normal that the life of any great community is enriched by the fact that it does not iron out all the differences within it, but accepts them and blends them into a whole larger than any one part could produce of itself.

In their relations with the majorities among whom they live, Jewish communities in the free world provide today an interesting example of this blending and adaptability into the conditions in which they find themselves. In fact many Jewish leaders fear that they will be so completely absorbed as to lose their identities ; and it is true that minorities are constantly disappearing in this way, so that only by family names or antiquarian researches can their history be recovered. The Huguenots today are such a minority in England. They were a large and easily identifiable society of their own when they arrived from France in the 17th century. They brought new industries and skills, which have survived ; but they were themselves slowly absorbed into the pattern of English life.

It has only rarely happened that a Jewish community of any size has completely disappeared. But the two books I have written on this subject illustrate, at any rate so far as England is concerned, the speed with which a minority passes from ' foreignness ' to identification with the society of which it is a part. When I began to be concerned with this problem in the '30's and when I was writing on antisemitism in 1944 and 1945, I was confronted with a number of problems arising out of the foreign quality of much Jewish life, either obvious or revealed under the stress of war. Reading through the pages in which these problems were discussed, I cannot find a single subject which it would be possible to transfer unchanged to the present chapter. Some have disappeared, and others are presented in a way which would be quite misleading today. An example of the last category is particularly illuminating for the study of group prejudice. It concerns what could be then described as a primarily ' Jewish ' tendency which was definitely irritating to the host society. It showed how this tendency had a perfectly normal human origin, and suggested that time would cure it. Now the ' cure ' has taken place but it has been an unexpected one.

Up to 1945 one could still speak of the Russian immigration to the West as being a ' recent ' event, and it was emphasised, rather than replaced, by the smaller immigration from Hitler's Europe. One of the charges against Russian Jews most frequently encountered was that they practised a lower commercial morality. It was not a charge which one could prove statistically, and for this reason I was criticized by Jewish organisations for even mentioning it, when I admitted frankly that I could not prove it. For it was not a charge that Jews broke the law, but that many of them were extremely expert in sailing very close to the wind. I met the charge —or suspicion—too often in talking to business men of all kinds, or people in official and public life, for it to be honest to ignore it. But, in fact, it would have been very surprising if it had not been true.

It would have disproved my fundamental thesis that Jews have had an abnormal history, but that their reactions to it are those of ordinary human beings.

The attitude of a community to its laws depends on the attitude of the lawmakers to the community. In the western democracies we have for long made the laws ourselves; they have not been imposed on us from outside. When a king and an archbishop behaved in an arbitrary fashion to us in the 17th century, we executed them. Now we grumble at the lawmakers and obey the laws ; and we do not particularly commend and admire those who indulge in sharp practice in evading their obvious intention. So I argued rightly in 1935 and 1945. But these Jewish immigrants came from a country where they lived under laws framed and administered, nationally and locally, in such a way as deliberately and maliciously to make life as unpleasant for them as possible. A much quoted example concerned Jewish girls who wished to, and had permission to, attend Moscow University in Tsarist days. For they had to have also permission to reside in Moscow ; and this the police would give them only if they registered as public prostitutes. Some did so, thinking it only an unpleasant formality, and were then arrested, convicted of not practising their profession, and expelled. Or a town would suddenly be declared a village in which Jews might not live, so that a convalescent mother coming from hospital would find that she could not return home to her family.

It was a normal human reaction to such a situation to admire the man who could find a way round such laws, and live a decent and prosperous life in spite of them. His skill in sailing close to the wind without committing an offence for which the ever-watchful police could catch him, his adroitness in knowing exactly whom to bribe, and with how much, these were admirable qualities for which his neighbour envied him. It was natural then, when very large numbers of refugees from such conditions came to another country, that it should take them a couple of generations to appreciate that they needed to develop a new attitude to law. The first and natural reaction of the settlers from Russia was that western laws, judged by the standards of the Russian laws to which they were accustomed, were extremely safe and easy to evade. They lived in close communities, in voluntary ghettoes in the big cities, and only slowly came into close contact with their non-Jewish neighbours. But their children and, still more, their grandchildren, went to ordinary

British or American schools ; they became integrally, often passionately, English or American citizens in their social and political
loyalties. Against them the old charge could not be, and was not,
made, and it would be abnormal if there were an exceptional
proportion of native born Jews who so regarded their legal and
social obligations.

What is the situation in 1962 ? It is that the landed nobility and
propertied class are giving us convincing evidence that, when a law
becomes sufficiently onerous, there is social approval for its evasion.
In this case there is no question of the law being hostile or malicious ;
for we all know that two world wars have to be paid for. But the
result of them has been that all forms of taxation and death duties
have reached so high a level that these leading English citizens are
behaving exactly like Russian Jewish immigrants. They devise
every form of evasion which just keeps the letter of the law, and the
courts themselves have admitted that it is the duty of the government to stop the bolt-holes, and not of the citizen to keep the spirit
as well as the letter.

Apart from the understandable sensitivity of a people who have
known in a single generation such appalling losses, with the personal
memories of such searing tragedies, Jewish communities of today
are astonishingly ' normal.' They are ' normal ' in the sense that
they have ceased to be foreign, not in the sense that they have
ceased to be Jewish. They have become normal Englishmen or
Americans or Danes, because there is a Jewish element in the cultural
amalgam which represents today England or an American or
a Scandinavian state. But the contribution whereby they have
enriched the amalgam of that state comes from their Jewish experience; and a close analysis will find it in innumerable subtle
ways, just as it can trace other elements in the amalgam to different
elements out of which the society is built up, elements which very
possibly originally grew in isolation from each other, and depended
on that isolation.

The common feature of all Jewries is urbanisation. Centuries of
exclusion from the land had made the Jews town-dwellers before
other Europeans. The 19th century intensified the drift to the towns
among the whole population, and the 20th century witnessed the
growth of mammoth capital cities. Both these movements are
reflected in Jewry, to the extent that before Hitler about a quarter
of all the Jews of the world lived in the nine capital cities of

New York, Budapest, Buenos Aires, Kiev, London, Moscow, Paris, Vienna and Warsaw. Each of these communities was over 100,000, and that of New York around 2,000,000. In many of these cities Jews, especially the more recent arrivals, were usually concentrated into certain districts. As an urban population Jews show the normal urban preference for the white collar professions. Among them also there is the normal practice whereby the son tends to follow in the social grade, if not the actual profession, of his father, or to seek to rise to a higher grade.

In every country outside Israel the most popular professions are law and medicine. For this one reason has already been given. Unlike the army or civil service, they were everywhere *free* professions, in which a man could make his way by his own personality and talents; and they thus attracted Jews in countries where access to government employment was impossible or extremely difficult. But they were also professions to which Jews took easily. The intense intellectual life of Jewry in the days when nearly all Jews were ' orthodox ' and students of the Talmud, was a good preparation for the subtleties of the law ; while medicine was a profession they had practised in the days when their Christian fellow-practitioners still dealt in every kind of spell and superstition. It was a common practice of medieval princes, when they expelled their Jewish subjects, to make an exception of their own doctors! Jews are not only numerous among doctors, they are also prominent in every field of medical research, and no antisemitic argument is more foolish than that which pretends that their presence in a profession automatically implies a loss. Jewish names are to be found among the greatest in every field of modern medicine and psychology. The list of winners of the Nobel prizes for medicine and scientific research would reveal that.

Jewish association with finance goes back only to the Middle Ages, and the licensed usurer of the medieval prince. The Biblical promise that Israel should ' lend unto many nations but should not borrow ' does not refer to the modern type of international loans! It is a promise of prosperity among the mixed population of Palestine—the Jew would not have to borrow a pruning hook from his Philistine neighbour, he would have a spare one to lend him. A medieval background was, however, enough to give some Jews a good start in the immense commercial expansion of the 19th century; and the need to find new ways of earning a living encouraged Jews to be adventurous speculators and entrepreneurs. In our present day, this is noticeable in the group of Jewish names at the centre of the real estate business. It is a new source of wealth, based on the fact that money falls rapidly in value when it is expended unproductively in war, so that property, especially commercial and urban property, comes to possess a higher money value than its pre-war owners are apt to calculate. It is, however, important to register that it is wealth earned by individual Jews, not by ' the Jews.'

All this may lead to immense fortunes for the lucky few, but it does not lead to that control over the financial and economic policy of nations of which antisemites still accuse them. In the institutions which make financial policy, the great joint-stock banks, the national banks and national treasury departments, there is hardly any Jewish influence at all. In Great Britain they have almost no place in the directorship of the five great private banks or in the Bank of England. In the United States the same is true. In the three banks which controlled German banking policy before 1933 Jews were without influence. Similarly Jews are not found in heavy industry, mining or transport, which determine employment policies and the general picture of industrial life.

If the adventurous and speculative spirit among Jews has caused a number of Jewish financial crashes and scandals in which non-Jews have sometimes lost money, it is still more true that Jewish initiative and imagination have been responsible for many developments in social and economic life from which the whole society has profited. The ' sweat-shops ' of Jewish tailors of the East End of London and of New York are extinct, but not the solid achievement of Jewish tailoring which still puts well-made and well-cut clothes within the reach of all sections of the population, men and women. Almost the whole of that industry has been built up by Jewish energy. What is true of clothing is equally true in the furniture and catering trades. Jews have pioneered in these trades all through the Western world. But a pioneer cannot generalise. He must know his actual field. So there are trades which are particularly Jewish in in some countries, but are not Jewish in others.

The real characteristic of the Jewish community is the immense mass of little—often ' one man '—businesses which take the place of the much more varied middle and lower-middle class occupations of non-Jewish national life. Skilled artisans and small shopkeepers,

little family factories producing some specialised article—these are
the real characteristics of Jewry in pre-war Poland as much as in
contemporary Leeds, Buenos Aires or New York. There are particular branches of special trades where Jews form an exceedingly
high proportion of the whole. This came out in some of the studies
made of the ' Black Market ' during the war. In one or two trades
Jewish names appeared to fill a distressing proportion of the
offenders—in one case over half. But an enquiry showed that in that
particular trade not half but three-quarters of those engaged were
Jews. And, in defence of both Jews and non-Jews concerned, it can
be added that the offenders altogether constituted a fraction of
1 % of those engaged in the trade.

No study of the Jewish community would, of course, be complete
which took no account of the Synagogue. Individually Jews may
attend worship as rarely as Christians, but the religion of the
Synagogue has created the pattern of their lives as much as Roman
Catholicism, Orthodoxy, or Protestantism have moulded different
sections of European civilisation.

Two thousand years ago, before the coming of Christianity, Julius
Caesar gave extensive privileges to the Jewish communities of the
Roman Empire because he had decided that Judaism made good
citizens. The Empires of the Nile and Euphrates valleys did the
same. More, they used Jewish soldiers to guard their most dangerous
frontiers, because they found them especially reliable. In the Middle
Ages the Princes and the Church permitted Jews to practise usury
because they considered that it was permitted by the Jewish
religion (actually they were wrong, and based their view on a mis-
translation) ; but the medieval public went to Jewish usurers
because they found them more honest than the Christian. Beneath
all the froth and scum created by modern antisemitism, and after
taking into account all the qualifications due to history and environment already discussed, it is still true that the evidence from all
countries is that Judaism makes of its adherents good citizens.

The first interesting feature of Judaism is that after the loss of
Palestine it did not meet the dispersion and persecution of its people
with a religion of comfort, resignation and escape. It is true that in
eastern Europe in the 18th and 19th centuries, and in corners of
England or America today, there are to be found Jews living a life
apart from the bustle of everyday activity, and wrapped in Talmudic
argument or mystical speculation. But the characteristic of Judaism

is activity. When independence was finally lost after the disastrous wars with Rome, the religious leaders set out to make their religion a 'portable Homeland' for the Jewish people. On the one hand they emphasised those ritual and ceremonial loyalties which ' made a hedge about the Law,' and kept the whole significance of Jewish life clear-cut and distinct. On the other they insisted that the ' righteousness of God ' would be vindicated in this world, and that Jews must so live that the name of God would be honoured. While Judaism accepts life after death, there is no tendency to make a future life iron out the inequalities of this one. In every generation the rabbis emphasised that righteousness is to be sought for here and now. This blending of ethical and ritual teaching into a single whole would appeal to a modern psychologist who knows how much our daily actions count in our total make-up, and how small the value of moral generalisations can be.

The second characteristic is its tremendous interest in questions which the ordinary Christian would not consider to be specifically ' religious.' There are to be found in the Talmud and in rabbinic writings of all centuries, discussions of education, courts of justice, laws of evidence, laws of contract, and all sorts of economic and cultural questions which affect daily life and practice. Most non-Jewish scholars, especially Christian theologians, have failed to see the significance of this because rabbinical writings are extremely difficult to understand, and apparently filled with extraordinarily unimportant details. They are not secret, but they are obscure.

The third characteristic is its democracy. The western Jewish world has a social ' aristocracy ' consisting of the Spanish or Sephardic Jews ; but Judaism has no place for authority of interpretation other than in the moral authority of the interpreters. It has no popes or bishops, and worship is ' congregational.' The rabbi is not a priest.

Fourthly there is its optimism. Judaism is throughout an optimistic religion. It is not a superficial optimism, and it is balanced by the fact—or rests on the fact—that the one day of the year which is observed by nearly all Jews is the Day of Atonement, the day of penitence, of self-examination and of spiritual ' stocktaking '.

Finally, it must be emphasised that there is nothing *secret* in Judaism. The usual antisemitic charges of secret practices, of double meanings, of ritual concealed from Gentile observers and so on, rest only on imagination. Nor need this be accepted on the word of Jewish authorities only—Jewish books have been too often confiscated by Christian censors, Jewish activities too often scrutinised by hostile examiners familiar with Hebrew, too many reputable Jews have become converts to Christianity, for sinister practices to have been kept secret by a people so dispersed for centuries among a non-Jewish population.

Although there are profound differences in the nature and structure of Judaism and Christianity, in the majority of cases these play no part in the creation of popular feeling. But the intensely democratic nature of Judaism, in which religious argument of the freest kind had a prominent place even in the traditional use of the synagogue, naturally created a temperament different from that created by the Christian tradition, where authority is much more prominent, and where the very idea of arguing in church seems irreverent. As another example of the way in which religion affects the situation, we can see that there is nothing in the Jewish conception of the Sabbath which could create ill-feeling. But the fact that it is celebrated on a different day from the usual day of rest in the non-Jewish community can create trouble, especially in districts which are half residential, half commercial.

A combination of religion and history accounts for another feature which exists in any Jewish community, and which, as soon as it attracts unfavourable attention, is labelled clannishness. Jews have been so often dependent on the help and support of their co-religionists that it is natural that a Jew who has found his own feet should turn to help others to the security he has found for himself, and this helps to intensify Jewish concentration, geographically, socially and economically. The statement that once a Jew is established anywhere he will bring in all his relations is sometimes true ; it is also frequently true of other, especially immigrant, groups ; and it is often heard in connection with the West Indians in various parts of Great Britain. In times of economic depression and unemployment, when it is easy to stir up enmity against any ' foreign ' group, the belief that the ' foreigners ' in question all hang together in order to deprive the ' native ' of work may provide a fertile breeding ground for political violence. And in times of international insecurity it is the breeding ground whence grow beliefs in international plots and manoeuvres.

It is unfortunately part of normal human nature that when any of these matters causes friction within a minority, whether Jewish or any other, members of the majority will say : ' Why does not the Jewish community, or the High Commissioner from Pakistan, or somebody else in authority, do something about it?' The brutal answer has already been given: 'Why should they?' A more sensible answer, perhaps, would be that many such matters will be solved by time, and that to make them the subject of official action is just psychologically wrong.

There is one point which is worth making, both about Jews and about all other identifiable minorities. The vastly more powerful trend today is towards a world-wide uniformity based on the mass media of cinema, broadcasting and television. Unchecked and unbalanced it could lead humanity in a not very distant future to become one unrelieved, grey, uniform *lumpenproletariat*. All those separate traditions which make for variety and distinction are more valuable today than they have ever been. Of course, there are differences which inevitably conflict with each other; but in this chapter we have not been dealing with such. In a democracy normality does not mean total surrender; and acceptance of membership—full membership—of a larger community ought not to mean the destruction of roots which are particular to any identifiable minority and its individual members.

All the preceding pages apply to the position of Jews as minorities in non-Jewish communities. But the most striking difference between this book and its predecessor is that, in its original form, this chapter contained no special reference to the community in Palestine ; whereas today the Jewish nation in the State of Israel is a very central part of the whole picture. In relation to Adolf Eichmann it, for the first time, assumed a responsibility on behalf of the Jewish people as a whole; for the crimes of Eichmann were committed before the State was born, and none took place on the territory of the State. This fact, which inevitably gave rise to a good deal of criticism of the role played by Israel in the whole matter, indicates the potential significance of the State in the relations of the Jewish people as a whole to the non-Jewish world. To a very large number of Jews elsewhere, and to most Israelis, it appears natural that the State of Israel should intervene on behalf of Jews in other countries who are suffering injustice ; to other Jews it appears to raise the bogey of ' dual loyalties'. They feel that such intervention should come from voluntary Jewish international organisations, such as the World Jewish Congress, or ' through the usual channels ' deepened over many generations by the excellent relations between such bodies as the Board of Deputies of British Jews and the British Foreign Office. A body of citizens does not normally approach a foreign state of itself, but through its own government ; and there is this advantage in such an approach in relation to antisemitism, that the disease is a non-Jewish problem, and that an exclusively Jewish approach can appear to place all responsibility on Jewish action.

Nevertheless, from any standpoint, the emergence of Israel introduces a new and important factor in the total situation. It has produced in the Israeli a new image of ' the Jew'. It has not fulfilled the expectations of those traditional Jews who saw in a Jewish state the fulfilment of Talmudic Judaism and the restoration of ancient ritual ; on the other hand it has provided much more than a refuge from persecution. Yet the expectations of those who saw in it a return of Jews to ' normality ' as a people have been even more falsified. The state of Isrel is an extremely lively and modern state, but it is anything but a normal one. For it survives only by the continual vigilance and determination of its own citizens and the support, especially financial, of the Jewish people throughout the world. If either failed, it would disappear, not because of its inherent artificiality, as we shall see in the next chapter, but because of its present dependence on world security and economic order.

The Israeli—especially if he is a native of the country—is immensely proud of the fact that he owes his independence to his own military victory, against immense odds, over the combined— but not united—forces of the Palestinian Arabs and the Arab States ; and in his thoughts he is more apt to see himself as the successor of the Maccabees and the desperate fighters against the Roman empire than as the descendant, removed by one generation only, of the ghettoes and emancipated communities of Europe. He is facing problems no Jewish community, however powerful and extensive, has faced for close on two thousand years, problems of international politics and of attitudes towards a non-Jewish minority, and he feels confident in his ability to overcome his difficulties. He resents the attempt of Jews in the Diaspora to adopt any kind of paternal attitude towards him ; and his reaction to the attack of the Arabs was so spontaneous and universal that he finds it difficult to understand how six million Jews in Europe came to be murdered almost without resistance. He finds more satisfaction in the stories of the battle of the Warsaw ghetto than sympathy with the victims.

To a considerable extent this attitude came as a surprise to the Zionist of the older generation, whether settled in Israel or in the Diaspora. He is delighted that Israel is already in a position to help the developing countries of Asia and Africa through its know-how, and he sees this expertise as the natural end-product of emancipation and his experience of the intellectual life of Europe and America. But he is puzzled by the determination with which the younger generation wishes to turn its back on the sources abroad of that experience. What is a surprise, alike to the European and the native born, is that within less than twenty years of its foundation, Israel is passing from a European to an Asiatic state, with a population the majority of whom have no knowledge of the two millenia of Jewish European experience.

Israel has already absorbed something like nine-tenths of the former Jewish population of Syria and Egypt, and almost the whole of the Jewish communities of Iraq, Yemen and Libya. It looks as though the majority of the Jewish communities of what was once French North Africa will also ultimately find their homes in Israel. These Jews from Muslim countries are younger, and have a much higher birth rate, than the Jews of European origin. At present, and in consequence of this, the Israelis are facing a problem entirely strange to Jewish history, the danger of a dual level of citizenship, with the Asiatic and African Jews rising with difficulty from the position of helots in the Land of Israel. Almost all the positions of intellectual, political and social responsibility are in the hands of Jews of European birth or descent. The more subtle and intangible values also are in their hands ; and, so long as the very existence of Israel rests on awareness of these values, their maintenance and survival constitute a unique problem. The abnormality of Jewish history has reappeared in a totally unexpected place!

X

ISRAEL AND THE ARAB WORLD

No DISCUSSION OF the problem caused by antisemitism would be adequate which did not take into account the unresolved issue between Israel and the Arab world. One may recognise the sincerity of Christians who say that they are not antisemitic, but that they are anti-zionist ; and they may quote certain Jewish elements which support them in the distinction. One may recognise likewise that there is an historic difference between the treatment of Jews within Christendom and within Islam—which means primarily within the Arab part of it, since outside the Arab sphere of penetration, and of the Arabic language as a vehicle of communication, only the Persian Jewish community is of historic importance among the fascinating peripheral Jewries of Asia and Africa. But a main centre of anti-Jewish propaganda throughout the world today is found in the Arab Offices in various countries ; and a good deal of the material disseminated by these offices is of direct or indirect Nazi origin, since a number of prominent Nazis are employed in their service. Consequently the attempt to distinguish anti-zionism from antisemitism rarely succeeds.

In recent years Arab denunciation and abuse have been monotonously violent and untruthful at the United Nations and elsewhere ; and hostility to Israel has provided the only subject on which all Arab states are unanimous. But disgust at the constant repetition of untruths must not blind us to the reality of the issue which lies between Jewry and Araby on the subject of Israel ; nor can it lessen the conviction that time will not solve unaided a problem in which there is on each side so passionate a conviction of right and so deeply outraged a feeling of justice.

From any humanitarian standpoint the non-absorption of approximately a million human victims of the conflict, more than a dozen years after the termination of warfare, is a deeply distressing event. But in relation to fundamentals the Arab refugee is a red herring ; and these human beings are being used as a kind of scapegoat to emphasise the more fundamental problem and the world's responsibility for it. But because they are so used, it is necessary to get a clearer view of their position than often appears in the partisan literature of the subject.

In 1948 Arabs west of Jordan outnumbered Jews by more than two to one, and they had had the same opportunities as Jews for acquiring arms clandestinely—perhaps greater opportunities, for it was in Arab-populated countries that the largest stock-piles of half-forgotten weapons were to be found, and there were Arab countries across all the frontiers of mandatory Palestine where they could be kept in reserve with complete safety. Financially there was certainly more money on the Arab side than on the Jewish ; since the Arab governments, rich in oil royalties, had declared their solidarity with the Palestinians, whereas the Jews were up to their eyes in meeting the financial needs of the resettlement of the survivors of Hitler's Europe. The odds appeared so much in their favour that most British military experts familiar with the Middle East were convinced that the Arabs would defeat the Jews within a matter of weeks, and that the practical need would be to prevent the whole Jewish edifice from destruction. A kind of papal state around the town of Tel Aviv was the most favoured suggestion. It is because this was the general expectation that the reality, when it came, was such a shock to experts on the Middle East and to the Arabs themselves.

The Arabs suffered an overwhelming defeat because they did not stay and defend their homes, but listened to many different voices which urged them to flee, although all the advantages of terrain and situation were on their side. They made practically no advance preparations for their own defence, because the kind of warfare in which they found themselves involved was not a natural part of Arab history. In many parts of the European countryside, especially near frontiers, coasts and the great routes, medieval villages are little walled towns, such as we can still see in Provence, South Germany or along the lake-sides in Switzerland. But an Arab village is a huddle of houses on a hillside or hilltop, protected mainly by position and by the closeness of the houses to each other. Their traditional experience of warfare was of the sudden and violent *razzia* from the desert bedouin, and this they had not met by resisting to the last man, but by flight to the nearest rocky fastness where they could hide, or to some larger village where their combined forces might be too large to tempt bedouin attack. The whole thing lasted a matter of hours, for the bedouin, having collected what loot they could and done what damage malice suggested, departed. The villagers were not accustomed to the kind of sustained defence and attack which was called for in 1947 and 1948. It is also true that they are not natural-born fighters ; and in this case they were deprived of the leadership which the more educated class could have given them. Their natural leaders had in too many cases already removed themselves to a safe distance.

Faced by this combination of facts, the majority fled ; although most of those who were unable to, or had the wisdom not to, are still in possession of their houses and fields in Israel, economically the most prosperous Arab peasants in the whole Middle East. There is no single reason why they fled, no single agency whose advice or compulsion they listened to. In some cases British officials encouraged them to go (being under the illusion already described) ; in some cases Arab urging, led to their flight, backed by the promise that they could return in a few weeks, not only to their own villages, but to take the Jewish lands beside them ; in some cases it was simply panic, probably based on rumour ; and in some cases it was directly due to the Jewish advance and attack, and the compulsion of the Jewish military on the spot. It is, in fact, easy to make a relatively accurate approximation of the proportion of responsibility among the different elements described. But this has no practical purpose provided that it is understood that the pretences of *any* of the parties to *complete* innocence are quite unsupported by evidence or, indeed, plausibility. ' The Jews' did not ' drive out a million Arabs ' ; nor did *all* Arabs leave at the instruction of the Arab Higher command.

The question of the numbers involved has also a propaganda importance, but only as long as complete blame is placed on one side or the other. All experts are agreed that the figures given from the beginning have been inflated ; but the main cause of inflation is the extreme poverty of the peasant and proletarian Arab neighbours of the refugees. Even at the meagre standard which relief could provide, refugees were often as well off as, and sometimes better off than, other Arabs who were in no way the direct or indirect victims of the Palestine war.

Finally, it is significant that, on the accepted basis on which the League of Nations, and its successor the United Nations, have dealt successfully with the problems caused by the presence of many millions of refugees since the first World War, the Palestinian Arab ' refugees ' would not be accepted under the international definition of ' refugees ' at all. Other victims of the cruelty of man to man have been refused official international help although they were in need similar to that of the displaced Palestinian Arabs. But they have been referred to the governments of the countries where they were living, and to voluntary organisations, such as the *Red Cross* or the *Save the Children Fund*, willing to help them. The League of Nations set up a High Commission to assist refugees, mostly Jewish refugees, from Nazi Germany ; but it limited itself at first to conferring official status on the High Commissioner. All the expenses of his office, as well as all funds to help the refugees, had to be provided by those who sympathised with them. The usual contribution of the League, as of the United Nations, to the refugees themselves is diplomatic protection, in cases where they have no citizenship, no government, and so nobody to speak for or assist them. The bulk of the displaced Palestinians, on the contrary, have either been received as citizens in neighbouring Arab countries or they are at least among people of their own ethnic group, religion and culture ; and they are constantly spoken for by the Arab states. It was because similar mitigation of their need covered the Pakistani and Indian refugees when the British withdrew in 1947 that the United Nations refused to assist them.

On the other hand, there have been small groups which have received special treatment, because the United Nations regarded their existence as in some way consequent upon United Nations' action or decision. The League had dealt specially with the Assyrians ; it felt itself in some degree responsible for their plight, because it was caused by the passage of Iraq from being a Mandated Territory of the League to independent status ; similarly the United Nations accepted some responsibility for South Korean refugees (though still in South Korean territory) because their international resistance to what they considered North Korean aggression had led to the existence of these homeless sufferers. Though in neither case has any action of comparable duration and expense resulted, it is as victims of action taken under the authority of the United Nations itself, rather than as ' refugees ' in the accepted sense, that the displaced Palestinian Arabs should be regarded.

Every other group of refugees, or of privileged displaced persons, has been resettled and restored to independent existence in much less time and at much less expense. They are in a *unique* category both because of the funds expended and because the problem shows signs of increasing rather than diminishing as time passes. This interminability of delay is not due to any inherent economic impossibility of solution, though there are here, as in all other cases, many actual difficulties. The problem rests insoluble because the Arab states are determined that it shall be so. And they are determined that it shall be so because they see the Palestinians, and parade them, as evidence of a basic injustice done to the Arab people as a whole.

It is well to recognise this, and to approach it coherently, and not through the wild and frequently untruthful statements which are the commonplace of Arab politics at the United Nations, and are echoed, often with additional violence and ignorance, by Europeans or Americans, especially Christians who have been occupied with relief work. Jews pride themselves on their long memories. It is for them a matter of legitimate approval that they have never forgotten the Land of Israel through two long exiles. It is probable that Arabs have equally long memories. We may hope for a change in the political climate of the world from which Arabs, as well as others, might benefit. We may hope for a time when it is possible to discuss on a reasonable and scholarly basis the position of Jew and Arab, Jew, Christian and Muslim, in the Middle East. That is a reasonable hope. But it is unreasonable utopianism to think that Arabs will get tired of denouncing Israel, or that they will of themselves change their reaction to the presence of Israel as an independent state in their midst, before the issue of justice has been fairly faced.

At present it is probably impossible to present a reasonable case to Arab leaders themselves. They are caught in the web of their own violence and their mutual antagonisms. At the moment of writing it is popular with the Syrians and the king of Saudi Arabia to accuse Nasser of being pro-Israel. By the time these words are published it may be the opposite. For in neither case do the charges bear any remote resemblance to reality. But it should be possible to bring home to some of the Europeans in the Middle East the evil they are doing to the Arabs by the ignorance and violence of their anti-Israelism, which is quite indistinguishable from antisemitism.

It is argued that one cannot do business in an Arab country, unless one openly shares the Arab point of view ; and relief workers say that they could have no influence with the displaced Arabs unless they endorsed their hatred of Israel. Of course it is more difficult now than if both groups had taken a firm line at the beginning, and had acquired some knowledge of the facts before they aired any opinion, *pro* or *contra*. But the same applies to them as to the other parties in the conflict. Untruths will no more become truth by the passage of time, than injustice will become right.

Just as the unfortunate ' refugees ' are a side issue, for the Israelis could either take them all back, or pay enormous sums in compensation, without softening Arab enmity ; so the legality of the Balfour Declaration is a side issue, and cannot of itself bridge the possible gulf between the ' legal' and the ' just', between the Israelis and the Arabs. It is only one more complication fogging the basic issue. But it needs some explanation, just as did the position of the ' refugees'.

It was natural, indeed inevitable, that Jews should pay immense attention to the legal aspect of their growing settlements in Palestine. Throughout both Christendom and Islam Jewish permission to live in any particular city or province had for more than a thousand years depended on an authoritative and legally binding document of some kind. In Islam their rights were set forth in the Quran and its commentaries; and, provided they accepted a humble status of inequality, these were generally respected. An expulsion or persecution was an act of violence against Islam. Such things did happen but, relatively to the situation in Christendom, rarely. In western Christendom, from the ninth century onwards, Jews were completely rightless, until they had obtained from the local prince, or his suzerain, a written charter, precisely defining their rights, and the length of time they should enjoy them. These conditions only disappeared with emancipation; and in 1917, when the Balfour Declaration was issued, there were few Jews among whom real political freedom was a tradition going back as much as a single century. And those who had such a tradition of freedom were aware that their political equality with others was the consequence of a precise Act of Parliament; and that Acts of Parliament were capable of revocation. Perhaps few western Jews would have thought this revocation possible in 1917. They learned to be less optimistic in 1933.

To say that the legality of the Balfour Declaration is irrelevant to the fundamental issues does not, of course, mean that the Declaration is an illegal document; or that the subsequent act of the United Nations in voting the partition of the country was an illegal decision. Both acts, in terms of the international situation at the time of their issue, were legal acts. What I mean is something different. Both acts affect others as well as Jews. The British issued the Balfour Declaration, and the partition was an act affecting all Palestinian residents, Arab as well as Jewish. But neither the Arabs nor the British have the reverence for, and reliance on, a legal document which has been the natural consequence of Jewish history. There are two legal documents in British history—*Magna Carta* and *Habeas Corpus*—and it is doubtful if one Englishman in a thousand could describe them or define the rights he enjoyed under them. As to Arab history, I doubt whether there is any legal document deeply engraved on the heart of the fellaheen. The ' legality ' of the two documents has never seemed to Arabs to counterbalance what they feel to be their injustice.

However, both Arabs and British immensely venerate tradition, and both are deeply affected by the sense of belonging to, and being rooted in, a geographical entity. But in historical fact this is precisely the basis of the Jewish relationship with the strip of land on the eastern Mediterranean seaboard wherein their earliest ancestors first became an identifiable and permanent social unit nearer four than three thousand years ago. The Balfour Declaration did not try to create any Jewish right; it recognised that one already existed.

There are certain things which have been done and which cannot be undone. At the time when the Declaration was issued it was a one-sided affair. It had not the prior consent of any Arab representatives from the area affected. One must say ' area affected ' because there was no political unit, and there were no political representatives, in ' Palestine ' whence Arab agreement could have been derived. As soon as they could, the Zionist leaders secured the conditional agreement of Prince Faysal, who was the internationally accepted Arab leader; but he was not a Palestinian, or accepted as a spokesman for their future by the Palestinians. For it must be recognised that Palestinian Arabs, as soon as they could, repudiated the action of Faysal and declared their hostility to the Declaration.

From the moment when Palestinian Arabs, both Muslim and Christian, could express their opinion, the overwhelming majority have continuously and consistently demanded of anyone in authority—the British government, the Palestine Administration, or the League of Nations—that the basis of Jewish settlement be re-examined. As continuously they have been told that their position will be sympathetically considered provided they recognise the Balfour Declaration. From their point of view the clash between legality and justice has been absolute. The British and international acceptance of the passage of the Jewish community in the '30's from an absorbable minority to a potential majority was to them a further intolerable injustice; the attempt to put them on an equality with those whom they regarded as interlopers could only add fuel to the fire of their anger. When the position was reached that their refusal to accept a basic injustice was to be remedied by the division of ' their ' country into half, their reply that they would meet such an outrage with armed resistance was inevitable.

So long as the conflict appeared to be between an imposed legality and a fundamental natural right, it is not surprising that many British and others sympathised with the Arab case. The British would, in all probability, have behaved with the same outraged determination to resist in similar circumstances. Of course it remains true that there are times when men in an imperfect world have to accept a legal decision which goes against them. The appalling tragedy is that this decision to issue the Balfour Declaration and all that ensued in the following thirty years, should never have been put before them as a legal decision. This was the second mistake. The reality, that the Jewish claims rest on tradition and continuous residence, was not the argument put before the Arabs. I do not say that they would instantly have accepted the Jewish thesis. But the ground between them would have been common ground : reverence for tradition. The Jewish case would have rested on evidence of the kind with which they were familiar, and on which they rested their own case to be allowed to continue undisturbed. It would have been the justice, not the legality, of the Declaration, which would have been the issue.

As the inter-war years passed, yet a third misfortune accentuated the division between them. Zionist leaders were constantly seeking to respond to a Jewish pressure of which the Arab inhabitants were totally ignorant; and it has to be added that most of the

British administrators were quite unfamiliar with the conditions which caused it. For the pressures were in central and eastern Europe, and the administrators were chosen from the Colonial Service. The failure of the Minority treaties, the growing economic collapse of the late '20's, the rising antisemitism in Poland, Hungary, Rumania and, above all, Nazi Germany, these were the facts which were making Zionist leaders demand a maximum response from the Mandatory Government; and no Jewish leader could have acted otherwise. But an increase of the tempo and pressure of Jewish immigration was the last thing which appeared intelligent even to those officials who recognised the rightness of the basic conditions of the Mandate. They felt that Arabs were not being given time to understand what was happening, that Jews were too impatient and had too much influence in London, which in turn had too little understanding of the difficulties in Jerusalem.

On such a background the decision of the United Nations to effect a partition of the country could not appear anything but a crowning injustice. That on top of this injustice should have come the bitter humiliation of defeat is enough to explain the irreconcilable Arab rage of today, a rage which affects all the Arab peoples alike, whether they did or did not partake in the attempt to stop partition by an ' illegal ' war. To take up arms for an ideal of justice and to be crushingly defeated is not an event which any people would accept with equanimity, and Arabs are a proud people. It would be a great help if it were generally recognised in Israel that, without in any way belittling the magnificent courage and skill of the Jewish victory, the Arab effort was based on a generous and worthy instinct, even though it turned out that most of the Arab governments involved, especially the Egyptian government of King Farouk, behaved with pusillanimous inefficiency.

All these things would sink into insignificance, and the displaced Palestinians might be restored to a creative and self-respecting life, if the argument could be shifted from fallacious to genuine issues. Arabs are not to that extent so unrealistic that they cannot accept that the past cannot be unwritten; but they will go on refusing to accept the existence itself of the State of Israel until they are met in argument along lines which they consider just and right.

This real argument turns around two points; the rightness or wrongness of increased Jewish settlement within the boundaries of the ' Promised Land ' under international guarantee; and the rightness or wrongness of an area of Jewish political control within the framework of that settlement.

There is not a ' Zionist ' and a ' non-Zionist ' interpretation of Jewish history, although there are Jewish scholars and religious leaders who have reacted against Zionist exaggerations by stressing the universalist and religious significance of Judaism to the exclusion of the particular and historical significance of the Jewish people. Historically Judaism survives because the Jewish people have survived; and the Jewish people have survived because they have always looked forward to a future happiness and fulfilment which will balance the strain and humiliation of the present. This has always in their history been expressed in the contrast between ' exile ' and ' restoration'. No land outside Israel, however prosperous or apparently permanent their settlement in it, has been accepted as the land of ' restoration'. Some Jews, especially in the enthusiasm of emancipation, postponed the restoration indefinitely, or joined the Christians in positing it in the ' next ' world; some, under the influence of an escapist mysticism, rejected any human action towards its achievement, and so demanded visible evidence of the arrival of the Messiah first. The main line of Jewish consciousness left the time undefined, while convinced of its reality in history; but no Jews ever left the geographical site undefined.

So long as the ghetto walls preserved an adequate unity, and even uniformity, throughout the whole people scattered in all the continents, Jews could accept their religion and its way of life as a ' portable Homeland'. But as soon as emancipation, even of the small western European and American communities, broke the enforced unity, it was inevitable that the need for a current and actual expression of that unity should take a geographical, in place of a literary and mystical, form. The Talmud, and the Torah which it interpreted, could be a ' portable Homeland ' only as long as Talmudic Judaism was the universally accepted norm of Jewish life. With emancipation it became instead *one* expression of Jewish life, disputed by other secular and religious attractions. That Zionism emerged was inevitable; that it took forms comparable to other contemporary nationalisms was natural.

The historical evidence on which Zionism rested had been forgotten even by most Jews themselves. The long period of stagnation under Turkey, in contrast with the excitement of European and American opportunities, made them overlook the continuity of

Jewish life in Palestine. But, once looked for, it was unanswerably impressive. Jews continued to be the majority of the Palestinian population for several centuries after the two defeats by Rome. They had a semi-autonomous Patriarch until the fifth Christian century. Then conditions became much harder. Forcibly baptised by eastern monks or imperial decree, massacred in successive wars, looted and killed by bedouin raiders, despised by both Muslims and Christians, sometimes reduced to a few thousands, forced to live within walled cities and terrified to pass beyond the walls, even so the Jewish communities had never abandoned the land, had never thought of themselves as anything but representatives of the whole people ' in exile'. So deeply rooted was this representational feeling that a poverty-stricken and half-starving Jew of Jerusalem, living on a miserable pittance of charity from Jewish communities elsewhere (a pittance of which the Muslim authorities took considerably more than half in bribes), felt himself to be more fortunate than the Jewish millionaire of London or Paris who had the privilege of supporting him.

The stream—or sometimes trickle—of Jews from communities of East and West into the ghettoes of the four holy cities of Israel, Jerusalem, Safed, Tiberias and Hebron, was continuous; the willingness of other Jewries to support them in the greatest measure possible was also continuous. But what is more relevant to the discussion with the Arab and the Muslim is that *this right of Jews to ' return ' to, and live in, this little area of land was accepted by all the successive Muslim rulers of Palestine from the Muslim conquest right up to the end of the nineteenth century.* Islam always made this interesting distinction. Apart from brief periods of fanaticism, the right of Christians to *visit* the country as pilgrims was always recognised. But a defined term was set to the length of pilgrimage. Except for specially privileged persons such as the Franciscans, any Christians who were not subjects of the Muslim ruler had to leave the country at the end of their pilgrimage. But Jews had the right to enter it and to live in it, until at the very end of the 19th century Zionist settlement became entangled in European *Weltpolitik* and the rival ambitions of Russia and other powers. Even then, Sultan Abdul Hamid, in refusing their right to purchase land in Palestine, emphasised that there were no limitations on their right to live in every other part of his realm. Before this happened, two special facts have a bearing on the present issue. Jews formed the largest

element in the population of Jerusalem well before the birth of
Zionism. Even Christians outnumbered Muslims, so that it was
accepted as tolerable in the third holy city of Islam that both
Jews and Christians should outnumber the Muslim inhabitants.
In other words, Islamic tradition recognised the rights of both
Jews and Christians in Jerusalem. The second fact extends this
special situation. Until a disastrous earthquake wiped out almost
all the Jewish population early in the 19th century, Safed was an
almost wholly Jewish city, and the holy places which surrounded
it were accepted Jewish holy places. And in the south of the country,
the city of Hebron, with the immensely holy Muslim shrine of
the tombs of Abraham and Sarah, was a city with a large Jewish
population, though Christians were not allowed to live in it until
the nineteenth century.

In the discussions which went on during the mandatory period,
and in the proposals for a permanent regime which were mooted
at that time, most Arab spokesmen were prepared to admit a
Jewish minority to have a right to continue in the country under
Muslim Arab rule. Jews, in the same way, were willing to accept
a very large Arab minority with much autonomy. But the condition
was that a Jewish political authority existed which should, at the
least, give them the ability to develop their position in the country
in such a way that it contained a really Jewish ' national ' centre
large enough and self-governing enough to receive those Jewish
immigrants whom desire or necessity brought to their shores.
There was, in fact, a certain recognition on both sides that this
strip of territory belonged historically to no one people *exclusively*,
and in this they were perfectly correct. Over at least four millennia
there never has been a century in which only one people inhabited
the country, and only one religion prevailed in it. All three religions
have had brief periods of imperialism, Judaism under the Maccabees,
Christianity under Justinian, and Islam under the mad Fatimid
Calif, al Hakim. But in no case had the imperialism endured.

The Jews argue that this recognition of a historical reality is
legitimately expressed in twentieth-century conditions in the possession by both Jews and Arabs of an area in which they are political
masters ' in their own house.' It may be asked why the third group,
the Christian group, is not included, but the answer is that the
settled Christian element is for historical reasons in the Lebanon,
and that the Lebanon has its own problems, but does try to recognise

its complex religious identity. The relation of the Christian world to the ' Holy Land ' has always been one of pilgrimage, never one of settlement. The problem has been exacerbated by one prime factor for which neither Jews nor Arabs are responsible, or could have modified or controlled. The ' Arab ' world, united in general culture and way of life, religion and language, was carved up during the first World War by France and Great Britain into separate territories over which each exercised a colonial government; and this gave rise in turn to Arab sovereignties over artificially created areas. Much the same thing today is happening in Africa, where states are created whose frontiers bear no relation to African tribal realities, but follow lines determined by what nineteenth-century Europeans could grab from each other.

The desire of Jews to control a homeland within the wide area of the Middle East would have had quite a different perspective, had Britain and France not carved up Syria, creating separate mandated territories. There would have been adjustment here, accommodation there; some Jews from elsewhere in the Middle East would have preferred to move in, some Arabs to move out. But this movement would have been a normal part of the Middle East's long history. Many of the ' Arab ' inhabitants of the mandated territory of Palestine were very recent immigrants from Egypt, from northern Syria, from the Caucasus, even from the Muslim Balkans; but it was the separation of southern Syria from its northern half which created the quite artificial picture of floods of Jews dispossessing and driving out Arabs who had for millenia cultivated the same soil, and turning a minority into an artificial majority by the creation of a million refugees. But ' the floods of Jews ' have come, and come above all from Arab lands. That also is a factor to be considered.

To get the real picture back into its true perspective is undoubtedly more difficult today than it would have been half a century ago. But it is still the true picture which has ultimately to be seen, a picture of the Middle East in which no one people or religion possesses a monopoly of land or government; and in which there are areas in which each has control over its own life. Today that means forms of sovereignty. But it may not mean that tomorrow. Today present Arab politicians will undoubtedly reject it, and denounce it as either colonialism or imperialism—probably both. But if it is true, it will in the end move into the foreground of discussion, to become in time the basis of a lasting peace.

From the very beginning of the conquest of the area by the Arabs in the seventh century, Jews and Christians were permitted to live with their own autonomy as ' millets ' under their own religious leadership. The development from millet to state is a development appropriate to the passage from the seventh century to the twentieth. In the twenty-first we may have again discovered that the fostering of cultural and religious variety leaves areas of political and economic activity in which larger groupings are the most serviceable. But for today the natural development of this long tradition is a variety of independent states. All the international proposals for partition desired that there should be economic unity over the area west of Jordan covered by the Mandate. Actually an area which included also the present kingdom of Jordan would be of great benefit to that kingdom. Were real peace to come to the Arab states of the Middle East, the final result might well be a federal system wherein there was one Jewish and one Christian member, though neither would be without Muslim fellow-citizens; and one Muslim member, (or, with Syria, two) likewise with Jewish and Christian minorities. For such a solution would meet the demand for justice which is legitimately made by Jew, Christian and Muslim alike.

XI

ANTISEMITISM IN THE SOVIET UNION

THERE IS UNHAPPILY little doubt that Mr. Krushchev's attitude towards the Jews was illustrated when he expressed his anger with the governing group of his Polish satellite by saying that 'it contained too many Abrahamoviches', a singularly uncommunistic comment. It is unfortunately neither surprising nor unique, for Nikita Krushchev, born in the Ukraine in 1894, passed all the impressionable years of his youth in the atmosphere created by the antisemitism of the Tsarist government, the Black Hundreds, and the Orthodox Church. Impressions thus created are not destroyed by a change of government, or even by a revolution. What we have learned to be true of Germany since 1945 is also true of the older generation of Russians, and it is only too easily transmitted by them to their successors. The background of Krushchev explains one of the bitterest experiences of eastern European Jews during the war. The partisans in Poland and the Ukraine were often as antisemitic as the Nazis whom they were fighting, and freely betrayed Jewish fugitives, and even Jewish partisans, to the Germans. There is not much evidence that Krushchev, who had become the most powerful figure in the government of the Ukraine just before the war, dissented from this policy.

It is true that the Communists reacted very strongly against the injustices of Tsarist rule, and that a law labelling antisemitism 'bourgeois' and making any expression of it illegal, was passed quite early after the Revolution. But ancient prejudices cannot be suddenly eliminated by a law, and Russians were indoctrinated with hatred and contempt for Jews for a much longer period than Germans. Moreover Russian Jews had their bitterest enemies in Russian Jewish Communists. For the majority of Jews were reformists rather than revolutionaries; and, if they were socialists, were members of the Jewish *Bund* rather than the Russian Social Democratic Party. Two of their most respected leaders were Henry Erlich and Victor Alter, who were prominent in the first revolution in the Spring of 1917. But, when Lenin seized power in October (November by the western European calendar), Erlich and Alter moved westward to Poland. There they remained as socialist leaders until they fled before the German armies in 1939. Stalin at first imprisoned and then released them as part of a general agreement with the Polish government in exile. He asked them to form a World Jewish Anti-fascist Committee, but when they submitted its proposed programme to him, it was returned by Stalin to his Police Chief, Beria, with the crude message on it, *Both to be shot*. The order was forthwith carried out though for years the Soviet Government denied any knowledge of their whereabouts.

The contempt of the Bolshevik for the social reformer was echoed in the contempt of the Jewish Communist for the Jewish *petit bourgeois*; and most Russian Jews fell into that category. Few were genuine proletarians, for their religious scruples made it impossible for them to work in any but Jewish-owned factories, and there were not many such. They were traders, pedlars and artisans. Moreover they were intensely attached to their religion, and Jewish schools were all religious schools, incapable of being turned into Communist proletarian schools. Finally, they were conscious of belonging to a single people scattered throughout the world, and the October Revolution took place within a few days of the issue of the Balfour Declaration. The final crime of many Russian Jews was that they saw in the Declaration, and its hopes of a Jewish Palestine, something which the most successful revolution on Russian soil could not give them.

Jewish Communists, organised in the Yevsektsia, in addition to sheer persecution, had two main lines of attack. They could make it impossible for a Jew to observe the Sabbath or the High Holy Days and Festivals without appearing to be disloyal to the new Communist society. And they outlawed the teaching of Hebrew, which they saw as a shrewd blow aimed at both Zionism and the worship of the synagogue. Yiddish, for the first period at least, they encouraged, and towards the end of the '20's and the beginning of the '30's there was a very flourishing Yiddish culture in the Soviet Union. There was a lively Yiddish theatre, there were a number of Yiddish newspapers. Yiddish authors, actors and musicians abounded. There was an extensive system of Yiddish schools, and in one or two districts where Jews were particularly numerous, Yiddish was even the official language.

This culture, however, was entirely secular. As a religion Judaism suffered perhaps even more than Christianity; for it is possible to conceal one's beliefs, but impossible to disguise one's practices. Such a situation weighs heavily against Judaism. Not only is it easier to baptize in secret than to circumcize, but Judaism contains so many practices which are easily detected, or made impossible to observe, that the campaign of the Jewish godless was quite easy to maintain. Moreover, partly by tradition and partly by Communist action, each Jewish community was much more isolated than a single parish or diocese of the Orthodox Church. Judaism has no hierarchical organisation whereby a centre could sustain its limbs, or balance defeat in one area with victory in another. Nevertheless in the first years of the Soviet régime there was an outstanding Jewish personality who was able to do much for Jewish religious life. This was ' the Lubavicher', Joseph Isaac Schneerson, rabbi of the little 'shtetl' of Lyubavichi near the river Beresina in the Province of Minsk. Schneerson came of an old Hassidic dynasty which enjoyed a wide reputation among the Jews of the Pale. Operating first from Rostock and then from Leningrad, he was able to promote illegal religious education, to support rabbis in distress and need, and to inspire a general resistance to anti-religious decrees among Jewish artisans.

The authorities arrested him in 1927 and condemned him to death. But his saintly character was so well known abroad that an immense outcry resulted, and he was not only released but allowed to leave the country with his family. He finally settled in New York, where he died in January, 1950. He spent this last period of his life in organising throughout the Jewish world schools and academies which preserved the traditional piety of the old eastern European Hassidic communities. But in the Soviet Union itself there was no outstanding Jewish personality who could carry on his work.

Not only was Jewish life made difficult by the inevitable survival of Tsarist antisemitism and by the persecution of the Yevsektsia, but it was complicated by the fact that the Soviet leaders had evolved a theory of nationality which Jews did not fit, since they had no established territory where they were the main population. Many years before he reached the summit this was the particular field in which Joseph Stalin specialised. Since *ex hypothesi* they could not admit a legitimate bond in the religion of Judaism, Jews had no representative or local organisation like other nationalities. They were finally made a pseudo-nationality in 1928, when an artificial " autonomous republic " named Biro-Bidjan was created by the Amur river in the extreme east of Siberia on the frontiers of Outer Mongolia and Manchuria. The area has rich timber and mineral resources, but an intolerable climate. In any case few Jews wanted to displace themselves to that extent, and the Republic did not provide, as the Soviet authorities hoped, a counter-attraction to the Land of Israel. The overwhelming majority of Jews remained in European Russian provinces, and distributed themselves more widely, both in occupation and in residence. Many found work in the administration from which they had, of course, been hitherto excluded. Those who accepted " secularisa-tion " found work in factories rather than agriculture, though there was for a time an agricultural settlement of Jews in the Crimea which was looked on with great favour. It also was supposed to supply an alternative to the collective agricultural villages in Palestine. What survived of these farms was entirely wiped out by the Nazis.

Although Jews had no territory, and had none of the basic right to their own culture which other nationalities enjoyed, for the flowering of Yiddish was no more than an interlude in the half-century of Russian Communism, Jews were from the beginning, and still are, obliged to register themselves on all official documents, from birth certificates onwards, as " Hebrews". When Yiddish writers, together with the Yiddish press, the Yiddish theatre and all separate Yiddish schools were liquidated in the terrible purges of the '30's by which Stalin ensured his absolute autocracy, Jews were left simply with the invidious distinction that they still had to inscribe " Hebrew " on their birth certificates and passports, might still be asked whether they were Jews when applying for work or an official position, but possessed no corresponding ad-vantage as a recognised nationality with a recognised language and nominal autonomy. They were also, of course, not allowed to solve their problem by emigration to Palestine or any other country. During the years of furious anti-Nazi propaganda before the infamous Nazi-Soviet Pact, Soviet antisemitism reached the absurd peak of arresting and condemning a number of prominent

Jews for spying on behalf of Nazi Germany! When Nazi Germany
became an ally, it was, of course, only " bourgeois " and " cosmopolitan " elements among the German Jews that the Nazis
were compelled to eradicate.

When the war came, the Nazis overran all that part of Russia
and the Ukraine which had been the traditional centre of Jewish
life. Together with several million Russians and Ukrainians, over
a million Jews were murdered by the special squads of the S.S.
Although the sites are known where tens of thousands of Jews were
killed in a single massacre, no monuments or other commemorations
have been allowed by the Soviet authorities; and, wherever possible,
Jews are not mentioned among the victims of the Nazis. Jewish
life during and since the war has had to be built up in new centres,
and this weighs especially heavily on Jews who wish to preserve
their religious identity since they are not allowed to build new
synagogues, and ancient ones do not exist where they now live.
As the Germans advanced, many Jews managed to escape eastwards
together with other inhabitants to work in the great munition
factories in the Urals. Many Jewish centres are still in those regions;
but the story that Stalin had particularly assisted Jews to escape,
because of their special danger, was one of the fables put forward
in the period of the Soviet-Western alliance of the war years.
The short-lived Jewish Anti-fascist Committee belonged to the
same period, and its information was often equally unreliable. Its
particular task was to win the sympathy of American Jews, but it
did not survive the war. It was the irony of history that it was
destroyed just when the Soviet Union was giving its recognition
to the new State of Israel; but this recognition was anti-British
and anti-colonial and not pro-Jewish.

As soon as their value had passed, the leaders of the war-time
Jewish Anti-fascist Committee were all treated with the contemptuous hostility which had already destroyed Erlich and Alter. Its
most outstanding member, the actor-manager Salomon Mikhoels,
was mysteriously murdered early in 1948. Isaak Feffer, a leading
Yiddish poet, and many other Jewish intellectuals were either
executed without trial or sent to Siberia. Sometimes there were
trumped up charges, but often it was without any explanation.
Many tens of thousands of ordinary Jews, especially from the areas
which the Soviet Union had taken from the Baltic States or from
Poland, were also deported to Siberia, often without any warning

whatever. Stalin made no secret of his hatred and his contempt for Jews; and there could be no question of a Yiddish revival so long as he lived.

In fact it soon became evident that the status of ordinary Jewish citizens was itself in danger, and so began an almost classic example of the use of Jews in all the ways described in Chapter Two on *The Psychology of Prejudice*. In this matter at least Krushchev has continued with little change the attitude of his predecessor. The immensely costly victory of the Soviet Union, the contact with western allies which gave many ordinary Russians for the first time a knowledge of the " capitalist " world, the unrest and malaise which reacted against the privations of wartime, all these things produced a disquiet in the Russian spirit which was met, partly at least, by appropriate diversions against Jews. Anything in the Russian attitude which Stalin disliked was projected onto them.[1] Did peace bring a desire to travel? Cosmopolitanism was a typically Jewish vice, and 'in the various forms by which it could be made illegal, two thirds of the publicised ' criminals ' had Jewish names. Were there in Russia, as in the West, problems of employment for demobilised officers and technicians? It was time that Jews should end their disproportionate occupation of political, administrative or scientific office. ' Once we needed them, now we have our own intellectuals,' said a high Soviet official, echoing the attitude of Stalin.

Jews were also attacked directly, as well as being scapegoats for general difficulties. Did they demand recognition of their Jewishness, this was ' bourgeois Zionism,' and criminal on that account. Local officials were encouraged to find every pinprick to harry Jews who still wished to practise their religion. Their synagogues were taken from them, their ritual drinking of a glass of wine at the close of the Sabbath became public drunkenness. Even petty spite, akin to the Nazi blotting out of Jewish names on war memorials of the 1914 war, found its parallels in these last years of Stalin. A new edition of the great Soviet Encyclopaedia omitted as much as possible the references to distinguished Jews which had found a place in the original edition of 1927.

The hatred of Stalin did not stop at the borders of the Soviet Union. He ensured that the same hostility was practised in the Soviet satellites, and he had little difficulty in fanning the antisemitism already existing in countries like Poland and Rumania. His most surprising success was in Czechoslovakia, where the disease had not been prevalent except in the more backward eastern parts, and where an unusually large proportion of the highest Communist officials were of Jewish origin. Like most Communist Jews they had either never had, or had long broken off, any contacts with Judaism or the Jewish community.

In 1949 Rudolf Slansky, Secretary General of the Czech Communist Party, was suddenly arrested, together with more than a dozen of his closest associates, and charged with treason. Most of those arrested were Jewish, and many other Jews were at the same time dismissed from their posts. The accused were kept in prison for more than two years, and submitted to extremely brutal torture and brainwashing. Other Jews were denounced and seized from time to time, notably two Israeli visitors of some political importance from the Marxist wing of Mapam, Mordecai Oren and Simon Ohrenstein. It was thus possible to claim that a conspiracy had been unveiled in which the whole Jewish people was implicated. When the trial opened in the late autumn of 1952, the prosecution produced ' evidence ' of the involvement of American and Israeli Jews, and the existence and sinister designs of secret ' Elders of Zion ' such as had been invented by 19th-century antisemites and enshrined in *The Protocols*. Slansky and his colleagues had been subjected to such treatment that they ' confessed ' whatever was desired of them, and their conviction and execution at least put an end to two years of intolerable torture and humiliation.

Three months later, in March 1953, Stalin died. In June there were riots against the Russians in Czechoslovakia and East Germany, which were not easily suppressed. Hungary was also restive, though there the smouldering anger took another three years to explode.

The death of the dictator was followed by a period of uncertainty while different personalities manoeuvred for power. It fairly soon became clear that Nikita Krushchev dominated the Party. By 1957 he had ousted his rivals, and was also the leading figure in the government, and in March 1958 he took over the office of Prime Minister.

There was undoubtedly a period of *détente* for all Soviet citizens after the death of Stalin. More contacts with the outer world were permitted and even encouraged. Religious leaders of other countries were allowed to visit the Soviet Union, though this profited Christians more than Jews. For Jews still had no central organisation, so that when a visitor reported that he had seen a full synagogue in Moscow or Leningrad, it told nothing about the situation in Kiev or Georgia. From time to time promises were made that Jews who wished to would be able to purchase the necessary ritual articles of their religion, or to print a new edition of their Prayer Book; but these promises were primarily made for the benefit of external propaganda. They were supposed to prove that there was religious freedom in the Soviet Union. At the same time foreign Jewish visitors were constantly assured that the Jews of the Soviet Union wanted nothing so much as to assimilate themselves completely into the environing communist society. Of their own free will they had abandoned all traditional religious practices.

Yet it was this assimilation which was precisely impossible. Jews were still compelled to inscribe ' Hebrew ' on all official documents, even though they enjoyed nothing at all of the advantages of being a recognised nationality. The inscription could, on the other hand, be quickly used to their disadvantage whenever a scapegoat of any kind was needed. Indeed it became commonplace in the Soviet press that in any criminal proceedings a Jewish name should be attached where possible to the accused; but, according to the normal law of group prejudice governing an identifiable minority, his or her Jewishness was never mentioned in recording praise or the award of some Soviet distinction to a Jewish citizen.

At the 20th Congress of the Communist Party in February 1956 Stalin was officially and publicly denounced by Krushchev as an insane criminal, who had wrought terrible evil in his lust for personal power. But the detailed list of his offences made no mention of his destruction of Yiddish or his many multiple and individual murders of Jews. The denunciation of Stalin inevitably produced, both in the Soviet Union and in its satellites, a feeling of insecurity as well as of relief. An established god was shattered, and had no immediate replacement. From then onwards there is a visible dualism in the Soviet attitude to its Jews. On the one hand Krushchev quite clearly wanted to liberalise the regime, to make more provision for the emergence of affluence in Soviet society, to encourage intellectual and cultural life, and to stand well with the non-communist world as the very fount from which world peace and tranquillity were anxious to flow. On the other hand, there is no evidence that he had in any way abated his inherited dislike of Jews, and his unwillingness to take any steps to ease their position, and to assist them to obtain their share of these new advantages. Moreover the Soviet Union was entering into a period of comparative affluence as the scars of war were healed, and such a period brought new kinds of moral problems in its train. Soviet citizens began to have time to criticize as well as to produce. The immensely complicated and overcentralised machinery of production in industry and agriculture continually raised new difficulties; and new opportunities of obtaining wealth continually opened new doors to individual greed and envy. It was still extremely convenient to have a scapegoat who was powerless to answer back.

The increase of foreign travel of Soviet citizens, and the increase of foreign visitors to the Soviet Union, made it prudent to grant a minimum number of concessions to bolster the claim that ' religion was free ' in the Union. In 1957 the rabbi of Moscow was allowed to create a rabbinical academy, the first to exist openly since the Revolution. At one time it had as many as thirty-five students enrolled, a pitiable number if it was intended to help the religious members of between two and three million Soviet citizens to practise their faith. But the number rapidly dwindled, by the simple process of the refusal of the local police, whence the student came, to grant him a travel permit. By 1962 the academy was empty, and it was closed. From time to time an inadequate supply of some ritual object would be made available, or Jews would be permitted to import it from abroad.

The standard objective in this game of cat and mouse is the provision or refusal of unleavened bread, *matzos*, for Passover. It is illegal to bake it privately for sale or gift, and it is easy to prevent its supply from abroad. A Jewish community never knows whether it will have *matzos* for Passover or not. If its supply from abroad has been licensed, it is always possible to delay it in the post till it is no longer ritually needed. In one year a few thousand copies of the Prayer Book were allowed to be printed, but these were quite inadequate to meet the demand. At another time one number of a Yiddish periodical was actually allowed to appear. There were still many Jewish writers who wrote in Yiddish, and the Yiddish classics were, after all, a significant part of the Russian literary heritage. So both contemporaries and classics were allowed to appear—in translation.

All these concessions, however, were but trifles when set against a steadily increasing current of anti-Jewish prejudice. It would be wrong to compare it with the Nazi policy of annihilation, or even with the Tsarist policy of solving the Jewish problem in Russia by death, emigration, or conversion. It is a meaner and more petty persecution. But it is too consistently noted by knowledgeable visitors, foreign residents, and extracts from the Soviet press itself, to be accidental. There were still in 1957 an enormous number of Jewish scientists of all kinds throughout the Union; but in that year Jewish students began to find it difficult to gain admission to the universities and higher schools. There were many Jewish administrators, but few could reach the top. After Kaganovich, there was no Jew in a top ranking position in the government. It steadily became the common practice to ask an applicant for a place to produce his papers, and the damning inscription ' Hebrew ' ensured refusal.

The local press was, as it had been before, a particularly useful medium for spreading an atmosphere of distrust and hostility. Attacks on Judaism as reactionary and bourgeois were to be expected. It became commoner to find the attacks directed, not against the Jewish religion, but against the Jewish character. Jews were described in feuilletons and articles as swindlers, speculators, and financial crooks. In reports of a trial only the Jewish accused would be pin-pointed. If there were no Jewish accused, the trial would probably get no mention. This spreading of a pervasive atmosphere through the press reached a culmination in 1960 in a Muslim paper in Daghestan, which asserted that religious Jews regularly needed to obtain Muslim blood for ritual purposes. The charge had been completely unknown in the history of Islam and, in any case, the mountain Jews of Daghestan had been deprived of all relics of synagogue life and practice for many years.

In the same year, Jewish communal leaders, first in Leningrad, then in Moscow, and then in smaller communities, were suddenly charged with illegal trafficking in foreign currency, and given heavy prison sentences. The increase of travel certainly brought more Soviet citizens into contact with the complexities of currency exchange, whether at home or abroad; and any country which maintains so artificial a rate of exchange between its own currency and that of other countries invites all kinds of evasion. Jewish communal leaders, visited by Jews of more prosperous countries, or acting on behalf of great Jewish charities such as the American

Joint Distribution Committee, would be extremely likely to be involved in the exchange between roubles and dollars or pounds; but they would be the least likely of men so involved to be dishonest.

It is very probable that in this somewhat unconvincing attack upon the religious leaders of Judaism the Soviet Government was displaying a form of antisemitism which has been noted in other countries and situations. This is manifested in an attack upon Jews and Judaism, when the real objective, recognised or unrecognised, is the Christian Church. From the moment when Stalin found it supremely important to call for the traditional defence of ' Holy Russia ' against her adversaries in organising resistance to the Nazi invaders, and from the moment when the Orthodox Church responded whole-heartedly to that call, the Soviet Government has been careful and, indeed, generous by its standards in its treatment of the Orthodox clergy, and in allowing Christian visitors to make contact with Orthodox circles. Yet by its very rigid Marxist-Leninist ideology it cannot but resent the fact that religion was essential to the successful defence against the Nazis, and that their own ideology has not proved a secure moral foundation in the successive changes in the Soviet situation. It had been fundamental to Marxist thinking that morality was merely the servant of a changing economic situation. The unchanging morality of religion had been sneered at as an obvious weakness. The firm ' thou shalt ' and ' thou shalt not ' of the Ten Commandments had seemed matter only for the ribaldry of the godless. It was both humiliating and perplexing that each advance in the economic stability and variety of the Soviet society brought new moral problems, which appeared just as difficult to solve as the old. In place of new triumphs, there resulted an increase of ' nihilism', a word which covers every form of hostility to the régime from hooliganism to deviation.

A typical example of the doctrine of changing morality in changing circumstances has been provided by the Marxist-Leninist attitude to marriage, brilliantly described by the late Walter Kolarz in *Religion in the Soviet Union*.[1] Each phase of the development of the Soviet society, each campaign of its battle with the Orthodox Church, had produced a new decree tightening or loosening the union of husband and wife, apparently brilliantly

[1] Pp. 26ff. and 32f.

adjusted to the needs of that precise moment. But the result had been confusion instead of admiration, satisfaction and conviction, and had only made it more difficult to prove to the women of Russia that 'Communism is women's greatest friend and religion their worst enemy'.

Here, in the attack upon Jewish religious leaders for unscrupulous financial behaviour, the underlying cause was, on this interpretation, envious anger and frustration at the unchanging and unswerving morality of religion in a situation in which convinced Communists were evincing anything but an unchanging and unswerving morality. Financial speculation and dishonesty simply increased in the proportion in which opportunities for speculation and dishonesty increased. It was becoming more and more impossible to maintain that Marx and Lenin had provided a blueprint for the solution of all the problems in the future history of human societies.

All through 1961 Krushchev was doing battle with the corruption of the vast centralised bureaucracies of Soviet production. The fact that there was large scale graft and corruption in these administrations was so well known that it was openly admitted in the Soviet press. But it was a humiliating confession for the leaders. New laws were passed, making embezzlement and graft on a large scale capital offences; and a series of dramatic trials began and were widely publicised. But again, in almost every case, attention was fastened on Jewish names. Doubtless there are Jewish knaves among the knaves of the Soviet Union. But Jews form at most one and a half per cent of the Soviet peoples. There are simply not enough Jews in the Union to be responsible for all the crimes attributed to them. We are, in fact, witnessing again the old technique of diversion of a general failure to a scapegoat. It is an attempt to conceal the painful truth that, after nearly half a century of socialism, there is not merely wide-spread dishonesty and inefficiency, but that there is no sign of these 'capitalist' evils diminishing. In western countries the real enemy whom the Nazis and Fascists wish to attack is not Jews but democracy; in the Soviet Union the victim is the same but the intention is different. The pretence that it is the inherent Jewish character which is to blame veils the unwanted truth that a fixed Marxist-Leninist ideology has failed to produce the happy and honest society in which state and even family could usefully and painlessly wither away.

XII

THE STERILISATION OF PREJUDICE

In *An Enemy of the People: Antisemitism* the last chapter was entitled *The Elimination of Prejudice*. The change in the present book reflects a change in perspective. In 1945, with all the horrors of the Death Camps still present to our minds and imaginations, men felt that while the present generation lived there could be no danger of a recrudescence of the violent antisemitism of the Nazis. Even if there were people so perverted as to believe that Hitler's policy towards the Jews had been right, they would be prudent enough to keep the feeling to themselves. They could win nothing but loathing from others if they proclaimed their views. The task, then, seemed a long-range one, a task of education in school and Church, supported by wise literature and competent organisations which would cope with local ignorance or manifestations of irritation. We believed then that the political malady had been exorcised by the kind of shock treatment which would be applicable to an individual psychosis.

Today there can be no such optimism. The fantastic nonsense of 'racial purity' has been made again into a political slogan. Trafalgar Square has seen in the summer of 1962 a huge placard bearing an appeal to free Britain from Jewish control. But elimination of a prejudice still remains a long-range task of education and wise application. There is therefore the preliminary problem of its *sterilisation*. The process might be described as preventing people from becoming fascists except by genuine conviction. As far as possible it is undesirable to censor freedom of opinions, and their discussion and the communication of them to others, even when the opinions discussed or communicated seem to the majority, or to authority, undesirable. But there is already a distinction between holding opinions and expressing them. We may feel riotously blasphemous inside, but we must not say so openly. We can shout fire in the middle of Jones Beach, but we shall certainly commit an offence if we shout it in the middle of a crowded theatre. The idea that at some point liberties must be limited in order that reasonable life may continue is well established in the codes of all communities. The need today is to ensure that traditional liberties could only be swept away if a majority of citizens, after due consideration, and with as full a knowledge of the facts as possible, decided that their own interests demanded such an action. But the totalitarians of Right and Left have learned from modern psychology and advertising many tricks for deceiving people. It is these adventitious advantages that should be stripped from them; and the stimulation of group prejudice is undoubtedly in the forefront of the tricks well tested by experience. It is this process which I have called *sterilisation*, and it needs to be considered from legal, educational and social standpoints.

We have already seen that anti-democratic movements are reviving all over the world under the widest variety of slogans. At the moment they are rarely a national danger. In any country with a democratic tradition they are apt to be dismissed as ' harmless crackpots'; it is probably true that none of the British and few of the American or European movements have a thousand members. But they will not necessarily stay like that of themselves. There are many dangers in the political climate of the world which might well favour them; and the time to ' sterilise ' them, and to set barriers to their advancement is when they are numerically feeble and ideologically unpopular with the general public.

It may well be true that there was a time when the advancement of the National Socialist Movement in Germany could have been brought to a halt, or so impeded that the danger of the legal election of Hitler to supreme political authority would have been very substantially lessened. The crucial moment came when Hitler and his followers were first being brought before the courts of the Republic for provoking violent ' breaches of the peace'. But too often complaisant and anti-republican magistrates saw in him and his fellow orators patriotic German nationalists who were keeping the courage of the German people alive. They allowed them to turn court proceedings into theatres and lecture halls for the expression of Nazi views, and either acquitted them or gave them ridiculously inadequate sentences, while no sympathy was shown to their victims especially if they were Jews or Socialists. The immense publicity which has been given to an unknown Coventry ex-school-master with a couple of hundred obscure followers, because of violence in Trafalgar Square and a few uniformed drills in the summer of 1962, reminds one uncomfortably of that period in German history.

There is at least one lesson which can be learned from the failure to sterilise the Nazi Movement while it was weak, which is as applicable to Americans or the British today, or to any other people tomorrow, as it should have been obvious to German believers in democracy forty years ago. And that is that *the campaign against group prejudice of any kind should not be left to the victims of that prejudice.* This is true of Jews in America, West Indians and Pakistanis in England or any subjects of prejudice elsewhere. The ultimate objective of Nazi and fascist movements, however they may camouflage it, is not the solution of some particular minority problem but the destruction of democracy and the substitution of some form of ' the leader principle'. The Coventry ex-schoolmaster provides an excellent illustration of the truth of this. He is anti-Jewish and anti-coloured immigrant; but he assures his audience that these people are simply and courteously to be sent back to their own countries. For Jews presumably ' their own country ' is the State of Israel, and he sees no inconsistency with this in asking for extensive financial support from Cairo. Nor does he seem aware that to send all the coloured workers in England ' back to their own countries ' would create rather than solve employment problems in both England and their own countries. He is not, in fact, interested in either Jews or coloured labourers, but in achieving political supremacy over the British people by pandering to the prejudices of its more ignorant representatives.

When group prejudice is being aroused, it is obviously foolish to conduct a campaign against it without the co-operation of those who are being victimised by it; but it is still more foolish to consider that it is the prime responsibility of the victims to decide upon and lead the campaign. And that is precisely what was done with regard to antisemitism between the wars in every country where it was rampant. It was the Jewish Board of Deputies, and the Defence Committee which it created, which felt itself obliged to besiege the British Home Office with requests that the law might be so strengthened as to cope more effectively with the menace of Mosley in London's East End, where tens of thousands of Jews then lived and were nightly subject to threats and violence. In Germany it was the equivalent organisation of German Jews which importuned the aged President Hindenburg to recognise that Hitler meant seriously to implement the threats he was daily pouring out against the German Jews. In the United States it is the Anti-Defamation League of the Jewish B'nai B'rith which has for many decades assiduously kept track of all the trouble-makers and rabble-rousers scattered over the continent. It was the American Jewish Committee which, at great expense, employed non-Jewish scholars to undertake the specialised research into the antisemitic personality, and the whole range of problems he created, which was published in five substantial volumes.[1] Even when one finds neutral titles to organisations created to fight racialism or fascism, it often proves on examination that Jewish persons are giving their time to organise and their money to support these defences of a common democracy.

It would ill become a non-Jew, especially a professing Christian, to denigrate this immense Jewish activity. It exists, and has existed, because Jews have found by unhappy experience that they cannot entrust their defence to others, even when the ultimate good of the others is what is really at stake. It has been said repeatedly in previous pages that antisemitism is a smoke screen for an attack on democracy. The most infuriating aspect of the whole matter is that, on the present evidence, the smoke screen has been effective. Once a Hitler or a Mosley or a Rockwell attacks the Jews, others sit back and expect Jews to cope with it. It is useless to implore Jews ' not to make themselves conspicuous as this just plays the game of the fascists' when non-Jewish bodies and prominent individuals are not really taking the matter seriously, or are doing absolutely nothing about it.

What is true of Jews is equally true of any other group which is made the object of deliberately roused group-prejudice. It is foolish as well as unjust to lay upon them the responsibility for initiating or sustaining the campaign against the common enemy; even if it is equally foolish to conduct a campaign in defence of common ideals or interests without the co-operation of those who are made the scapegoat for an attack upon those interests and ideals.

There is this further, but very important, point. The appeal to prejudice is an appeal to the majority, not to the minority. There

[1] See note 3, p. 8.

may be a few Jews who are antisemitic, a few West Indians who are prejudiced on the subject of colour. But they are no problem to anybody except themselves. It is ' the Gentile', ' the white man', the member of the majority group whatever it may be, whom the fascists want to win by appealing to his prejudice. It is only when they can convert him to their views that they constitute any real danger to society. This also is a memorable factor in the whole story of group prejudice: it is his resistance to the appeal to prejudice that is alone decisive. For it is as true today as ever that the moral temperature of a community can be measured by the treatment which the majority accords to its minorities. It would probably be true to say that in 1962, less than twenty years after the last fires in the Death Camps were extinguished, the normal Jew has more profoundly recovered his moral balance than the normal German. Terrible as was the measure of suffering borne, the suffering witnessed and inflicted has left a still deeper scar on the moral personality of Germans. That is of the basic nature of humanity. No Hitler, however powerful, no Reich though it survives a thousand years, can alter that aspect of human nature. You cannot persecute a minority without damaging your own spiritual integrity. Even in the six years of Hitler's rule which preceded the war, the rest of the world observed the rapid decline of German scholarship, science, culture and spiritual values.

Trends in America, England, Germany and elsewhere, and all developments from the swastika daubing in Cologne in 1959, have made people in all continents troubled as to the safeguards of our freedoms. They were yet another reminder of how fragile is the barrier between a free society and a tyranny; and there was, naturally enough, a general questioning as to whether the legal and political safeguards already in existence were adequate to the needs of the time. For it is by legal and political means that a destructive movement can be sterilised before its poison is eliminated. Of course every community already possesses various disciplines embodied in its laws, which control the public expression of the differing opinions of a democracy. Police can act where a breach of the peace is intended, or is obviously in danger of occurring. Courts provide remedies if sedition is preached, if a citizen is libelled or defamed, if the public standards are shocked by blasphemy or obscenity. All this is embodied in the twentieth century legislation of every community. But there is still debate on these alternatives: *Are these safeguards still adequate, provided the police and courts are determined to use to the full existing laws?* or *Has the general atmosphere and condition so changed that further safeguards are needed?*

The case for the *status quo* was so admirably expressed in a Leader in *The Times* of London of August 25 that it is printed (by permission) as an Appendix. It presents a case worthy of every respect, and presents it with a judicial moderation. Briefly stated, the argument runs thus: To make incitement to racial hatred or prejudice a crime ' would be sharp deviation from the direction in which the control of public discussion has evolved in Britain during several centuries. The tendency has been for the criminal law to intervene only for the purpose of keeping the peace and maintaining public tranquillity and the stability of the state'. After stating the traditional exceptions to this freedom, and noting their limitations, the Leader goes on to say that ' the state has never hesitated to equip itself with powers to preserve the public peace; and it has progressively relinquished the power to censure particular opinions. Nor has the state sought to combine these principles, by using the prohibition of specified classes of extreme opinion as a means of preserving the peace—by, for instance, prohibiting the preaching of racial prejudice in order to insure against civil disturbance. For, once the criminality of an utterance comes to be judged by direct reference to its content, insoluble difficulties of definition and interpretation arise'. It then discusses, and rejects, the idea that the unpleasant opinions of neo-fascism justify an exception to this trend, since one must not claim that ' it is the business of the criminal law to articulate the conscience of society'. It sums up its argument by saying that ' the whole development of modern domestic British history is towards a position of political maturity, in which people are left to weigh for themselves the opinions, policies, and creeds that are publicly proclaimed before them; treating with contemptuous disdain those that are deserving of contempt; resolving their differences by argument and by constitutional machinery; and refusing to be stampeded by fools, charlatans, and psychopaths'.

The weakest point of the argument is the apparently majestic phrase that it is not ' the business of the criminal law to articulate the conscience of society'. In the correspondence which followed the Leader this sentence was seized upon by Lord Walston, who pointed out that all our legislation about sex was precisely an articulation of the conscience of society; and that, if all matters of principle had to be excluded from legal consideration, laws would be concerned only with material benefits, and would be entirely indifferent to moral corruption. The point is well made. On this point the argument of *The Times* does not stand. But what of the rest? Is there such a change in the nature of contemporary society, and are the dangers to which it is exposed so increased, as to justify what *The Times* claims would be a deviation from the development of centuries?

It is salutary, in considering this question, to reflect upon the effect of the Public Order Act of 1936 to which reference is made. This Act was passed in December 1936 at the time when Mosley was daily increasing the national attention concentrated upon him, by the violence of the anger which he attracted to himself and his views in London's East End, with its large Jewish population and its thousands of unemployed. The method which he used had nothing to do with any possible excellence of his political programme or practical value of his political advice. It was simply a technique for attracting attention, and it was adopted from Fascist Italy and Nazi Germany—openly and avowedly, for it had no roots in English political history. He put a corps of his supporters into fascist uniform and marched with them through the streets to the place where he intended to hold his meeting. And he chose the streets where the opposition to his views and conduct would be most certain to provoke violent reactions.

As *The Times* rightly says, the Act expressed no views on his opinions. It simply authorised the appropriate authorities to forbid him, or anyone else, to organise processions for political purposes, especially processions in uniform, through the streets. And this simple prohibition did in fact, in a very short time, reduce Mosley and his speakers to their actual stature of irresponsible rabble-rousers. It put an end to the growth of his influence, because it removed him and his activities from the front page of the newspapers. He ceased to be interesting.

If *The Times* had published its leader of August 25, 1962 in December of 1936, it might well be that it would have claimed that the Public Order Act was a retrogression from the position achieved by centuries of development. It had never been necessary to have such an Act before. But the reason was that no political party in

England had before used uniformed thugs or (though this has happened in Northern Ireland) political processions in order to provoke opposition. Once the government had seen this new development, and had been convinced of its danger, it had been prepared to pass a new Act of Parliament.

The real issue then is: does the situation today warrant another innovation?

The Times itself in some measure provides the answer. Earlier in the summer of 1962 it published a series of articles, closely reasoned and based on extensive observation, which analysed *The Pulse of Britain*. The result was a somewhat pessimistic assessment of our state of mind seventeen years after the ' successful ' ending of the second World War. A basic ingredient of a widespread malaise was the feeling that Britain had suddenly fallen from her former pre-eminence. Her empire had gone, or was obviously going; her influence in world affairs was waning; anybody could insult her; she was a nobody. The result was a yearning after strong leadership, after something which would bring back ' the Dunkirk spirit'. Men were disillusioned with both the major parties; material comfort was unsatisfying; there was a general feeling, especially among the young, that nothing was worth-while. In fact there was just the kind of vacuum which a fascist leader, with his fictitious promises of greatness, his appeals to patriotism, discipline and sacrifice, might well fill. It was the same atmosphere in the Germany of the '20's which gave Hitler his opportunity.

The argument that there is justification for considering whether new safeguards are needed rests on the disturbing fact that, just at the time when we are bound to become more deeply involved in our neighbours' affairs and less able to isolate ourselves from other streams of contemporary life (whether we are in the Common Market or not), this same malaise is everywhere apparent. In many countries the moral breakdown is much more serious than it is here. In some, which lack our tradition of

> ' Freedom broadening slowly down
> From precedent to precedent '

democratic government is already proving too weak to control it. Moreover the evidence is quite clear that the human material which is most dangerously exposed to this malaise will grow and not diminish in quantity. For the greatest danger arises from the passing of control over those territories of Europe's colonial empires and entanglements in which tens of thousands of white settlers and professional men were living. Dutchmen from the East Indies, Belgians from the Congo, Frenchmen from North Africa and Indo-China, Englishmen from Egypt, the Middle East and East African territories, members of colonial armies and police forces from anywhere, are coming back to Europe, very many of them embittered and unemployed, more conscious than those at home that they have been the object of personal injustice, less conscious of the inevitability of the ' winds of change ' in the world's climate of opinion.

In the particular form described in the preceding paragraph the contemporary malaise has been related to the passing of the European empires. But elsewhere, and in Communist as well as other countries, there are phenomena which are not very different. The truth is that a period of violence and stress, of instability and thwarted expectations, such as the whole world has known for nearly half a century, is not likely to produce a stable, tranquil and restful atmosphere. The young will be particularly conscious of their environment, but they will find many older men and women to share their apprehensions.

The disunion of the various Nazi and fascist movements at the present time may give the impression that the enemies of democracy are less dangerous than they really are. Not all who despise them do so because they believe in democracy. Some are contemptuous when they hear and see self-styled Leaders who mouth the doctrines, and ape the struttings, of men who, like Hitler and Mussolini, have already proved a failure. They have been attracted by new and more expert forms of mastery and violence. At one moment OAS in France was attracting many men of this type, men to whom the image of the ruthless and athletic paratrooper had a much more potent appeal than the German SS or the Italian Blackshirts.

In this post-colonial world one thing is certainly clear. Side by side with the old prejudice which could be aroused against Jews there is a new and imminent danger in the prejudice which can be aroused about colour; and the white and coloured peoples of the world are being thrown together into a new intimacy, an intimacy in which those countries which had a previous relationship of white dominance and coloured subservience incur an added danger. For the past provides an area of resentment ready to poison, from either side, the atmosphere of new contacts and obligations.

There was a time when one could reasonably guess at the attitude of an individual or group to questions of colour if one knew their political allegiance. A man of the Left would be impatient of 'colonial' attitudes of superiority, would despise 'the typical sahibs', whereas a man of the Right would be a believer in Empire and in 'keeping people in their proper place'. But today colour enters into questions of Trade Union membership and employment as readily as into the Suburban Country club. One is as likely to meet it on the Left as on the Right; and the Trade Unionist is just as likely to be seduced by facile appeals to his prejudices as the employer—perhaps more likely. More than once men have threatened to strike just because the management wanted to employ a man who was otherwise completely appropriate and competent for the work wanted, but who was to them the wrong colour.

Finally there is a quite definite element in the population which simply finds in violence an enjoyable recreation. It is to be found in all parts of the country, in the small towns and rural areas as much as in the big cities. In England, the case for Nuclear Disarmament —whether one agrees or disagrees with it—has been complicated by the existence of this element. Once the genuine members of the movement had begun to employ tactics which brought them into violent conflict with the civil or military police, then numbers of other people joined in, people with no interest in favouring or opposing Nuclear Disarmament. It was often these who were in the forefront of the crowd, and fomented violence just for sheer pleasure. The same has been true in Nazi or fascist meetings which have ended in the same way. In some cases, indeed, one can say 'which have begun in violence', for rioting has begun before any speaker has had the opportunity to open his mouth. These 'toughs' form an added difficulty in the whole issue. They are often physically very fit (in London many come from the dockers and workers in the big markets), and the restoration of order is made doubly difficult by their presence. It is unrealistic not to recognise that there is a new lack of moral principle, a new contempt for law and order, a new uninhibited enjoyment of destruction, which immensely complicates the decision as to whether ancient safeguards and established disciplines are adequate to meet the present need.

All these different and novel elements in our situation would be rendered much more dangerous if there were a period of wide-spread unemployment, nationally or locally. The appeal to ' trust a leader ' would become almost irresistible among tens of thousands of sober men of all ages and classes, who were disgusted with the emptiness of life and the failure of the accepted political solutions. And there would be many more young thugs with nothing to do except to enjoy whatever violence there was.

In a situation which is not confined only to the British Isles, these are the novelties which justify a fresh consideration of whether we already possess all the legal safeguards which are intelligently applicable to the preservation of democracy, or whether new ones should be added. And in considering them it is well to take note that in some other countries, especially in countries which the Nazis overran, new safeguards have already been incorporated in their laws.

So far as legal measures are involved, there are four fields to be examined in which additional legislation might be advantageous:

(i) *The prohibition of Racial Discrimination in hotels, places of public resort, and employment;*

(ii) *The extension, to the protection of a group, of the laws against libel and defamation already in force for the protection of an individual;*

(iii) *The exclusion, from the traditional liberty of speech, of opinions and policies designed to destroy that liberty;*

(iv) *The prohibition of marching or wearing uniforms for political purposes.*

Legislation dealing with one or more of these issues is already in force in at least one country.

Two arguments which are commonly used against new measures in this country may be dealt with first; for they would apply to all the measures concerned. One is that ' they would be very difficult to apply'; and the other is that 'you can't make men good by Act of Parliament'. As to the first, there is no reason why legislation in this field should be held to be more difficult to apply than in any other field. I doubt whether any modern state has an income tax law which is not difficult to apply. But so far no state has abolished income tax for that reason. Certainly the laws under consideration would need judgment in their application. But so do many others. Certainly the police could not be always on the spot for their enforcement; and sometimes they would be difficult to bring home to a suspected culprit. The same is true of many others—especially for example those defining motoring offences—but the situation would not be improved by their abolition. As to the second argument, that ' you can't make men good by Act of Parliament,' nobody would propose that the dangers of group prejudice should be tackled *only* at the legal level. But it is probably not even always true that men cannot be helped to be good by a wise law; and it is certainly false to claim that legal prohibitions cannot help to protect them from indulging in crime or moral turpitude. In any case the legal is only one aspect of the whole issue.

There is one argument which is particularly irritating, because it would be both true and convincing, if only human nature were different. It is the argument that the right way to treat these people is to abstain from their meetings, to pay no attention in the press to their activities, and to refuse them the publicity of open trial in the courts. What ruins the argument is the old French saying that ' *Cet animal est très méchant: quand on l'attaque, il se défend* '; that when it does so the consequence is ' news '; and that then the net result is bound to be an appearance in the courts, if only because a considerable number of toughs will go to the meetings, not in the desire to obtain guidance on their political opinions, but in order to ' have a good scrap'. We have to accept the fact that, in a country with an ancient tradition of law and order, these things are news, and that many consequences flow therefrom. Moreover, this being so, we have to avoid the repetition of what happened in Germany when Hitler and his movement were weak; when an appearance in the courts meant only an excellent new piece of publicity and, even if there were to be a conviction, so trifling a sentence that it could be accepted with equanimity, indeed with pleasure. It combined the aura of martyrdrom with the aura of power; and no would-be dictator could ask for more.

For the control of that section of the population which enjoys violence the measures already contained in the Public Order Act, 1936, are the most effective. Processions are not a necessary part of freedom of political expression, and the form in which the Act deals with them[1] is sufficiently elastic and clear to enable full use to be made of it, but only when it is judged necessary. It lies with the local authorities, civil and police, to decide whether in the interests

[1] The relevant parts of the Act are printed as Appendix II.

of order processions should be prohibited for a period, and it lies with them also to decide how long the period should be. Because the prohibition applies to *all* political processions, they do not have to discriminate for or against any particular organisation.

The same Act prohibits the wearing in public places of ' uniform signifying association with any political organisation '; and this also is probably the most effective way in which the law can assist in impeding the adventitious increase of assaults upon our freedom. For uniforms also are not necessary to express political opinions, but they exercise a very potent spell over many unstable, obscure, or neurotic personalities. On the one hand they absorb him into a larger whole and take away the sense of loneliness and isolation; and, on the other, they lift from his shoulders the personal responsibility for actions which might otherwise cause him to have a queasy conscience, or be too frightening to undertake. The evidence from Nazi Germany for both these arguments is overwhelming. The private possession and display of uniforms for any political purpose is a thoroughly undesirable right in any civilised society.

Beyond this point the issues on which legislation is needful and helpful demand the most exacting scrutiny. It might, for example, appear logical and obvious that a democracy should protect itself from destruction by a law making it illegal for a party to demand its overthrow. Is it right to have allowed the Nazis in Germany before 1933, or contemporary Nazi and fascist parties, openly to proclaim that they will refuse to allow the freedom to others which others at present allow to them? They make use of democratic freedoms to destroy democracy. But a hundred years ago France voted away its freedom, and placed itself in the hands of Napoleon III; and it has done the same in our own day in despair at the inability of a democratic government to solve the Algerian crisis. In neither case would a law have protected the democratic process, because the majority of vocal citizens considered that it was precisely the process itself which had broken down. This is not a field which can be directly approached by legislation.

There is a more profitable approach in the attempt to discover what are the reasons which the fascist groups put forward to justify their destruction of ordinary democratic freedoms. It is never because the general population is such a collection of nitwits and criminals that they are not capable of looking after themselves.

Not at all. The general population over whom the fascists wish to become dictators is described as the highest manifestation of humanity. But their nobility and excellence need to be protected from lesser breeds which take advantage of their generosity to corrupt and destroy them. Their goodness makes them overlook the subtle way in which these evil elements gain complete power and then, remaining in the shadows themselves, let criminal and racially inferior elements debauch them and their womenfolk. This is the universal line of approach; and this is the reason why antisemitism and similar movements to incite prejudice are an essential weapon to the rabble-rousers. It is, therefore, along the line of impeding the use of group prejudice in order to win further support from unwary citizens that legislation can best protect democracy itself.

Such legislation might have two prongs which, to mix the metaphor, might usefully interact upon each other. To protect democracy it would make use of the prong which forbade group libel, and to improve relations between the majority and the minority it would discourage various forms of discrimination against minority groups. This is an indirect way of achieving the objective, but it may well be the wisest. If it cannot easily be claimed that the majority is endangered by various abominable practices which are falsely attributed to a minority, then a strong argument for limiting the normal democratic freedom of the minority is removed. If every effort is made to remove discrimination, so that majority and minority meet in as many ways as possible and on a level of equality, then it will be more difficult to claim that the minority possesses dreadful characteristics and indulges in dangerous practices which make it a menace to others. It will be seen for what it is: a group of citizens, good, bad, and indifferent, just like other groups of citizens.

Legislation about libel (written attacks) and defamation (spoken attacks) on a living individual already exists in all civilised communities. There is also legislation making it an offence to speak or write obscenities and blasphemies. There is, therefore, already a recognised limitation upon freedom of speech. It seems difficult to claim that there is so enormous a difference between the attacking of an individual and the attacking of a group, or between sexual obscenity and racial calumny, that laws about the one are possible, and about the other are impossible. Many countries already have such laws. One of the most elaborate is in the German Federal Republic. Article 130 of the Penal Code enacts that[1]

'Whoever attacks the human dignity of others, in a manner capable of disturbing public peace, by

1. incitement to hatred against parts of the population,
2. calling for violent or arbitrary measures against them,
3. insulting them, maliciously exposing them to contempt or slandering them,

shall be punishable by imprisonment of not less than three months. In addition, a fine may be imposed.'

A wide variety of phrasing in the laws of different countries may reflect the need for careful definition and the difficulty of finding it. But they do not suggest that the task is an impossible one. In the British Parliament the phrase ' words inciting hatred of any racial group of Her Majesty's subjects ' has been proposed. Italy says simply ' engaging in racial propaganda '; India goes furthest in definition by prohibiting the promotion of feelings of enmity or hatred ' on grounds of religion, race, caste, language or community'. The Swedish definition covers ' threats, calumnies, or insults against an official national group of a certain descent or religion'. The words ' official ' and ' national ' would not apply in many countries, but they are not essential to the identification. ' Threats, calumnies or insults against an identifiable group of the population of a certain nationality or descent or religion ' would cover Jews, coloured immigrants from the Dominions, and immigrant workers from Europe. It would remain possible to argue against the presence or practices of such groups, provided one kept to the facts. But it would give the group concerned protection against ' threats, calumnies and insults '; and it is precisely these exaggerations which form the main part of the fascist armoury. Facts have never been of much service to them.

There remains the question of discrimination against—let us use the same definition—' an identifiable group of the population of a certain nationality or descent or religion'. The discrimination is principally practised in one of three fields: employment, recreation (that is: private clubs and associations), and board and lodging (that is: hotels, common lodging houses and restaurants). The

---

[1] Quoted, together with comparable legislation of other countries, in *World Jewry*, V. 5 for September/October 1962, a number dealing with *The Law and Race Hatred*.

second of these is almost certainly not a suitable object of legislation. In a club or similar institution citizens are entitled to choose their own environment and companionship. It is only when public money is involved, for example in a Municipal Golf Club, that discrimination against a rate-paying resident on the grounds mentioned above becomes objectionable. The reasons for the exclusion of recreation would apply to private educational establishments such as the British ' public schools'. They are private bodies, often of religious foundation. Some behave reasonably and some don't; but one would not make any progress by trying to control them with the thick stick of legislation.

There remains discrimination in employment and in ' board and lodging'. The United States is the main country with evidence on the former subject. Anti-discrimination laws have been in force in a number of States for some years. Since the tendency is to increase both the number of States and the number of prosecutions, the prevention of discrimination in employment has evidently proved an appropriate subject for legislation. Negroes, Roman Catholics, and Jews have all at one time or another had the advantage of the protection they offer. It is, of course, not always possible to pin a refusal of employment down to a cause covered by the law. But at least it has made impossible the public advertisement that ' No negro—or Jew, or this or that—need apply '; and it has served to combat intolerance in both employers and fellow-workers. Its successful application probably depends on the presence or absence of something equivalent to sympathetic factory inspectors or welfare officers of the type described below (p. 174). The law, if lacking all moral backing, would by itself probably be relatively ineffective. But if it were the potential fellow-workers who were unreasonably hostile, the law would strengthen the hands of the employers, and *vice-versa*, provided there was someone with understanding and authority to support the purposes of the law.

To some extent the same applies to hotels, common boarding houses and restaurants. If there were no one interested in good relations, the law could probably be so easily evaded as to be often ineffective. The proprietor or restaurateur could produce a reason, and the potential client would have great difficulty, as well as expense, in disputing it in court. On the other hand the law would immensely strengthen the hands of a liberal-minded person on either side against prejudice on the other. But again, it would do so only if the reason for refusal appeared to be such as the law described. It would not protect a person whose personal conduct was objectionable, or enable him to obtain rights not available to ordinary citizens; but it would make it more difficult for fictitious reasons to be advanced for an exclusion, or for the exclusion to be based blankly on race, colour or religion.

Legal action by itself will never be enough. Indeed it has already been suggested that the satisfactory enforcement of such laws as may be enacted will in itself depend on extra-legal conditions being fulfilled. These can be, indeed should be, of various kinds. In the United States, where the cities are more cosmopolitan than in most parts of Europe or Great Britain, it is becoming increasingly common for there to be attached to the personal staff of the Mayor, or to the Municipal Council, a *Community Relations Officer*, with an adequate staff of his own. He is usually a trained sociologist or psychologist; and his task is to know all the different communities of which the city is composed, to gain their confidence, and to intervene where injustice and ignorance mar the harmony of the city. Where such an officer exists, the power for good of the various possible laws here described is immensely enhanced. It is his particular task to see that frivolous or malicious cases are avoided, and that the law is used effectively where prejudiced action needs correction. But always he is concerned more with the positive task of creating harmony than with the negative one of preventing hatred and injustice. There are probably a number of cities in England where the costs of such an officer and office would be less than the present police costs of fighting a necessarily negative battle against the violent effects of prejudice after they have been manifested.

Of particular value in the communal field is work centred in the schools of the community. Eastern prep schools may pick and choose among those who seek entrance; but the elementary and secondary schools which are state controlled will reflect accurately the mixture of citizens in the community. For education is both compulsory and universal. Here an intelligent group of people concerned with the harmony of the community is invaluable, for prejudice can start in the young and become almost ineradicable by the time the child is an adult. *The Council of Citizens of East London* is a voluntary body which has made an immense contribution to understanding by devoting a great deal of expert knowledge, time and thought, to ignorance and prejudice at the school age. It was founded while Mosley's evil work was making East London a nightly hell; it drew together East Londoners of all kinds, and it provided just that kind of moral backing which has already been commended, and which makes the enforcement of law a creative activity. In the United States there have been a number of such councils, and there have been many experiments in combatting prejudice in education.

Allied to such possible communal assistance are many other forms of voluntary activity. The recent *Yellow Star Movement* in London is experimenting with the power and effect of non-violent resistance. Its members intervene between a fascist speaker and the minority whom he desires to attack, either by anticipating him on his chosen pitch and keeping up a continuous meeting during the period in which he had planned to speak, or by surrounding the speaker in large numbers, and preventing him from reaching the audience he wishes to whip up to a fury. This likewise prevents members of the audience, or persons present just to enjoy violence, from attacking the speaker or his supporters.

That is a particular technique for a particular situation. Of more general application are all the national and local associations for mutual understanding and education, such as the *Council of Christians and Jews* with its many local councils, the groups which definitely set out to bring people of different colours together, and the local Churches and Synagogues.

The rôle of Synagogues is perforce limited. It is impossible for them to take the initiative against a prejudice which is directed against Jews; and, unless they are part of a larger religious activity, it is difficult for them even to help in understanding between other minorities, such as coloured settlers or immigrant workers. The prime responsibility rests on the Churches.

Seventeen years ago I wrote[1], in profound distress, that 'with many notable exceptions, their ignorance is both dishonourable and disgusting. There is nothing whatever to be said in their defence. They maintain missions to convert the Jews, while at the same time they will not spend a penny of either time or effort to see that Judaism and the story of the Jewish people are fairly presented to their congregations. This might not matter if they could ignore the Jews. But references to them are bound to crop up continually in

[1] *An Enemy of the People: Antisemitism*, pp. 143ff.

sermons, lectures and books; and nine-tenths of those references are ill-informed, often to the point of being definitely untrue. They don't mean to be prejudiced; they are not conscious of antisemitic feeling; but the share that they bear for providing a fertile breeding ground for every kind of antisemitic misrepresentation is an exceedingly heavy one; and a few resolutions of sympathy with the victims of Hitler's massacres do not square the account. Innumerable ministers of religion preach sermons on the Pharisees; and know nothing whatever about them. They talk of ' the Law '; and they have not the slightest idea what ' Torah ' (the Hebrew for Law) means to a Jew. They speak of ' the Jews ' when they describe the less attractive activities of the early Israelites, with complete indifference to the fact that the congregation will relate their words to the conduct of a contemporary 20th-century Jewish community. This is particularly the case in their ignorant contrasts between the ' Jewish ' and ' Christian ' ideas of God. I have met ministers who believed that 'Love thy neighbour as thyself' was an entirely New Testament idea, and are unaware that Jesus is quoting and endorsing the teaching of the Mosaic law (Lev. xix. 18), not giving original teaching himself in the passage. With sublime indifference to the evidence of the Synoptic Gospels themselves (which contain no mention of the Pharisees in the events of the arrest, trial and death of Jesus) they lay the blame for the crucifixion on Pharisaic shoulders. As to the post-New-Testament developments of Judaism they know nothing; and they preach to their people as though the less attractive beliefs of Old or New Testament times contained the sum total of the Jewish religion for the last two thousand years. And all these things are doubly abominable when they occur in Sunday School lessons to the young'.

There is unhappily nothing in the history of the past seventeen years which would make me modify this condemnation. All that can be said is that it is possible to specify more clearly ' the notable exceptions'. In the forefront of these I would place the Conference at Seelisberg in Switzerland at which Roman Catholics, Anglicans, Protestants and Jews were present in August 1947 from many national organisations of Christians and Jews. At the tail would come the World Council of Churches which has just, but only just, begun to move.

The reason why the Churches are still of very great importance, in spite of the fact that they obviously have extremely little direct or indirect influence in the affairs of adult life, is that they still play a considerable part in the education of the young. Millions of families throughout the world, where the parents never go to Church, desire that there shall be a religious element in the teaching of their children. Thus at the most impressionable stage of their existence generation after generation imbibe prejudice against Jews from the Gospel stories of Pharisaic hostility to Jesus, or from carelessly told stories of the crucifixion, stories which their parents and teachers are too indifferent and ignorant to present with sufficient knowledge and historical accuracy to ensure that they will not result in the creation of a fertile seed-bed for antisemitism.

The *National Conference of Christians and Jews* in the United States has worked hard on religious text books. Under the influence of the terrible evidence, produced by Jules Isaac in *Jésus et Israël*, that statements were constantly being made in Protestant and Catholic teaching in France which had no biblical warrant or justification, but were simply the product of antisemitic prejudice, Catholic groups have attempted to see that the worst text books are eliminated, and that the grossest inaccuracies are no longer taught. This is written before the present Vatican Council has had time to consider its agenda; but Pope John has already taken official action to eliminate certain prejudice-creating phrases from the Liturgy; and the atmosphere seems favourable to further progress. Little can yet be recorded of the World Council of Churches, save that they have begun, very late in the day, a study of the text books used in schools.

The most important Christian statement on the subject of the teaching of Christian children about the New Testament picture of the Jews remains the ' Ten Points of Seelisberg'. They are concise clear, and unequivocal. After a careful preliminary summary of the needs, they read as follows:

1. Remember that One God speaks to us all through the Old and New Testaments.
2. Remember that Jesus was born of a Jewish mother of the seed of David and the people of Israel, and that His everlasting love and forgiveness embrace His own people and the whole world.
3. Remember that the first disciples, the apostles and the first martyrs were Jews.
4. Remember that the fundamental commandment of

Christianity, to love God and one's neighbour, proclaimed already in the Old Testament and confirmed by Jesus, is binding upon both Christians and Jews in all human relationships, without any exception.

5. Avoid distorting or misrepresenting biblical or post-biblical Judaism with the object of extolling Christianity.

6. Avoid using the word *Jews* in the exclusive sense of the enemies of Jesus, and the words *the enemies of Jesus* to designate the whole Jewish people.

7. Avoid presenting the Passion in such a way as to bring the odium of the killing of Jesus upon all Jews or upon Jews alone. It was only a section of the Jews in Jerusalem who demanded the death of Jesus, and the Christian message has always been that it was the sins of mankind which were exemplified by those Jews and that it was the sins in which all men share that brought Christ to the Cross.

8. Avoid referring to the scriptural curses, or the cry of a raging mob: *His blood be upon us and our children,* without remembering that this cry should not count against the infinitely more weighty words of our Lord: *Father, forgive them, for they know not what they do.*

9. Avoid promoting the superstitious notion that the Jewish people are reprobate, accursed, reserved for a destiny of suffering.

10. Avoid speaking of the Jews as if the first members of the Church had not been Jews.

In most issues of group prejudice the record of the Churches is increasingly admirable. To find a prejudice against colour is extremely rare. But in dealing with the very tap root of group prejudice, antisemitism, they have not yet faced the fact that, whether any manifestation of it may be primarily political or economic in character, the responsibility is theirs that generation after generation of children first hear of the Jewish people in their Scripture lessons, learn that ' *the Jews* ' killed Jesus, make no distinction between Jews of that day and Jews of this, and so grow up disposed to credit the outpourings of a Hitler or his successors.

The battle against prejudice is a battle which needs to be fought as much for the sake of the majorities as for that of the minorities. It is a battle which needs to be fought from every vantage point, of education, of scholarship, and of political and social life. If the well-being of innumerable minorities is involved in its successful issue, the spiritual temperature of every majority is still more deeply at stake. The world is so interdependent, life has become so complex, the desire of ordinary men for guidance and leadership is so right and natural, that it is foolish to allow the charlatan and the fanatic the adventitious benefits which he can secure by the encouragement of prejudice among the ignorant and the self-seeking. More than ever before we need honest politics honestly presented.

FREEDOM OF SPEECH

First Leader in *The Times* of London for August 25 1962
(Reprinted by permission)

SHOULD INCITEMENT TO racial hatred or prejudice be made a crime? Mr. George Brown thinks so, so do the National Council for Civil Liberties, the L.C.C., the Communist Party, and the members of Parliament who supported the Bills introduced last session by Mr. Brockway and Mr. Iremonger. Such a provision is to be found in the penal codes of other states. The Home Secretary is considering during the recess whether to introduce legislation of a like kind here.

It ought to be understood that any such legislation would be sharp deviation from the direction in which the control of public discussion has evolved in Britain during several centuries. The tendency has been for the criminal law to intervene only for the purpose of keeping the peace and maintaining public tranquillity and the stability of the state. There are exceptions to this, the law relating to defamation, blasphemy, obscenity, and sedition, but the exceptions are more apparent than real. In blasphemy, for instance, the law nowadays is interested in the manner rather than in the matter of what is said, with an eye out for breaches of the peace; while in defamation the courts are inclined to look askance at indictments, as opposed to civil actions for damages, in cases where no threat to public order arises. As for sedition, the following judicial observation is worth quoting:

> Every man has a right to give every public matter a candid, full and free discussion; something must be allowed for feeling in men's minds and for some warmth of expression, but the intention to incite the people to take power into their own hands and to provoke them to tumult and disorder is a seditious intention.

Here too the law is concerned not with the merits of what is said but with its calculable effects on public order. That was in 1839, and the emphasis has certainly not been reversed during the intervening years.

The Public Order Act, 1936, the latest reinforcement of this department of the law, was introduced to put a stop to mob violence in the East End of London—in which it succeeded. It was not introduced for the purpose of stamping out fascist or communist doctrines. From all this two principles clearly emerge. The state has never hesitated to equip itself with powers to preserve the public peace; and it has progressively relinquished the power to censure particular opinions. Nor has the state sought to combine these principles, by using the prohibition of specified classes of extreme opinion as a means of preserving the peace—by, for instance, prohibiting the preaching of racial prejudice in order to insure against civil disturbance. For, once the criminality of an utterance comes to be judged by direct reference to its content, insoluble difficulties of definition and interpretation arise.

Those who now advocate a deviation by making the preaching of racial hatred or prejudice an offence are moved by a variety of considerations. Four beliefs are prominent: (i) that this is a way of squashing neo-fascism; (ii) that it would put a stop to the recrudescence of violence at public meetings; (iii) that the multiracial character, or ideal, of British society requires some form of overt recognition in the statute book; (iv) that racial animosity is so odious that there ought to be a law against it.

As for the first of these considerations, a law of the kind proposed would not put paid to, for example, Sir Oswald Mosley's political activities—not, that is, unless his hand were suddenly to lose its cunning, or unless the statute were so widely drawn and so searchingly enforced as to amount to an inquisition bearing heavily on serious political argument. The second belief is dubious: in so far as violence is attributable to provocative utterances the provokers are already liable to prosecution under the present law—witness the case of Mr. Colin Jordan, which is now subject to appeal; and in so far as the violence is factitious the proposed new law would have no contribution to make. The third and fourth propositions presuppose that it is the business of the criminal law to articulate the conscience of society. Certainly it should be closely related to the dominant moral feelings of society, otherwise it forfeits respect and support. But it is quite another thing to argue that even the strongest and widest disapproval of a certain disposition is a sufficient reason for adding its manifestations to the list of crimes.

The whole development of modern domestic British history is towards a position of political maturity, in which people are left to weigh for themselves the opinions, policies, and creeds that are publicly proclaimed before them; treating with contemptuous disdain those that are deserving of contempt; resolving their differences by argument and by constitutional machinery; and refusing to be stampeded by fools, charlatans, and psychopaths. These are the conditions demanded by the way of conducting public affairs to which Britain is committed—competitive persuasion and the free passage of ideas, bad as well as good, pernicious or beneficial, silly or wise. The comportment of the people has well justified this course, and that might be expected to be a cause of legitimate pride. Why should we be deflected from this course by the ranting of a handful of exhibitionists, by the sporadic violence of factions which thrive thereby, and by the honest fury of a few citizens who have lost control of their feelings in public?

Extracts from the PUBLIC ORDER ACT, 1936

An Act to prohibit the wearing of uniforms in connection with political objects and the maintenance by private persons of associations of military or similar character; and to make further provision for the preservation of public order on the occasion of public processions and meetings and in public places.

(18th December 1936.)

Be it enacted by the King's most Excellent Majesty, by and with the advice and consent of the Lords Spiritual and Temporal, and Commons, in this present Parliament assembled, and by the authority of the same, as follows:—

1.—(1) Subject as hereinafter provided, any person who in any public place or at any public meeting wears uniform signifying his association with any political organisation or with the promotion of any political object shall be guilty of an offence:

Provided that, if the chief officer of police is satisfied that the wearing of any such uniform as aforesaid on any ceremonial, anniversary, or other special occasion will not be likely to involve risk of public disorder, he may, with the consent of a Secretary of State, by order permit the wearing of such uniform on that occasion either absolutely or subject to such conditions as may be specified in the order ....

2.—(1) If the members or adherents of any association of persons, whether incorporated or not, are—

    (a) organised or trained or equipped for the purpose of enabling them to be employed in usurping the functions of the police or of the armed forces of the Crown; or

    (b) organised and trained or organised and equipped either for the purpose of enabling them to be employed for the use or display of physical force in promoting any political

183

object, or in such manner as to arouse reasonable apprehension that they are organised and either trained or equipped for that purpose;

then any person who takes part in the control or management of the association, or in so organising or training as aforesaid any members or adherents thereof, shall be guilty of an offence under this section...

3.—(1) If the chief officer of police, having regard to the time or place at which and the circumstances in which any public procession is taking place or is intended to take place and to the route taken or proposed to be taken by the procession, has reasonable ground for apprehending that the procession may occasion serious public disorder, he may give directions imposing upon the persons organising or taking part in the procession such conditions as appear to him necessary for the preservation of public order, including conditions prescribing the route to be taken by the procession and conditions prohibiting the procession from entering any public place specified in the directions:

Provided that no conditions restricting the display of flags, banners, or emblems shall be imposed under this subsection except such as are reasonably necessary to prevent risk of a breach of the peace.

(2) If at any time the chief officer of police is of opinion that by reason of particular circumstances existing in any borough or urban district or in any part thereof the powers conferred on him by the last foregoing subsection will not be sufficient to enable him to prevent serious public disorder being occasioned by the holding of public processions in that borough, district or part, he shall apply to the council of the borough or district for an order prohibiting for such period not exceeding three months as may be specified in the application the holding of all public processions or of any class of public procession so specified either in the borough or urban district or in that part thereof, as the case may be, and upon receipt of the application the council may, with the consent of a Secretary of State, make an order either in terms of the application or with such modifications as may be approved by the Secretary of State...

5. Any person who in any public place or at any public meeting uses threatening, abusive or insulting words or behaviour with intent to provoke a breach of the peace or whereby a breach of the peace is likely to be occasioned, shall be guilty of an offence....

BIBLIOGRAPHY

General

Coudenhove-Kalergi, Count H., *Antisemitism throughout the Ages*, Hutchinson, 1935
Valentin, H., *Antisemitism: historically and critically examined*, Gollancz, 1936.
Zuckerman, N., *The Wine of Violence: An Anthology*, Association Press, New York, 1947.

Psychological Causes of Prejudice

See Books mentioned in Footnotes on pp. 8 and 18.

Christian Roots of Antisemitism

Hay, Malcolm, *The Foot of Pride*, Beacon Press, 1950 (reprinted as paperback with title *Europe and the Jews*).
Parkes, James, *The Conflict of the Church and the Synagogue*, Soncino Press, 1934 (reprinted as paperback by Meridian Press).
Parkes, James, *The Jew in the Medieval Community*, Soncino Press, 1938.
Simon, Marcel, *Verus Israel*, Boccard, Paris, 1948.
Trachtenberg, Joshua, *The Devil and the Jews*, Yale, 1943.

Modern Antisemitism

Parkes, James, *The Emergence of the Jewish Problem* 1878-1939, Oxford, 1946.
Sachar, Abram L. *Sufferance is the Badge*, Knopf, New York, 1940.
Sachar, Howard M., *The Course of Modern Jewish History*, World Pub. Co., Cleveland, 1958.

Austria

Jenks, William A., *Vienna and the Young Hitler*, Columbia Univ. Press, 1960.
Steed, H. Wickham, *The Hapsburg Monarchy*, Constable, 1913.

France

Byrnes, R. F., *Antisemitism in Modern France: I. The Prologue to the Dreyfus Affair*, Rutgers Univ. Press, 1950.
Chapman, Guy, *The Dreyfus Case: A Reassessment*, Hart-Davis, 1955.

Germany

Massing, P. W., *Rehearsal for Destruction: A Study of Political Antisemitism in Imperial Germany*, Harper, New York, 1949. (See also below, *Nazism*.)

Poland and Russia

Dubnow, S. M., *History of the Jews in Russia and Poland*, Jewish Publication Society, Philadelphia, 1916. (See also books under *Modern Antisemitism*, above.)

Rumania

Winestock, Earl, *The Seven Years*, Dutton, New York, 1959.

185

Nazism

Wiener Library, *Persecution and Resistance under the Nazis:* Catalogue Series No. 1,
2nd ed. Vallentine, Mitchell, 1960.
Roberts, Stephen H., *The House that Hitler built*, Methuen, 1937.

Hilberg, Raul, *The Destruction of the European Jews*, Quadrangle Books, Chicago,
1961.
Reitlinger, Gerald, *The Final Solution*, Vallentine, Mitchell, 1953.

The Influence of the Nazis

Artucio, H. F., *The Nazi Octopus in South America*, R. Hale, 1943.
Cross, Colin, *The Fascists in Britain*, Barrie and Rockliff, 1961.

The Soviet Union

de Grunwald, *The Churches and the Soviet Union*, Macmillan, 1962.
Leneman, Léon, *La Tragédie des Juifs en U.R.S.S.*, *Questions Actuelles*, Paris, 1959.
Kolarz, Walter, *Religion in the Soviet Union*, Macmillan, 1962.

Israel and the Arabs

ESCO Foundation, *Palestine, a Study of Jewish, Arab and British Policies*, Yale
Univ. Press, 1947.
Goitein, S. D., *Jews and Arabs: Their Contacts through the Ages*, Shocken, New York,
1955.
Kaplan, Deborah, *The Arab Refugees: An abnormal Problem*, R. Mass, Jerusalem,
(Israel) 1959.
Parkes, James, *A History of Palestine, A.D. 135 to Modern Times*, Gollancz, 1949.

INDEX

QUADRANGLE PAPERBACKS

American History

Frederick Lewis Allen. *The Lords of Creation.* (QP35)
Lewis Atherton. *Main Street on the Middle Border.* (QP36)
Thomas A. Bailey. *Woodrow Wilson and the Lost Peace.* (QP1)
Thomas A. Bailey. *Woodrow Wilson and the Great Betrayal.* (QP2)
Charles A. Beard. *The Idea of National Interest.* (QP27)
Carl L. Becker. *Everyman His Own Historian.* (QP33)
Ray A. Billington. *The Protestant Crusade.* (QP12)
Allan G. Bogue. *From Prairie to Corn Belt.* (QP50)
Kenneth E. Boulding. *The Organizational Revolution.* (QP43)
Gerald M. Capers. *John C. Calhoun, Opportunist.* (QP70)
David M. Chalmers. *Hooded Americanism.* (QP51)
John Chamberlain. *Farewell to Reform.* (QP19)
Alice Hamilton Cromie. *A Tour Guide to the Civil War.*
Robert D. Cross. *The Emergence of Liberal Catholicism in America.* (QP44)
Richard M. Dalfiume. *American Politics Since 1945.* (NYTimes Book, QP57)
Chester McArthur Destler. *American Radicalism, 1865-1901.* (QP30)
Robert A. Divine. *American Foreign Policy Since 1945.* (NYTimes Book, QP58)
Robert A. Divine. *Causes and Consequences of World War II.* (QP63)
Robert A. Divine. *The Illusion of Neutrality.* (QP45)
Elisha P. Douglass. *Rebels and Democrats.* (QP26)
Felix Frankfurter. *The Commerce Clause.* (QP16)
Lloyd C. Gardner. *A Different Frontier.* (QP32)
Edwin Scott Gaustad. *The Great Awakening in New England.* (QP46)
Ray Ginger. *Altgeld's America.* (QP21)
Ray Ginger. *Modern American Cities.* (NYTimes Book, QP67)
Ray Ginger. *Six Days or Forever?* (QP68)
Gerald N. Grob. *Workers and Utopia.* (QP61)
Louis Hartz. *Economic Policy and Democratic Thought.* (QP52)
William B. Hesseltine. *Lincoln's Plan of Reconstruction.* (QP41)
Granville Hicks. *The Great Tradition.* (QP62)
Dwight W. Hoover. *Understanding Negro History.* (QP49)
Stanley P. Hirshson. *Farewell to the Bloody Shirt.* (QP53)
Frederic C. Howe. *The Confessions of a Reformer.* (QP39)
Harold L. Ickes. *The Autobiography of a Curmudgeon.* (QP69)
Louis Joughin and Edmund M. Morgan. *The Legacy of Sacco and Vanzetti.* (QP7)
William Loren Katz. *Teachers' Guide to American Negro History.* (QP210)
Burton Ira Kaufman. *Washington's Farewell Address.* (QP64)
Edward Chase Kirkland. *Dream and Thought in the Business Community, 1860-1900.* (QP11)
Edward Chase Kirkland. *Industry Comes of Age.* (QP42)
Adrienne Koch. *The Philosophy of Thomas Jefferson.* (QP17)
Gabriel Kolko. *The Triumph of Conservatism.* (QP40)
Walter LaFeber. *John Quincy Adams and American Continental Empire.* (QP23)
Lawrence H. Leder. *The Meaning of the American Revolution.* (NYTimes Book, QP66)
David E. Lilienthal. *TVA: Democracy on the March.* (QP28)
Arthur S. Link. *Wilson the Diplomatist.* (QP18)
Huey P. Long. *Every Man a King.* (QP8)
Gene M. Lyons. *America: Purpose and Power.* (QP24)
Jackson Turner Main. *The Antifederalists.* (QP14)
Ernest R. May. *The World War and American Isolation, 1914-1917.* (QP29)
Henry F. May. *The End of American Innocence.* (QP9)
George E. Mowry. *The California Progressives.* (QP6)
William L. O'Neill. *American Society Since 1945.* (NYTimes Book, QP59)
Frank L. Owsley. *Plain Folk of the Old South.* (QP22)
David Graham Phillips. *The Treason of the Senate.* (QP20)
Julius W. Pratt. *Expansionists of 1898.* (QP15)
C. Herman Pritchett. *The Roosevelt Court.* (QP71)
Moses Rischin. *The American Gospel of Success.* (QP54)
John P. Roche. *The Quest for the Dream.* (QP47)
David A. Shannon. *The Socialist Party of America.* (QP38)
Andrew Sinclair. *The Available Man.* (QP60)
John Spargo. *The Bitter Cry of the Children.* (QP55)
Bernard Sternsher. *The Negro in Depression and War.* (QP65)
Richard W. Van Alstyne. *The Rising American Empire.* (QP25)
Willard M. Wallace. *Appeal to Arms.* (QP10)
Norman Ware. *The Industrial Worker, 1840-1860.* (QP13)
Albert K. Weinberg. *Manifest Destiny.* (QP3)
Bernard A. Weisberger. *They Gathered at the River.* (QP37)
Robert H. Wiebe. *Businessmen and Reform.* (QP56)
William Appleman Williams. *The Contours of American History.* (QP34)
William Appleman Williams. *The Great Evasion.* (QP48)
Esmond Wright. *Causes and Consequences of the American Revolution.* (QP31)

European History

William Sheridan Allen. *The Nazi Seizure of Power.* (QP302)
W. O. Henderson. *The Industrial Revolution in Europe.* (QP303)
Raul Hilberg. *The Destruction of the European Jews.* (QP301)
Telford Taylor. *Sword and Swastika.* (QP304)
John Weiss. *Nazis and Fascists in Europe, 1918-1945.* (NYTimes Book, QP305)

Philosophy

F. H. Bradley. *The Presuppositions of Critical History.* (QP108)
William Earle. *Objectivity.* (QP109)
James M. Edie, James P. Scanlan, Mary-Barbara Zeldin, George L. Kline. *Russian Philosophy.* (3 vols, QP111, 112, 113)
James M. Edie. *An Invitation to Phenomenology.* (QP103)
James M. Edie. *New Essays in Phenomenology.* (QP114)
James M. Edie. *Phenomenology in America.* (QP105)
Manfred S. Frings. *Heidegger and the Quest for Truth.* (QP107)
Moltke S. Gram. *Kant: Disputed Questions.* (QP104)
E. D. Klemke. *Studies in the Philosophy of G. E. Moore.* (QP115)
Lionel Rubinoff. *Faith and Reason.* (QP106)
Paul Tibbetts. *Perception.* (QP110)
Pierre Thévenaz. *What Is Phenomenology?* (QP101)

Social Science

Nathan Glazer. *Cities in Trouble.* (NYTimes Book, QP212)
George and Eunice Grier. *Equality and Beyond.* (QP204)
Charles O. Lerche, Jr. *Last Chance in Europe.* (QP207)
David Mitrany. *A Working Peace System.* (QP205)
Martin Oppenheimer and George Lakey. *A Manual for Direct Action.* (QP202)
James Parkes. *Antisemitism.* (QP213)
Fred Powledge. *To Change a Child.* (QP209)
Lee Rainwater. *And the Poor Get Children.* (QP208)
Clarence Senior. *The Puerto Ricans.* (QP201)
Arthur L. Stinchcombe. *Rebellion in a High School.* (QP211)